About this book

"An incredibly helpful guide to investment success."
—John C. Bogle, Founder, The Vanguard Group

This is a guide for anyone in the academy – faculty member, administrator, or professional staff – at whatever point she or he may be along the career path.

Whether you are a newly minted Ph.D. landing your first job, at mid-career, or even already retired and concerned about how long your money might last, Ed Bridges offers you a straightforward, easy-to-grasp, and structured way to think about money, learn how it works, understand the priorities for your stage in life, determine your objectives, and develop a personal plan most likely to achieve them.

Why a book specifically for those who work in higher education? The chances are that your retirement funds are mostly invested in TIAA-CREF funds, and that the plans created by the different institutions where you have worked, or will work, impose sometimes-conflicting limitations on how you can manage your retirement money. This is potentially complex terrain with which many professional financial advisors are unfamiliar. This book provides ample guidance for you to manage your retirement funds, but if you do prefer to seek professional advice, it sets out the criteria for choosing a reliable advisor, and may even be a book from which your advisor can benefit if he or she is not fully conversant with TIAA-CREF's offerings, and the quirks of academic retirement plans.

What makes this book unique is that Ed Bridges shares with you his self-education about the risky business of investing and retirement planning. As he writes, "In schooling myself, I adopted the mindset that I had used as a social scientist for the past forty-six years. I distinguished between fact and opinion and scrutinized the evidence behind every author's claims; moreover, I searched for research that might corroborate or refute these claims. In the process, I learned a great deal about the route I should have taken to retirement from the time I accepted my first academic appointment to the time I submitted my intention to retire. Join me as I relive my long journey so that you may avoid my wrong turns and succeed in reaching your ultimate destination, a worry-free retirement, despite the risks and uncertainties you will surely face when you retire."

The book includes simple questionnaires and worksheets to help you determine where you stand, and think through your options.

About the authors

EDWIN M. BRIDGES, Professor Emeritus, Stanford University, has an extensive background in higher education. Prior to joining the Stanford University faculty in 1974, he taught at Washington University (St. Louis), The University of Chicago, and University of California (Santa Barbara). He is internationally known for his work on problem based learning and has worked with faculty from a variety of disciplines in China and the United States. During his thirty-five-year career in higher education, he has consulted with numerous organizations, including the World Health Organization, the World Bank, and the New York City Public Schools. Professor Bridges has received two lifetime achievement awards for his contributions to the field of educational administration and is listed in *Who's Who in America* and *Who's Who in the World*. At the age of twenty-six, he was appointed a high school principal; the following year he was chosen as one of the three Outstanding Young Men of Indiana.

Since retiring in 1999, Ed lives with his wife, Marjorie, in an historic home on the Stanford University Campus. In retirement, he has devoted much of his time to activities that he neglected during his career as a professor—investing and retirement planning. After reading hundreds of books and articles on these subjects, he decided to share the lessons he learned with friends, colleagues, family, former students, and others through his writing and public speaking.

BRIAN D. BRIDGES is a registered investment adviser in the state of California and a trained financial planner (University of California, Santa Cruz) with a background in counseling (M.A., Department of Counseling, Santa Clara University). Prior to entering the fields of financial planning and life-enhancement counseling, Brian provided engineering solutions to IBM, Sun Microsystems, and NASA's Jet Propulsion Laboratory.

As President of Rewarding Directions, Brian uses his rich background in engineering, financial planning, and counseling to develop solutions that enable others to experience fulfilling, prosperous lives.

THE PRUDENT PROFESSOR

THE PRUDENT PROFESSOR

Planning and Saving for a Worry-Free Retirement From Academe

EDWIN M. BRIDGES
BRIAN D. BRIDGES

STERLING, VIRGINIA

Published by Stylus Publishing, LLC
22883 Quicksilver Drive
Sterling, Virginia 20166-2102

The Prudent Professor is a revised, updated, and enlarged edition of *Retirement Roulette: May the Odds Be with You*, by Edwin M. Bridges and Brian D. Bridges, published 2007 by iUniverse, Inc.

Library of Congress Cataloging-in-Publication Data

Bridges, Edwin M.
The prudent professor : planning and saving for a worry-free retirement from academe / Edwin M. Bridges with Brian D. Bridges.
p. cm.
Includes bibliographical references and index.
ISBN 978-1-57922-467-7 (cloth : alk. paper) –
ISBN 978-1-57922-468-4 (pbk. : alk. paper)
1. College teachers–Retirement–United States.
2. College teachers–United States–Finance, Personal. 3. College Retirement Equities Fund.
I. Bridges, Brian D., 1965- II. Title.
LB2334.B65 2010
331.25′291378–dc22
2010017226

13-digit ISBN: 978-1-57922-467-7 (cloth)
13-digit ISBN: 978-1-57922-468-4 (paper)

Printed in the United States of America

All first editions printed on acid-free paper that meets the American National Standards Institute Z39-48 Standard.

First Edition, 2010

10 9 8 7 6 5 4 3 2 1

The information, ideas, and suggestions in this book are not intended to render professional advice. Before following any suggestions in this book, you should consult your personal accountant or other financial advisor. Neither the author nor the publisher shall be liable or responsible for any loss or damage allegedly arising as a consequence of your use or application of any information or suggestions in this book.

To my beloved wife and dearest friend, Marjorie,
who has brightened my life for more than
fifty-six years.

CONTENTS

PREFACE

If you participate in a defined contribution plan and are responsible for managing your own investments and planning your retirement, this book should be helpful to you. Unlike other books on saving and planning for retirement, this one is written by someone with a first-hand, bird's-eye view of defined contribution plans and what it means to manage your own investments and create a pension plan for yourself. I spent 33 years as a professor and administrator in private universities and am now completing my 10th year in retirement. Each of these universities offered defined contribution plans but provided no guidance on how to invest or create a retirement plan.

During my journey spanning more than four decades, I traveled without a road map or a GPS. As you might imagine, I encountered numerous roadblocks, detours, potholes, and forks in the road. Yes, I even made a few wrong turns. When I eventually reached the so-called Golden Years, I decided to spend my leisure time learning more about where I have been, where I should have gone, and where I should go in the future. This quest inevitably led me to read hundreds of books and articles about investing and retirement planning. Along the way, I discovered that no single book dealt realistically with all of the questions that arose during my journey. Therefore, I thought others might benefit from what I had learned so that they might create the road map that I lacked when I began my journey to the retirement phase of my life over four decades ago.

Now that the ink has dried on my manuscript, you can join me vicariously in reliving this journey. I expect you to benefit from the twists and turns of my life and to leave with a better sense of how to create a worry-free retirement. Since I have a long history with

Teachers Insurance and Annuity Association-College Retirement Equities Fund (TIAA-CREF), you can expect to discover whether this financial services company deserves a prominent place on your retirement road map and which of its products merit a lengthy stay.

The results of my efforts should be of interest and value to professors and administrators regardless of the stage in their career—beginning, nearing retirement, or planning to confront the risks and uncertainties during retirement. More specifically, you will learn how to:

- build a nest egg that sustains your standard of living when you retire,
- deal with the consequential decisions you will face prior to and during retirement,
- cope with the threats to your financial security in retirement,
- maximize your retirement income and financial security when you retire, and
- use financial planners wisely.

As you read this book, bear in mind that I am not a registered investment adviser. Before following my advice, check with a financial adviser. Although I believe that most of what I say is based on what is currently known about the topics I discuss, knowledge is dynamic and ever changing. Regardless of how it evolves over time, I am reasonably confident that this book will benefit those who manage their own tax-deferred retirement accounts, including the ones offered through TIAA-CREF, and increase the understanding of most people planning for retirement. You may find that this book becomes the most dog-eared and consulted book on your bookshelf.

Several people deserve a healthy share of the credit for my completing this work but none bear the responsibility for whatever errors may have crept into it. Henry Levin and Larry Cuban, longtime colleagues, have provided insightful comments on drafts of this work. Li Ping, a Visiting Scholar from Beijing University, provided valuable technical assistance in preparing this manuscript for publication. One of my sons, Brian, recently completed a program in financial planning at the University of California, Santa Cruz, and has made significant contributions to this book.

"Believe nothing, no matter where you read it or who has said it, not even if I have said it, unless it agrees with your own reason and your own common sense."—Buddha

INTRODUCTION

A Preview of Retirement

The estimates done by the pros typically assume your assets will get a certain average return, that you'll get a certain percentage each year—and that may be adjusted for inflation—and that you'll live to something like your actuarial expectancy... So assuming you save a certain amount, and if *you get the assumed investment return, and* if *you don't take out too much and* if *inflation doesn't take off, and* if *you don't get a horrible disease, and* if *you die on schedule, you'll be okay.*

—Crenshaw (2006)

Anything that's possible is inevitable!

On the final leg of my journey, I feel like I have just spent the past 10 years in a Las Vegas casino playing roulette. I no longer control my fate; the croupier does, with every spin of the strangest roulette wheel I have ever seen. Each of the black and red numbers on the roulette wheel represents a risk one might face during retirement. Whenever the silver ball stops on a number that I have selected, the croupier hands me a white risk card. On the first spin, the ball rolls round and round and lands on red 6. The croupier hands me a white risk card. I turn it over; in bold black letters, I see the following:

You face bear markets and lower returns in the future.

I flinch because my silver ball landed on one of the most dreaded risks in retirement. It's time to meditate and repeat my mantra. (Yes, I live in California.)

I retired on January 1, 2000, one of the worst times in market history. For the first three years of my retirement, the stock market dropped—10.6% in 2000, 11% in 2001, and 21% in 2002. A bear market at the outset of retirement substantially increases the odds of your going broke before meeting your Maker. In reality, your pension pot shrinks even more than the market declines suggest. Why? You are no longer contributing money to your account and buying shares at lower prices. Instead, you are withdrawing money from it and selling shares at lower prices. As a result, less money will be available to earn returns when the market recovers as it did beginning in 2003.

Fortunately, my retirement suffered little, if any, shrinkage during this period. By the time I retired, I had placed most of my retirement savings in the TIAA Traditional Account. It had positive returns during this three-year period. Besides this good fortune, I did not begin withdrawals from my Teachers Insurance and Annuity Association-College Retirement Equities Fund (TIAA-CREF) accounts until midway through the third year of my retirement. When I retired, Stanford granted me an early retirement bonus equal to two years' pay. (Nine years later, Stanford increased the bonus to three years' pay.) I managed to live for two and one-half years by using three sources of income: the bonus, Social Security, and the rent from two cottages we own.

Just when I began to relax, a second major bear market struck. By the end of 2008, nearly every asset class dropped 40% or more. Government-backed mortgages, U.S. Treasuries, and TIAA Traditional proved to be among the few safe havens. Because of the market decline, many people with 401(k) and 403(b) retirement accounts decided to delay retirement. Some retirees began to reduce their expenditures and contemplate a return to work.

The sequence of returns matters a great deal for retirees and preretirees alike. Milevsky and Salisbury (2006) show in their research

> how an early bear market during retirement can double or triple the ruin risk, compared to experiencing the same poor investment returns later on. The years just prior to retirement are equally important. Furthermore, this risk cannot be avoided by attempting to time the market nor can it be mitigated by transitioning to a conservative (i.e., bond) asset allocation. (Milevsky & Salisbury, 2006, p. 1)

By examining various return sequences throughout retirement, Milevsky and Salisbury (2006) demonstrated that the age of exhausting one's retirement assets varied by as much as 14 years. Simply by reversing two simple return sequences (−13%, +7%, +27% vs. +27%, +7%, −13%) over a retiree's lifetime, they discovered that a retiree went broke at age 81 for the first sequence and at age 95 for the second.

In another analysis, they explored how a bear market in the last preretirement year would affect how much longer a 65-year-old retiree would need to work to reach his financial goal (Table I.1). The revised retirement age depends on the severity of the bear market. For example, a retiree who suffers a loss of 10% needs to delay retirement for two years, whereas one whose portfolio drops 40% must delay retirement for five years.

Bear markets, depending on their timing, have meaningful consequences for both retirees and preretirees who learned this lesson the hard way in 2000 and again in 2008.

Your chances of encountering a bear market early in your retirement are much higher than you may imagine. Over the past

TABLE I.1
Revised retirement age for 65-year-old by bear market return the year before retirement

Investment Return Year Before Retirement (%)	Revised Retirement Age (Year)
−10	67
−30	69
−40	70

80 years, bear markets have occurred, on average, every three years according to Ned Davis Research (www.ndr.com). Since 1950, the bear has roared nine times; the declines in the stock market ranged from 20% to 49%. On two occasions the market dropped more than 30%; on two other occasions it declined nearly 50%.

Several years into my retirement, I learned that financial experts (e.g., Bogle, 2003) project lower returns from stocks and bonds in the future and offer some compelling reasons for their pessimistic forecasts. Historically, nearly 40% of the stock market total returns come from dividends, and dividends currently are near all-time lows. As for bonds, the total returns derive from interest rates (again near all-time lows) plus increases in the value of bonds. Because the value of bonds moves opposite to bond yields and interest rates are currently low, the value of bonds will decline as interest rates increase. Investors are unlikely to benefit from the strong stock and bond market returns that prevailed in the past. I have factored more conservative rates of return into my retirement planning; you should too.

Woe is me. Shortly after the end of the bear market, the croupier tosses my silver ball into the roulette wheel. The ball bounces around and eventually lands in the black 22 slot. My nemesis hands me a risk card, and I flip it over to read what appears on the back. I stare at the bold black letters and begin to sweat heavily. The fickle finger of fate has struck again.

Inflation lies ahead.

As if I didn't have enough to worry about in retirement, inflation looms around the corner. I suspected that it would hit me and other retirees harder than when we worked. Sure enough, the Labor Department's Bureau of Statistics reveals the grim picture I had expected. From December 1982 through September 2007, the Consumer Price Index (CPI)-E (for elderly) increased 124.9% compared with 108.1% for the CPI-W (for working). It seems that health-care costs have risen twice as fast as other items over the past 10 years, and the elderly spent twice as much of their income on medical costs as those still working did (Hamilton, 2007). The future for retirees drawing Medicare looks bleak. By 2025, Mulvey and Purcell (2008) expect the premiums for Medicare

Part B to rise substantially. In 2006, these premiums equaled 27% of the average Social Security benefit; they project that this percentage will rise above 50% by the year 2025.

Some experts (e.g., Phillips, 2008) question the accuracy of the U.S. government's CPI reports and accuse it of "creative" accounting. Because the CPI may vary from one locale to another, it makes sense to calculate your own personal inflation rate. You can use one of the money management software programs to set up your personal budget, monitor your expenses, and calculate the growth in your expenses for various categories (e.g., health care, housing, and transportation). With this information, you can more realistically estimate your personal rate of inflation. I use Quicken software to prepare these estimates and find them useful in planning for the future.

After stunning me with inflation, the croupier resumes his spinning. I see my silver ball roll around and eventually settle in red 28. I reach for the Excedrin as he hands me another risk card; turning it over, I see the following words:

Health problems await you.

Three years into retirement, my cardiologist delivers bad news. In somber tones, he says, "Cancel your trip to Costa Rica; I have scheduled you for a triple bypass." A month later the medical bills arrived. I stared at the figure on the bottom line; it was a staggering $137,000. Thank goodness, I had Medicare and a first-rate Medicare supplementary health plan. With only Medicare, I would be forced to pay 20% of the allowable costs and all of the nonallowable expenses. Because Medicare has no cap on how much one must pay for medical expenses in any given year, we could have found ourselves in bankruptcy court.

During my recovery, I counted my blessings and realized how fortunate my wife and I were to have purchased long-term care insurance when we turned 60. No telling what other health problems (e.g., Alzheimer's disease) might lie ahead.

My wife and I strongly support universal health care because we know firsthand the potentially devastating consequences of health problems for two of our children. Health expenses rank as a leading cause of personal bankruptcies. The leader of the Swiss government was asked this question recently, "How many people in your country declare bankruptcy due to health expenses?" He appeared startled by the question and replied, "No one; it would be a national disgrace if that happened." Personal insolvency due to health-care costs occurs in only one developed country—the United States. Until U.S. citizens become eligible for universal health care, retirees must take health care and long-term care costs into account as they plan for retirement.

Having recovered from my triple bypass surgery, I report on schedule for another spin of the roulette wheel. As I enter the casino, I mutter to myself, "Perhaps, this time I will be lucky, and the ball will land on 00 (no risks in store)." Unfortunately, the ball falls into red 26. The croupier hands me a retirement risk card that reads as follows:

The government raises taxes and reduces your Social Security benefits.

During the past few years, the U.S. government has piled up mountains of debt and a staggering trade deficit. Combine the debt and trade deficit with future commitments (Social Security and Medicare) to retirees, and we have a perfect storm brewing on the horizon. The perfect storm will leave in its wake higher taxes and/or reduced benefits, no matter which political party takes control of our government. I have already felt a bit of what lies ahead. Thus far, my Social Security cost of living increases have barely covered the increases in Medicare premiums. Many retirees with lower payments from Social Security have experienced a shortfall. The government has already begun means-testing Medicare premiums, and I fully expect that Social Security benefits will be means-tested as well. All of this reminds me of Ronald Reagan's famous quip, "The most dreaded words in the English language are, 'I am from the federal government, and I am here to help you.' " Rest assured the federal government is on its way to "help" you, and you need to plan for it.

With the future changes in the federal government's taxes and benefits in mind, I stare into the roulette wheel as the croupier resumes his spinning. When the silver ball slides into the black slot numbered 5, he hands me another retirement risk card; I flip it over and see the following words:

Financial crisis occurs.

The whole world seems to be in a financial crisis. Our government sought to avert Great Depression II by bailing out the banks and Wall Street. Interest rates plummet when the Federal Reserve lowers its short-term rates, and our country, like many others around the world, has "healthier banks and certainly poorer savers" (Editorial, 2010). I might add to this brief list poorer retirees who have counted on living off their bond yields. Before the crisis and the government's response, my bond yields were in excess of 6%. After the crisis, intermediate bond yields dropped to around 3% and short-term rates to less than 2%. This situation hurts retirees, and the Federal Reserve shows no signs of reversing its course.

Reeling from the financial crisis, I dread the next spin of the roulette wheel. Well, I should. My next retirement risk card reads as follows:

Relatives need your help.

I am now a full-fledged member of the Sandwich Generation. Early in my career, my parents needed financial assistance, and my wife and I helped them. Much later in life, two of our children experienced health problems and required our financial assistance. We are fortunate that we could provide it; at the same time, it wasn't something that we had planned for when I thought about retiring. Some retirees will be unable to provide such assistance; others might have been able to do so if they had planned for it; still others might be able to provide it but refuse. If you want to have the option of assisting your family in a time of need, plan for it before your silver ball lands on this number. By all means, prepare a will; if you have a sizable estate, work with an attorney to prepare a revocable living trust (see chapter 29).

It's time for another spin, and the croupier obliges me. He stares into the roulette wheel to see where my silver ball has landed, shakes his head, and then hands me a retirement risk card.

Large unexpected purchases await you.

During my working years, we often made large purchases such as a new car, a new roof for the house, a major remodel of the kitchen, or a new refrigerator. When I considered whether to retire, I failed to factor large purchases into my retirement planning; unfortunately, my financial planner didn't alert me to the problem either. Subsequently, I learned that many retirees overlook the need to plan for these purchases before retiring. Since retiring, I have made some major purchases—new furnace, new car, new paint job for the house, and bedroom remodel. To finance these purchases, I have withdrawn more money from my retirement account than I had planned and regard as safe. Belt tightening may be in my future, and yours too, if you don't plan ahead.

By now, my head is spinning along with the retirement roulette wheel. I can't bear to watch the next spin and close my eyes. When I hear the wheel stop, the croupier grabs my hand and thrusts a card into it. I open my eyes and see the following words:

Beware of predators.

The elderly, on average, apparently are better off than their younger counterparts. As a result, con artists target seniors. These con artists take various forms—relatives, yes, I said relatives, friends, financial advisers, and the like. One of my wife's aunts signed a document without reading it; her oversight cost her dearly. She signed away her right to her husband's pension when he died. She failed to follow the advice of a former president, "Trust, but verify."

What else can befall me? The roulette wheel reveals the answer after the croupier smiles and says, "This is your *final* spin." The silver ball rests on black 30. With trepidation I take the card from the croupier and begin to read the following words:

Congratulations, expect to live a long time.

I don't know whether to laugh or cry. With all the other risks in my future, now I learn that I must maintain my standard of living for 25–30 years. It may be a long, long time before I enter the checkout line. How can I manage that financially?

Most people are like me; they underestimate their life expectancy. As a TIAA-CREF (TC) participant, you can expect to live longer than the average person in this country. Take a moment to estimate how long you expect to live; now study the life expectancy table for TC annuitants (Table I.2). Women should expect to live longer than the average ages because the life expectancies listed are gender neutral.

If you are married, the chances are much higher that one of you will live past 90 (74% to be more precise). Longevity and inflation loom as two of your greatest risks in retirement.

As I leave the casino, the croupier follows me to the door. Outside he says, "Let me give you a tip. Never overlook the possibility that your own behavior might endanger your financial future." I nod my head in agreement. Studies of investors' behavior attest to the self-defeating proclivities of the average stock fund investor. From 1986 to 2005, the average stock fund delivered an average annual return of 11.3%; during this period, the average stock fund investor earned an average annual return of only 3.9% (Dalbar, 2006). Ten thousand dollars invested in the average stock fund in 1986 grew to $85,095; the typical investor left $63,601 on the stock floor and walked away with only $21,494. Investors who chased the hot performers and sold during bear markets played the loser's game while buy-and-hold investors reaped a full measure of the market returns. The same pattern appeared when Dalbar

TABLE I.2
2005 TIAA-CREF annuitant life expectancy table (gender neutral)

Current Age (Year)	Life Expectancy (Year)
60	87.8
65	88.4
70	89.3
75	90.5
80	92.0

(2006) examined the behavior of bond investors. Long-term government bonds produced a healthy 9.7% annual return, whereas the average investor in bonds eked out only a 1.8% annual return. Investors can't control the sequence of returns, but they do have control over their own behavior if they can learn to resist the tugs and pulls of the evil emotional twins—greed and fear.

Apparently, most TC participants have not succumbed to greed and fear. They seldom made changes to their portfolio holdings (Swensen, 2005). I suspect they, like me, were often too preoccupied with their careers and families to concern themselves with the ebb and flow of the market.

Dealing With These Uncertainties

Confronted with all these uncertainties, one can easily become depressed and decide not to retire. However, some forge ahead confident they can deal with the uncertainties. What do they do?

Rely on the Mutual Fund Industry

When I began saving for my retirement, my employer offered only one option—TC. I remained with this investment company throughout my career. I never questioned the integrity of this company or doubted that it was acting in my best interests. However, when I retired, I discovered that withdrawing money from TC to finance my retirement created a host of challenges and frustrations. You will learn more about this later in the book.

Since 1964, the year I began saving for retirement, the mutual fund industry, with a few exceptions, has been transformed from a client-centered profession serving the interests of the investor to a marketing business focused on salesmanship (Bogle, 2005). Now owned by conglomerates, the emphasis has shifted to creating and selling products that generate a profit for the corporation. As a result, investors have one chance in seven of owning a fund whose returns parallel those of the U.S. stock market. When I started saving for retirement, investors had much better odds—three of four.

What accounts for this underperformance compared with the past? According to Bogle (2005), there are several reasons, most notably the following:

- Soaring portfolio turnover (from 17% to 112%), meaning mutual funds now hold the average stock for an average of 11 months versus six years in 1945–1965
- Skyrocketing operating expenses that on the average have doubled the costs of investing

Unless investors are careful, they may wind up socking their money away in a mutual fund company that services their interests the way one critic describes as "Bonnie and Clyde serviced banks." As for me, I will stick with companies with a solid, long-term reputation for looking out for the interests of their clients.

Go It Alone

Over the years I've heard people say, "I prefer to manage my own investments even if it costs me money." Unfortunately, it does. As we earlier pointed out, many investors lack an understanding of investing and let their emotions rule their judgment. At times, greed overtakes them, and they chase the hot performers. At other times, fear overwhelms them, and they sell shares when they should have been buying more of them. As I have learned through my study of behavioral finance, this pattern of buying into rising markets, selling when markets fall, and repurchasing shares long after the market has risen is a common one. Consequently, the annual returns for individual investors have been far below what the market returned, as shown repeatedly in the research on investor behavior (e.g., Bogle, 2005; Creech, 2005; Dalbar, 2006).

Follow the Media

Because most investors lack knowledge of investing, they are inclined to do as I did. I obtained much of my investing information, better yet "misinformation," from television, media articles, investment newsletters, and analyses from the so-called financial gurus. Whenever I followed their advice, I often regretted it. Over time

I discovered that these false prophets are in bed with the media. The media lend these fortune-tellers a strong measure of credibility. One day, they feature the top performer in one or more sectors of the market; the next day, it is the market timer who called the most recent bear market. The media insist that these gurus tantalize viewers with a few hot sectors of the market or stocks on the move with the usual disclaimers about any potential conflicts of interest. An uninformed listener erroneously concludes that these so-called experts are bona fide fortune-tellers and acts on their recommendations. Volumes of research debunk forecasts that rely on technical analysis and attribute occasional investment home runs to luck, not expertise. Even stopped clocks are right twice a day. One correct prediction does not make someone a reliable forecaster.

Bear in mind that the financial media benefit from leading the investment public to believe that they are a credible source of the latest information. They appeal to the naiveté, greed, and fears of investors; those who succumb to this appeal rarely benefit from the advice. Don your skeptical hat whenever you hear one of these gurus advising you to place your bets.

A Better Way: Educate Yourself

When I finally realized that the options I had tried were as risky as the uncertainties I was trying to manage, I decided to educate myself about the risky business of investing and retirement planning. In schooling myself, I adopted the mindset that I had used as a social scientist for the past 46 years. I distinguished between fact and opinion and scrutinized the evidence behind every author's claims; moreover, I searched for research that might corroborate or refute these claims. In the process, I learned a great deal about the route I should have taken to retirement from the time I accepted my first academic appointment to the time I submitted my intention to retire. Join me as I relive my long journey, so that you may avoid my wrong turns and succeed in reaching your ultimate destination, a worry-free retirement, despite the risks and uncertainties you will surely face when you retire.

It's very hard to make predictions, especially about the future.
—Yogi Berra

Worksheet: Risk Analysis

As you approach retirement, you may wish to inventory the risks you may face in the future and assess their probability, as well as the magnitude of the personal impact. To facilitate your risk analysis, we have prepared a chart that lists the possible risks and asks you to estimate the probability and the severity of the impact on you and/or your beneficiaries. When you have completed this chart, consider how you may mitigate those risks with a high impact/high probability (Scatizzi, 2010), as well as those with a high impact regardless of the probability level.

Risk	Probability (High, Moderate, Low)	Personal Impact (High, Moderate, Low)
Bear Markets Immediately Prior to Retirement or After Retiring		
Lower Returns From the Stock Market		
Inflation		
Health Problems		
Higher Taxes		
Reduced Social Security Benefits		
Lower Bond Yields		
Relatives Needing Financial Assistance		
Large Unexpected Purchases		
Living a Long Time in Retirement		
Exhausting Financial Assets Prematurely		
Predators		

When you have completed the chart using admittedly crude measures of probability and personal impact, circle the risks with the highest probability and/or personal impact. As you read this book, actively look for ways that you can mitigate these risks. Bear in mind that some of these risks may be beyond your control.

PART ONE

Saving for Retirement

This section contains 10 chapters. When you finish reading these chapters, you will have an understanding of how to create a savings plan, set a savings goal, choose your investment vehicles, build an investment portfolio, and choose the types of investment vehicles that warrant inclusion in your portfolio. This section should be of special interest to early and mid-career professionals working in higher education institutions, as well as those nearing or in retirement who lack knowledge of investing.

Subsequent sections of the book foreshadow the consequential decisions, perils, and opportunities facing those contemplating retirement. When I began my career in higher education, my own retirement planning would have benefited greatly from knowing what lay ahead. Hopefully, by recounting my own past, I will enable professionals at any stage of their career to chart a brighter future for themselves and their families.

CHAPTER ONE

Getting There

A LOOK IN THE REARVIEW MIRROR

I see a winding road with hills and valleys behind me.

During most of my working years I was a disciplined saver for retirement. To be sure, I confined my savings to setting aside part of my salary in the 403(b) plan provided by my employers. Today that's called putting your retirement savings on autopilot. After a few years on automatic pilot, I ratcheted up my savings 1% a year until I reached 12%. Vanguard refers to this as a SMarT program, Save More Tomorrow. No one told me to do this; it seemed like the right thing to do in view of my tendencies to spend nearly everything I earned. Financial experts advise you to create a budget and live by it. Realizing that was easier said than done, I decided to protect myself and my family against my worst urges—the urge to spend most of what I earned and sometimes more. Autopilot savings and my own SMarT program literally and figuratively saved the day.

My employers (Washington University in St. Louis, The University of Chicago, and Stanford University) also contributed a healthy proportion of my income to my 403(b) account. For 33 years they contributed 10% of my annual income. Combined with what I had been contributing, the total amount of money that went into my retirement account equaled 16%–22% of my income. I later learned that financial experts recommend 15% annually if you intend to maintain a standard of living similar to the one you enjoyed when you worked.

Although my employers and I set aside money each year for my retirement, I, like most ordinary citizens, hadn't projected how much money I might need later and whether I was saving enough to meet the needs of me and my family. Moreover, the only things I knew about investing were the distinctions between a stock and a bond and between a load fund that charges a sales fee and one that doesn't, a no-load fund. As you will discover, that led me to make mistakes, and some were whoppers. But before getting to these valleys in my winding road to retirement, I'd like to begin on a more positive note—the hills.

The Hills

Without a doubt the most important contributors to my final destination were the aforementioned autopilot savings plan, my SMarT program, and the generous contributions from my employers, as well as my participation at a relatively early age (30 years). Even if you know as little about investing as I did, these four factors will stand you in good stead when you come face to face with retirement. With only a limited knowledge of investing, you can build a fat nest egg due to the magic of compounding.

Parenthetically, if you are fortunate enough to start investing during an extended bear market, your nest egg will grow even more. T. Rowe Price conducted a recent study that vividly demonstrates the powerful effect of starting in a bear market versus a bull market (Mont, 2009). Investors who began investing in 1929 and 1970 (bear markets) had accumulated nearly twice as much in their retirement accounts than those who started building their nest eggs during strong bull markets (1950 and 1979). Bear markets enable investors to purchase more shares at lower prices.

In addition to the four factors I mentioned earlier, I also benefited from the investment options that my employers provided. Every one of them used Teachers Insurance and Annuity Association-College Retirement Equities Fund (TIAA-CREF), a nonprofit provider. TIAA-CREF offered low-cost investments, which meant that most of the money in my retirement account was working for me. At the time, I didn't realize the importance of investment costs and could easily have wound up in investments that fattened the retirement accounts of the fund managers rather than mine.

TIAA-CREF benefited me in another way. Its retirement plan at the time consisted of only two investment options, so I wasn't paralyzed by a huge array of good and bad choices that are increasingly typical. Moreover, I decided to invest half of my contributions in each fund (actually they were low-cost annuities, something I hadn't noticed at the time). Without realizing it, I had developed a simple, low-cost portfolio, the type of portfolio which John Bogle, the founder of Vanguard and champion of the small investor, recommends. When spinning my preretirement roulette wheel, the odds certainly were with me.

At the end of each year TIAA-CREF mailed me a report showing how much my employer and I had contributed that year, what the balance was in each of my two funds, and how much I would receive in retirement if I continued my current contributions until age 65. Frankly, I just glanced at the report and filed it away. Occasionally, I would take note of the fact that there was much more in my stock fund than my fixed-income fund. For some inexplicable reason, I decided to equalize the amount in each fund when the amount in the stock fund was twice the amount in the bond fund. After I retired, I learned that my actions resembled rebalancing, a technique that limits your risk and increases your returns.

During the 33 years that I contributed to TIAA-CREF, I estimate that my annual internal rate of return was a little over 9%. Moreover, the return per unit of risk was quite high because the volatility of my portfolio was low to moderate due to half of it being invested in a stable-value fund like TIAA Traditional.

Before turning to the valleys, two other factors warrant mentioning. My wife and I financed the education of our four children. We were assisted by Stanford University's tuition benefit program—half of Stanford's tuition could be used to offset the cost of any accredited university's tuition. To cover the rest of the tuition, as well as the room and board, we borrowed the money. I later learned that borrowing made more sense than reducing retirement savings in order to set aside money for college (Fahlund, 2006). If you cut back on saving for retirement, you sacrifice the magic of compounding. Besides, you can borrow to finance college, but you can't borrow to finance your retirement.

Finally, our current home that we bought in 1974 with a 100% loan from Stanford University has figured prominently in financing our retirement and providing a cushion. Our 95-year-old home could star in the movie *The Money Pit*. Over the years we have spent substantial sums of money to remodel our historic home and the two rental cottages on our property. We considered these expenditures as investments that would provide income during retirement. They have.

The Valleys

Like so many young investors, I didn't understand the magic of compounding and didn't start saving for retirement until age 30. My wife and I graduated from college at the age of 20. If we had begun saving 10% of our income that year (roughly $600), continued saving that amount for only nine more years, and earned 9% until I retired at age 65, our retirement account would be nearly $186,000 greater. Starting a retirement savings program early really pays dividends. Too bad I didn't know that at the time.

My retirement portfolio also suffered from my ignorance of investing and conservative investment philosophy. If I had created an investment portfolio using a simple rule of thumb like 100 – your age in stocks, at age 30 I would have invested 70% in stocks, rather than 50%. Over time the more aggressive investment strategy would have made a substantial difference in how much we accumulated in our 403(b) account. I don't have the heart to calculate what might have been; it would simply be too painful.

Even though TIAA-CREF later increased its investment options, I didn't bother to examine any of these in depth. In retrospect, I regret not looking more closely at my options. One of the added options was Social Choice, a balanced fund consisting of 60% in stocks and 40% in bonds. Fifteen years before I retired, Stanford University offered a new fund family, Vanguard. Faced with so many investment options, I didn't bother to examine it and missed the opportunity to invest in an even better balanced fund, Vanguard Wellington, which I now own. Sometimes I think hindsight is a curse, but if others can benefit from my mistakes, my hindsight becomes your blessing.

For the “fixed” income fund in my simple portfolio, I chose TIAA Traditional, a stable-value fund as I recently discovered, instead of a bond fund. Although TIAA Traditional is an excellent fund with a guaranteed principal and interest rate plus dividends, it is subject to a number of restrictions. I invested too heavily in this fund, and it limited my ability to create a less conservative portfolio reflecting my newly acquired knowledge of investing and retirement planning.

I also regret using about 5% of my retirement portfolio to invest in narrow and risky sectors of the market—gold and technology. Yes, I was occasionally guilty of chasing the hot performers and lost money when I could have been making money following my Steady Eddy strategy. I learned firsthand the importance of having a simple investment strategy and following it even when the *greed* goblins whisper otherwise.

In last place on my list of regrets is my failure to establish a Simplified Employee Pension Individual Retirement Account (SEP IRA) for my self-employment income. I could have saved 10% of my consulting income over time and never missed it. Now I miss it, and it’s too late.

Conclusion

Although I reached my destination better off than most, I fully realize that my fate could have been much worse or much better. Through ignorance and inertia, I failed to capitalize fully on the opportunities that came my way. Hopefully, my look into the rearview mirror will spare you some of the pain I experienced when you look into yours.

CHAPTER TWO

How Much Do I Need to Save?

At least one-third of the faculty members in higher education do not have a good idea of how much they need to accumulate for retirement. Many college and university faculty members underestimate the amount of replacement income they will need in retirement.

—Yablonski (2006)

A sound retirement savings program should focus on adequate savings rates and early participation. These features are, if anything, more important and less risky than a program that encourages participants to chase investment returns.

—Hammond & Richardson (2009)

At some point during my late forties I asked myself, "How much money would I like to have in my retirement account when I retire?" After a long pause, I muttered something like, "One million dollars sounds about right." Not once did I consider whether this sum represented a realistic goal or whether it would prove to be an adequate amount for me and my wife to maintain our current standard of living. Later while talking to colleagues and friends, I learned that they had not devoted much time to setting a realistic goal either. It appears that we are not alone; less than half of the workers surveyed by the Employee Benefit Research Institute had tried to calculate how much they needed to save for retirement (Ruffennach, 2009). They, like me, guessed how much they might need.

Fortunately, we have entered the information age, and we now have access to the Internet. To set a realistic savings goal for retirement, we can use the "Determine how much to save" calculator on the Vanguard website. This useful calculator takes into account your age, current retirement account balance, and monthly savings to project your balance at age 65 and monthly withdrawal amount. The projection includes the underlying assumptions and a tutorial about the value of starting early to save. In addition, the website features a chart with a suggested lifetime savings rate for different income levels ($25,000–$150,000) and ages (27–47). The assumptions built into this calculator are worth reading.

To illustrate how this calculator might be used, I created two different scenarios based on my situation at age 30, the first year I contributed to my retirement account.

Current age: 30

Current salary: $10,500

Current account balance: $0

Monthly savings: $131 (15% of salary, including the 10% contributed by my employer)

The calculator projected my balance at age 65 in today's dollars to be $119,699 and a monthly withdrawal rate of $399, roughly 45.8% of my current salary. Retirement experts recommend a replacement rate of 75%–80%. If I assume that Social Security will replace 30% of my income, I move to the low end of the recommended range.

Not fully satisfied with the outcome, I decided to increase my monthly savings rate to $175 (20% of salary, including the 10% contributed by my employer). When I ran the new projection, I learned that my account increased to $159,903 in today's dollars and my monthly withdrawal increased to $533. My revised monthly withdrawal rate climbed to 61% of my current salary which, when combined with Social Security, brought my replacement rate to 91%, a more satisfactory outcome. The Social Security Administration annually provides you with your projected income in retirement; you can combine this information with the results of the Vanguard calculator to obtain a somewhat more accurate estimate of your future situation.

I found this calculator easy to use; moreover, it provided a more realistic estimate of how much I should save for retirement than the number I plucked out of thin air at age 30. In retrospect, this number should have been 20% of my then current salary, not the 15% I chose. However, this calculator did not take into account my personal circumstances. At age 30, I was supporting my wife, three children, and my mother. I felt strapped financially, and it seemed to make sense for me to adopt the Save More Tomorrow (SMarT) program. Consequently, I vowed to set aside 1% of future salary increases and continue that until I reached the maximum allowed by the federal government. You may find yourself in the same position and shouldn't feel guilty about postponing larger contributions.

As your salary increases, you should rerun the Vanguard calculator with the new information to assess where you are. If you discover that you are falling short of your goal, you should consider increasing your contributions, rather than becoming one of the many American workers (80%) approaching retirement who don't contribute the maximum to their defined-contribution plans (Ruffennach, 2009).

Many educational institutions that offer defined-contribution plans contribute roughly 5% of your income, and another 5% if you also set aside 5% of your income for retirement. I took advantage of this option and automatically received a 100% return on this money—the best investment for retirement or any other purpose that I ever made. I urge you to take advantage of this wonderful opportunity as well. Many Teachers Insurance and Annuity Association-College Retirement Equities Fund (TIAA-CREF) participants do, according to a recent study by this financial services organization (Hammond & Richardson, 2009). A sample of more than 70,000 TIAA-CREF (TC) participants revealed that the average participant was on track to replace from 70% to 90% of their total income when Social Security income was included. A major factor in this relatively rosy picture for TC future retirees was the average total employer and employee contribution rate of 17%. Income replacement rates also increased when participants weighted equities more heavily in their investment portfolio, but to a much lesser extent than increasing contribution rates.

As further evidence of the important role that contributions play in your achieving a financially secure retirement, consider these two scenarios. If you invest $10,000 for 20 years and earn 6% a year, your portfolio will be worth $386,959. Fifty-two percent of that amount comes from your contributions and 48% from market returns (Aim, 2009). In the highly unlikely event that your portfolio earns 12% instead of 6%, the value of your portfolio leaps to $832,623 (Aim, 2009). Even in this scenario, more than one-quarter of the ending value of your portfolio comes from your contributions. Most likely, you will be able to replace a large proportion of your total income in retirement through your contributions, not market returns, as the TC study of 70,000 participants also showed.

If you wish to save more for retirement and can, look into the 457(b) plan. Many colleges and universities now offer this plan because it enables employees to double their tax-deferred contributions. Although you still must pay the 7.65% FICA (Medicare and Social Security) tax, you can defer state and federal taxes on your 457(b) contributions. Moreover, you can delay paying taxes on the contributions and earnings until you take distributions. 457(b) plans are subject to the IRS minimum distribution requirements at age 70 1/2; however, withdrawals are not subject to the IRS 10% penalty for early withdrawals. Much to my regret, I did not have the opportunity to take advantage of this plan because I retired one year before the United States Congress enacted the legislation. If you decide to save more for retirement as your financial situation improves, the 457(b) plan enables you to increase your tax-deferred contributions. As we have shown, saving more pays off, especially in an era projected to generate below average returns on stocks and bonds.

TIP!

Use the form in Appendix P to perform an annual review of your savings and retirement plan to determine whether adjustments in your contributions and planning seem warranted. Place a recurring reminder on your calendar to perform this annual review.

CHAPTER THREE

Do Investment Costs Matter?

You get what you don't pay for.

—John Bogle (2005)

Now that you have settled on your savings goal, you are ready to shop for your investment vehicles. When you begin your search, you should look for investment vehicles with low initial costs and operating expenses, just as you would when shopping for a car. Few investors do. At a recent biweekly meeting of our retired old men eating out (ROMEO) group, one of my friends confided to me during a discussion about investing, "Ed, I never bothered to look at the operating expenses of a fund until you brought it to my attention."

Subsequent to my meeting with the ROMEO group, I spoke about planning for a secure retirement, and midway through the talk I said, "Raise your hand if you know what the operating expenses are for your mutual funds." No one did, and I confessed to the group, "Before undertaking my self-study of investments, I didn't pay any attention to investment expenses either."

Apparently we aren't alone. Three Ivy League professors studied the investing behavior of Harvard and Wharton students (MBA and undergraduates) with above average financial literacy (Hulbert, 2006). When given a choice among four S&P (Standard & Poor's) 500 index funds and information about their portfolios and fees, these students paid much higher fees than were necessary. Their indifference to investment fees inevitably would lead to lower returns because the stock portfolios were the same. The law of simple arithmetic embodied in this equation tells it all:

$$\text{Your return} = \text{market return} - \text{expenses}$$

Cost Matters

In one of his numerous writings on investment, Bogle (2005) advanced the CM Hypothesis (Cost Matters Hypothesis or CMH for short). The effect of expenses starts small but with the magic of compounding becomes substantial. After one year, fund costs explain only 0.5% of returns. By the fifth year, fund expenses explain 12.9% of returns. In 15 years, the effect of fund expenses on returns rises to 36%. Investment costs do indeed matter; they are the *single best predictor* of returns.

Costs come in lots of different flavors and are hazardous to your financial health. Let's look at some of the costs that you might face:

- Adviser fees (1%–2%)
- Annual sales load or redemption fee (1%–8%)
- Total expense ratios (1.28%, the average for large-cap blend funds)
- 12b-1 fee (for the fund company to advertise)
- Transaction costs (turnover of holdings)

The future returns for the market are projected to be much, much lower than the ones enjoyed by investors in the 1980s and 1990s. Bogle, one of the most trusted men on Wall Street, projects a 6.3% annual return for a 60% stock/40% bond portfolio (Bogle, 2003). If he is correct, costs matter even more than in the past two decades. For example, let's assume Bogle is right and examine the effect of costs on returns for several different expense scenarios. Glance at Figure 3.1, and you will quickly note how returns decrease as expenses increase. Regardless of whether Bogle's forecast is right or wrong, cutting investment costs represents a sensible strategy for increasing your returns.

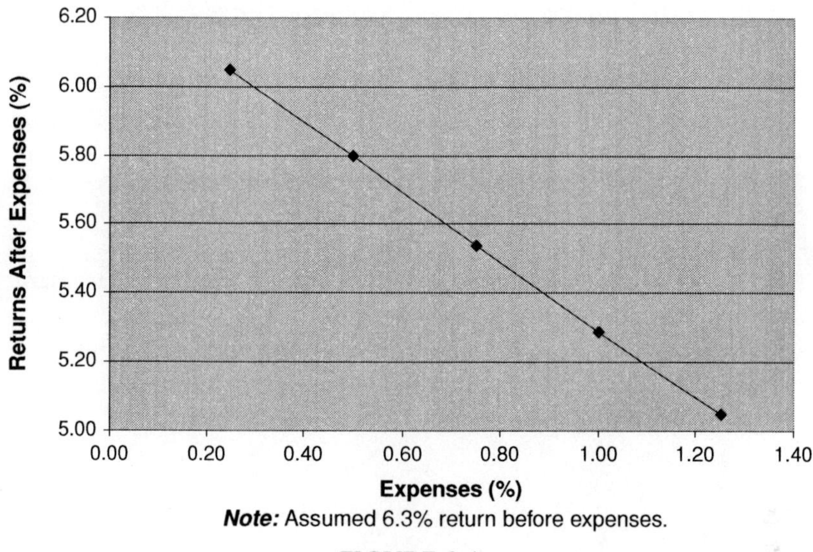

Note: Assumed 6.3% return before expenses.

FIGURE 3.1

Effect of mutual fund expenses on returns.

Impact of Costs on Income

To appreciate more fully the impact of investment costs in retirement, let's consider the potential effects on the income derived from one's investments. According to Bogle (2005), costs affect the income derived from stocks, bonds, and cash as follows:

1. Dividend income from stocks: Investment costs can consume anywhere from 7% to 225% of dividend income depending upon the mutual fund selection.
2. Yield from bonds: The average bond fund consumes 20% of the income (assumed yield of 4.5%) versus 3% for bond index funds.
3. Dividends from money market funds: Investment costs can consume 8%–38% of your dividends depending on your choice of funds.

By investing in lower cost mutual funds you can achieve the same returns with lower risk than if you had invested in higher cost funds with higher risk. In other words, if you invest in lower cost mutual funds, your returns for a 50/50 stock/bond portfolio will equal the returns of higher cost funds invested in a 75/25 stock/bond portfolio. That means you can lower your risk without sacrificing returns by simply lowering your investment costs.

Impact of Costs on Wealth Accumulation

To assess the impact of costs over time, I ran two scenarios with Jim C. Otar's Retirement Calculator software program. This retirement program uses 100 years of market data and inflation rates. Each scenario featured the same assumptions with one exception—the fees. For the two scenarios, I included the following assumptions:

- Age: 30
- Retirement age: 70
- Initial nest egg: $7,500
- First year contribution: $7,500
- Three percent annual increase in contributions
- Sixty percent in stocks and 40% in nominal bonds

The two scenarios differed 0.50% in annual fees. The program generated three different outcomes for each scenario—unlucky, median, and lucky. I have reproduced the results for the two scenarios in Table 3.1.

Lower fees pay dividends in several ways. The total accumulation for the lower cost investment surpasses that of the higher cost investment for all three outcomes—unlucky (below average returns), 9.3%; median (average returns), 9.2%; and lucky (better than average returns), 11.2%. When we translate these differences into monthly payments based on an initial "safe" withdrawal rate of 4% increased annually for the rate of inflation, the differences are dramatic. If you fall into the unlucky category, you receive an

TABLE 3.1
Portfolio value at age 69 for lower cost and higher cost investments

Cost Investments	Unlucky	Median	Lucky
Lower Cost Investments	$704,696	$1,452,504	$2,489,377
Higher Cost Investments	$644,700	$1,330,166	$2,238,343

initial monthly payout rate that is $200 greater for the lower cost investment. If you receive a median outcome, your monthly payout differential climbs to $408. Finally, if the odds fall in your favor and you enjoy the lucky outcome, your monthly payout shoots to $837 more than the higher cost investment. We only assumed a difference in fees of 0.50%; imagine what the payout differences might have been if we had assumed even greater disparities in the investment fees. To repeat what John Bogle maintains, "You get what you don't pay for."

Costs and Sustainability of Retirement Assets

If you still harbor some doubts about the importance of costs, let's look at their effects on the duration of your retirement assets. Vanguard makes a persuasive case when it comes to investment costs and the sustainability of your retirement account:

1. Most studies of withdrawal rates from retirement accounts find that an initial withdrawal rate of 4%–4.5% adjusted annually for inflation has a low likelihood of depleting the account before the retiree dies.
2. Initial withdrawal rates of 5% or more run the risk of exhausting the retirement account before the retiree dies.
3. The studies that seek to determine relatively "safe" withdrawal rates fail to account for investment costs; thus, they err on the optimistic side. Let's assume that retirees follow these guidelines, withdraw 4.5% the first year from their account, and incur investment costs of 1.5% of their assets. These retirees have inadvertently crept into the danger zone; their withdrawal rate represents an equivalent of 6% (4.5% plus 1.5%), an amount far in excess of a "safe" withdrawal rate.
4. Because investment costs threaten the sustainability of a retirement account over the lifetime of retirees, they must and can reduce this threat by lowering their costs.
5. If retirees encounter a bear market early in retirement, as happened to those retiring in 1968, 1973, or 1999, high

investment costs combined with early erosion of capital create a potentially lethal combination.

Costs and Estates

Finally, costs affect the size of your estate. If you want to leave more for your children and grandchildren, reduce your investment costs. Vanguard reports that a lower cost investor who retires at age 60 with a quarter of a million-dollar portfolio and withdraws 4% each year will have a balance of $283,094 at age 85 compared with $172,807 for a higher cost investor.

Conclusion

Numerous studies have shown that costs matter to investors, especially retirees. By limiting investment costs, retirees can lower their risk, increase their total returns, accumulate more wealth, and enjoy higher annual income from stock dividends, bonds, and money market funds. Moreover, they can reduce the risk of outliving their retirement accounts and leave more for their heirs. Costs are hazardous to your financial health, and it is imperative that you choose investments with low fees. In real estate, it is location, location, and location; in mutual funds, it is low costs, low costs, and low costs.

Worksheet: Fund Expense

You can obtain information about sales loads, redemption fees, total expense ratios, 12b-1 fees, and turnover on Yahoo.com by following these steps:

1. Go to Yahoo.com
2. Click on "Finance" www.finance.yahoo.com
3. Enter the ticker symbol of the mutual fund in which you are interested.
4. Click on "Profile."
5. Look under "Fund Operations" for information about turnover—the higher the turnover, the higher the transaction costs. Compare this figure with the average for the Category (similar funds).
6. Look under "Fees & Expenses" for information about the total expense ratio, the 12b-1 fee, front-end sales load, and deferred sales load. Compare reported information with the average for the Category (similar funds).

I look for mutual funds with expense ratios that are at least 50% below the average, turnover rates less than 50%, and no sales loads, redemption fees, or 12b-1 fees.

Name/ticker symbol of fund________________________

Check all that apply:

__Turnover less than 50%

__Expense ratio at least 50% below average—the lower the better

__No 12b-1 fee

__No front-end sales load

__No deferred sales load

__No adviser management fee

CHAPTER FOUR

Should I Invest in Index or Actively Managed Funds?

Once you have adopted cost as a major factor to consider when choosing your investment vehicles, you need to bear a few additional factors in mind. Investing is a risky business. An effective way to reduce risk is to buy mutual funds rather than individual stocks (certificates of ownership of a corporation) or bonds (certificates of corporate debt obligations). Mutual funds provide access to investment pools of stocks, bonds, or both. They can provide diversification *within* and *among* investment portfolios. When you shop for mutual funds, you will discover, as I did, that there are cap-weighted index mutual funds, dividend index funds, fundamentally weighted index funds, exchange-traded funds (ETFs), and actively managed mutual funds. Because cap-weighted index funds and actively managed funds have the longest and most-studied track records, I choose to ignore the rest. If you are curious about the recent wrinkles to index investing, take a look at Sonya Morris's (2006) piece, *What's the right way to index?*

Index funds, according to Bogle (1999), invest fully in a particular segment of the market. The oldest and most well-known index fund is Vanguard's S&P (Standard & Poor's) 500; it replicates the

S&P 500 Composite Stock Price Index. Stocks with the largest capitalizations are heavily weighted in this index; the current top five holdings are Exxon Mobil, Microsoft, General Electric, JPMorgan Chase & Co., and Procter and Gamble Co. Actively managed mutual funds try to beat the market through security selection and market timing.

Research consistently shows that index funds, on the average, outperform actively managed funds. Moreover, this pattern applies to domestic and international mutual funds alike, including large-cap funds, mid-cap funds, long-term government bond funds, and mortgage securities funds. For example, 88% of managers of emerging market mutual funds failed to beat the index over the past five years (Kollmeyer, 2006). There are numerous reasons for this consistent pattern. Index funds remain fully invested at all times, are generally more tax efficient, and have much lower operating expenses and turnover than actively managed funds.

If you went to Las Vegas and were given a choice of playing blackjack at a table where the odds were 85/15 in your favor versus a table where the odds were 85/15 against you, which table would you choose? Of course, you would play at the table with the odds stacked in your favor. Transferring from Las Vegas to Wall Street, you notice the same choice; only this time it is index versus actively managed funds. The odds are clearly in your favor if you choose index funds. You are virtually assured of capturing nearly all of the market returns and outperforming most actively managed funds.

"Wait a minute," you say. "Fifteen times out of one hundred I can actually beat the market. All I have to do is select an actively managed fund that does this. Although the odds are stacked against me in finding such a fund, surely there is a way for me to do it." I reply, "Yes, there is a way for you to increase your odds." Look for actively managed funds that have the following characteristics:

1. Low operating expenses (at least one-half of the category average—the lower the better)
2. Low turnover (preferably lower than 30%–35%)
3. Management with longevity (minimum of five years, preferably 10 or more)

4. Consistency of performance over a long period (preferably 10 years or more) relative to its benchmark in bull and bear markets

5. No extra fees (purchase, redemption, 12b-1, and load commissions)

If you look for high-performing funds without regard to the ingredients of their success (1–5 above), you may wind up with a hot-performing fund that flames out in the next market cycle.

Faced with approximately 10,000 mutual funds to choose from, how does one sort through this vast warehouse of investment opportunities? Well, the easiest way is to choose a set of low-cost index funds reflecting your risk tolerance and investment philosophy (see chapters 5 and 6). As we have mentioned elsewhere in this book, you can limit your risk by the percentage you invest in bonds. You should assume no more risk than you need to take. In retirement, *preservation takes precedence over growth.*

If you are willing to do your homework and invest in actively managed funds, you need to understand how these two types of funds can work together. Index funds generally, but not always, fall much farther in a bear market than actively managed funds while the reverse is sometimes true in bull markets. Given this pattern, you may choose to invest some of your retirement money in actively managed funds that match the five criteria cited above.

Should you choose to do the legwork necessary to find actively managed funds matching the criteria listed above, I recommend that you use the Vanguard mutual fund screening tool (see Appendix D).

TIP!

If you elect to use the Vanguard mutual fund screening tool to choose actively managed funds, follow these steps:

1. Log on to "vanguard.com."
2. Click on "Research Funds and Stocks" on the Vanguard website.
3. Click on "Mutual Fund Screener"—right-hand side of page.

4. When provided with a list of basic and additional criteria, select the following after choosing "Fund Type," "Fund Category," and "Fund Family":
   (a) Operating expenses: Check less than 0.5%
   (b) Turnover: Check less than 50%
   (c) Management tenure: Check five years, preferably 10
   (d) Total return: Check 5 and 10 years
   (e) Fees: Click on all listed (purchase, redemption, 12b-1, and load commissions)

CHAPTER FIVE

What Should My Mix of Assets Be?

The overwhelming determinant of portfolio performance is asset allocation; it dwarfs the two factors touted by many in the investment community—security selection and market timing.

With the costs of investment vehicles in mind, along with a preference for index funds, your search for specific investments begins. Investing *for* retirement, like investing *in* retirement, involves a number of important decisions. A major one I faced involved a decision about the percentage of my assets I should allocate to stocks, bonds, and cash—in short, my asset mix or allocation. To make an informed decision, I read extensively about the risks and returns of these three asset classes. The more I read, the more I realized that the risks and returns of investing are more problematic for retirees than those accumulating money for retirement. Because retirees must withdraw money to cover living expenses, they inevitably worry about the risks of inflation and volatility of returns. Unfortunately, no single asset class, as I will show, combats both of these risks. Choosing one's asset mix inevitably involves a tradeoff between increasing returns and lowering volatility. As I have learned, volatility really matters. "When stocks are blasting skyward, even the most steadfast can be sucked into the updraft. When they are cascading downward, keeping one's cool is almost impossible" (Bernstein, 2002).

Returns of Asset Classes

The annualized returns for stocks, bonds, and cash, as one might expect, differ. During the period 1926–1998, stocks were the hare, cash was the snail, and the tortoise (bonds) edged out the snail but lagged far behind the hare. In Table 5.1, note the nature of the differences for 30-day U.S. Treasury bills (our surrogate for cash), five-year U.S. Treasury bonds, large stocks, and small stocks.

Clearly stocks finished first during this period in the inflation-fighting derby, while cash and bonds trailed by a substantial margin.

Unfortunately, retirees are unlikely to receive the annualized returns reported in Table 5.1 for several reasons:

1. Annualized returns reflect the effects of compounding and assume that the investor has used dividends and interest income to purchase additional shares. By purchasing additional shares with the dividends and interest income, investors increase their returns over time. Most retirees instead of reinvesting their dividends and interest income use them to cover living expenses. As a result, their returns suffer because they do not benefit from the compounding that accrues when the dividends and interest income are reinvested. If retirees need to sell additional shares to cover expenses, they are further

TABLE 5.1
Annualized returns, 1926–1998, for Treasury bills, Treasury bonds, large stocks, and small stocks

Type of Asset	Annualized Returns (%)
30-Day Treasury Bills	3.77
Five-Year Treasury Bonds	5.31
Large Stocks	11.22
Small Stocks	12.18

Source: Bernstein (2001).

penalized. The net effect lowers the retiree's returns by approximately 0.5% annually.

2. Annualized returns assume that investors have adopted a buy-and-hold strategy. Unfortunately, few investors follow this winning strategy. Rather, they chase performance and sell when the market turns south. As a result, investors typically fall far short of the returns reported in Morningstar or Yahoo! Finance.
3. Annualized returns do not account for investment costs, a nontrivial omission as we discussed at length in chapter 3.
4. Scholars who study the market forecast much lower returns for the stock and bond market over the next decade or two. As a result, the actual returns of retirees may be 20%–30% less than those we reported for Treasury bonds and stocks.

In light of these four reasons, people contemplating retirement are well advised to use conservative estimates of returns in retirement projections. Unfortunately, most investors are likely to earn much less than the average returns recorded in the future, whatever they are.

Risks of Asset Classes

Sadly, retirees must also worry about volatility of returns and deadly drops in the market. When we consider these risks, stocks still finish first, though this time first is worst. Retirees want less of this kind of risk, not more. In Table 5.2, the volatility risk and the worst return for a single year are listed for the same time period, 1926–1998.

If you want to reduce your risk when investing, cash and bonds represent the asset classes of choice. They lower your volatility risk and limit the downside when the market drops.

Risks and Returns of Stock/Bond Combinations

To fight inflation and reduce the volatility of their investment portfolio, retirees need to invest in stocks and bonds, but how much

TABLE 5.2
Volatility of various asset classes 1926–1998

Asset Class	Risk (SD*)	Worst Return for a Single Year (%)
30-Day Treasury Bills	3.22	0.00
Five-Year Treasury Bonds	5.71	−5.13
Large Stocks	20.26	−64.23
Small Stocks	38.09	−87.98

Source: Bernstein (2001).
*SD, standard deviation, tells you how tightly your annual returns cluster around the mean. The lower the standard deviation, the more tightly the returns cluster around the mean. Sixty-eight percent of the returns will fall plus or minus the standard deviation from the mean. For example, the mean return of small stocks is 12.18%, with roughly two-thirds of the annual returns falling between + or −38.09% of the mean, and the remaining one-third showing an even greater distance from the mean.

in each is the 64,000-dollar question. Answering this question requires an understanding of the risks and returns for various combinations of stocks and bonds. In Table 5.3, we report the average annual return (1926–2008), as well as the worst annual loss, for seven different combinations of stocks and bonds.

When one examines the relationship between various stock/bond combinations and returns, annual average returns, and the worst annual loss, one begins to understand the sensibility of one rule of thumb for calculating the percentage to be invested in stocks (age in bonds, remainder in stocks). Once the percentage in stocks moves beyond 20%, the effects of one bad year in the market become evident. The worst annual losses increase

TABLE 5.3
Average annual returns and worst annual losses for different stock/bond combinations (1926–2008)

Stock (%)/Bond (%) Combination	Average Annual Return (%)	Worst Annual Loss (%)
100/0	9.6	−43.1
80/20	9.2	−34.9
60/40	8.5	−26.6
50/50	8.1	−22.5
40/60	7.7	−18.4
20/80	6.7	−10.3
0/100	5.5	−8.10

Source: Vanguard.com (2009). Model Portfolio allocations.

TABLE 5.4
Asset allocation and bear market cumulative returns

Asset Allocation Using Broad Indexes	Bear Market Cumulative Returns (%)	
	1/1/1973–12/31/1974	3/31/2000–9/30/2002
60% Stocks/40% Bonds	−25.42	−19.75
50% Stocks/50% Bonds	−21.07	−12.71
40% Stocks/60% Bonds	−16.60	−5.26

Source: Gordon, C. D., & Stockton, K. A. (2006). *Funds for retirement: The 'life-cycle' approach.* Vanguard Investment Counseling & Research.

much more than the average annual returns. Moreover, these annual losses don't take into account the withdrawals to cover living expenses.

Because most bear markets last longer than one year, the worst annual loss underestimates the potentially devastating effect of a bear market. To properly gauge the risk to one's investment portfolio, one should examine the performance of various combinations of stocks and fixed income over two or more years. Thanks to the efforts of the Vanguard Investment Counseling & Research group, we have data showing the relationship between returns and various combinations of stocks and bonds for the two multiple-year bear markets that have occurred during the past 36 years. These data are reproduced in Table 5.4.

When we consider two or more years of a bear market, the effects of different combinations increase substantially. Moving from 40% in stocks to 60% increases the loss in portfolio value from −5.26% to −19.75% in the 2000–2002 bear market, excluding the additional 4%–5% withdrawn to cover living expenses. As you increase the percentage of your portfolio allocated to stocks, expect your retirement account to shrink disproportionately when the market nosedives.

Bear Markets at the Outset of Retirement

Bear markets early in one's retirement increase the risk of going broke. Imagine the following scenario, the one facing a millionaire who retired on December 31, 1999, the date of my retirement:

Year 1

Beginning balance: **$1,000,000**

Withdrawal rate: 7%

Market performance: declined 10.57%

Year 2

Beginning balance: $824,300

Withdrawal rate: 7%

Market performance: declined 10.97%

Year 3

Beginning balance: $678,399

Withdrawal rate: 7%

Market performance: declined 20.96%

Ending balance: **$491,161**

At the end of three years, the million-dollar man has been transformed; the Incredible Hulk has become the Shrinking Man. Mr. Market and withdrawals have whittled away $571,600, and the retiree is left with only $491,161 to live on for the next 25 years. Even if the market reverses its trend and climbs 31.5% as it did the following year, the retiree's nest egg totals only $611,495 after withdrawing 7% for living expenses. This retiree bet on a highly risky mix of assets (100% in stocks) and chose too high a withdrawal rate.

The Sweet Spot

The Incredible Hulk who was transformed into the Shrinking Man had plenty of company during the 2000–2002 bear market. As I mentioned at the outset of this book, a number of my colleagues experienced substantial declines in their retirement accounts. I was more fortunate because I only had 20% of my total portfolio in stocks and experienced a modest decline of 5%. Although I slept well during this bear market, I realized that my allocation to stocks was too low to withstand the long-term erosive effects of inflation. As a result, I began the process of gradually increasing my allocation to stocks two years ago. Realizing that my wife is likely to live 20–25 more years, I am leaning toward an eventual asset allocation 100 – age in stocks and the balance in short-term and intermediate-term high-grade bonds. If I anticipated that our joint time horizon was 10 years or less, I would opt for an even smaller allocation to stocks. Given the diversified sources of income I have to finance my retirement, I do not need to assume more risk.

When considering my desired allocation to stocks and bonds, I didn't take into account Social Security, which functions somewhat like a fixed-income asset. If I had followed the advice of the pros, I would have incorporated Social Security into my asset allocation decision. The net result of adding Social Security, a company pension, or an immediate fixed-income annuity inevitably increases the allocation to stocks. Those who choose to adopt this expanded view of their portfolio when choosing their asset allocation could use the simple approach suggested by Bogle (Burns, 2003). Simply multiply your annual income from Social Security by 14 and add it to your retirement savings. Multiply the latter total by the percentage you plan to allocate to stocks. If you still remain uncertain about how to incorporate other financial assets into your portfolio, you probably should consult a fee-only planner to help you with your asset allocation decision.

As for me, I have chosen to keep it simple, assume no more risk than necessary, and select a reasonable and prudent mix of stocks and bonds without incorporating Social Security into this decision. Because asset allocation is the most important investment decision investors make, I can understand why retirees may choose to adopt an expanded view of their portfolio. Retirees who choose to follow the path I took would be well advised to consider the factors that I have taken into account: my time horizon, financial needs, personal goals, available assets, risk tolerance, and a conservative estimate of the returns to expect. In the event that future returns are 20%–30% less than in the past, as many serious students of the market forecast, I am prepared for that eventuality but, like you, not looking forward to that possibility.

Worksheet: Mix of Assets

Asset allocation is the single most important investment decision you will make. Before selecting your target asset allocation, review the historical returns and losses chart, along with John Bogle's rule of thumb.

Historical returns and losses

Stock (%)/Bond (%) Combination	Average Annual Return* (%) (1926–2008)	Worst Annual Loss* (%) (1926–2008)	Returns (%) (1973–1974 Bear Market)**
80/20	9.2	−34.9	—
60/40	8.5	−26.6	−25.42
50/50	8.1	−22.5	−21.07
40/60	7.7	−18.4	−16.60
20/80	6.7	−10.3	—

**Source:* Vanguard.com (2009). Model Portfolio allocations.

***Source:* Gordon, C. D., & Stockton, K. A. (2006). *Funds for retirement: The 'life-cycle' approach.* Vanguard Investment Counseling & Research.

John Bogle's rule of thumb: Your age in bonds.

My target asset allocation is Stocks____% Bonds____%

CHAPTER SIX

Why Should I Diversify?

> *Investment management provides only* one *dependable way to survive through uncertainty of the future:* diversification. *Diversification means owning assets that do not move up and down together—a portfolio designed to subdue volatility rather than to maximize returns while still exposing you to the widest possible range of positive opportunities.*
>
> —Peter L. Bernstein

In the preceding chapter, I discussed the critical importance of allocating investments across three asset classes (stocks, bonds, and cash). It plays an important role in managing volatility and increasing returns. In this chapter, I will show how diversifying investments *within* asset classes can also affect volatility and returns. Each of these major asset classes can be divided into a number of subasset classes.

Stocks

Stocks, like ice cream, come in different flavors. The most common subclasses of stocks are as follows: domestic (United States) and international (foreign)—roughly 50% in each category. Domestic and international stocks can further be divided by size of company (large, mid, and small) and investment style (value and growth).

Size generally refers to the level of capitalization of the company, which is determined by the number of outstanding shares times the price of each share. As for investment style, value refers to stocks with slower growth in earnings and assets exceeding liabilities while growth refers to stocks with above average increases in earnings and revenues. If one invests in these various subasset classes, they are said to be diversified. You can check your current level of diversification by going to http:///www.morningstar.com, clicking on "Tools" and selecting the "Instant X Ray" tool. This valuable tool can be used without registering or paying a fee. I have used it several times and find this tool helpful and easy to use.

Bonds

All levels of government and corporations issue bonds. These debt instruments typically are classified according to their *maturity* (short-term, intermediate-term, or long-term) and *credit quality* (low, average, and high). Maturity matters; as the maturity of a bond increases, so does its volatility. When interest rates increase, the value of the bond falls; conversely, when interest rates decline, the value of the bond rises. If you have trouble remembering how interest rates and the value of bonds behave, you may find it helpful, as I have, to think of a teeter-totter. On one end of the teeter-totter is the interest rate; on the other end is the value of the bond. When either the value of bonds or interest rates go up, the other goes down. If you stretch for higher yields, which you ordinarily receive by increasing the maturity of your bond holdings, expect to see much higher swings in the value of your bonds.

Credit quality refers to the possibility of default, that is, the issuer of the bonds will go bankrupt and be unable to redeem the bonds or pay the interest. U.S. Treasury bonds represent the highest credit quality because the investor can count on the federal government meeting its credit obligations fully; unlike corporations, the federal government can print money whenever it chooses. High yield or "junk" bonds run the greatest risk of default. I personally prefer bonds with high credit quality; that means I lean toward government-backed and high-grade corporate bonds.

Until recently, bonds provided little or no inflation protection. Several years ago, the U.S. government issued I-bonds and Treasury Inflation-Protected Securities (TIPS). Both guarantee a return that exceeds the rate of inflation; the amount the return exceeds inflation depends on the initial base rate. This base rate has fluctuated over time. Tax specialists recommend that I-bonds should be purchased for taxable accounts and the TIPS for tax-deferred accounts.

Benefits of Diversification

As you may recall, two of the major risks facing retirees are volatility risk (fluctuations of returns) and inflation risk (loss of purchasing power). Diversification can help retirees alleviate both of these risks. Diversification among and within asset classes affects the volatility and returns of an investment portfolio, because asset classes and subclasses do not usually move in lock-step with one another. For example, during the 2000–2002 bear market, value stocks outperformed growth stocks, and small-cap and mid-cap stocks outperformed large-cap stocks. By investing across these various subclasses of stocks, investors experienced lower volatility and higher returns than those who were invested heavily in large-cap growth stocks.

To more fully understand the benefits of diversification, I examined the performance data of several different asset classes and subclasses for a 20-year period (1984–2003). The seven classes included large-cap growth, large-cap value, small-cap growth, small-cap value, international, bonds, and real estate investment trusts (REITs). An REIT is a company that owns and manages income property. In chapter 9, I discuss TIAA (Teachers Insurance and Annuity Association) Real Estate, a unique variable annuity that enables investors to own a share of different kinds of property (e.g., apartments, malls, and office buildings). My analysis of the data for these seven different asset classes and subclasses follows:

- Each of the seven classes experienced losing years.
- Each of the stock classes lost money 20%–33% of the time.
- Each of the seven classes was the best performer in two or more years.
- All but two of the seven classes finished last in one or more years.

- Both of the funds that avoided finishing last experienced at least four negative years with their worst years ranging from −15.52% to −21.77%.
- All of the asset classes showed wide swings between their best and worst years (Table 6.1).

If a retiree is trying to limit volatility, preserve capital and grow it, betting on one asset class is not the way to go. Rather, one should invest in a basket of mutual funds that diversifies across all of these asset classes. Those who created an investment portfolio consisting of 15% large-cap growth stocks, 15% large-cap value stocks, 40% bonds, 10% international stocks, 10% REITs, 5% small-cap growth and 5% small-cap value stocks suffered losing years 20% of the time but never lost more than 5.70% in any one year. Moreover, the average return (11.74%) for this diversified portfolio was well above the inflation rate over the 20-year period. During this 20-year period, retirees with a diversified portfolio like this made their withdrawals for living expenses and actually increased the size of their investment portfolio.

If you are tempted to predict which stock asset class would be the best performer each year and put all of your retirement eggs in that basket, resist the temptation. No one has been able to forecast the market or performance of an asset class, whether it be stocks or bonds, with any consistency. Walk, no run, away from anyone who tells you otherwise!

Diversification has provided a systematic approach to building a retirement portfolio that has beaten inflation and reduced the volatility of returns, two major risks facing every retiree.

TABLE 6.1
Asset class performance, 1984–2003—best and worst years

	Performance (%)	
Asset Class	Best Year	Worst Year
Large-Cap Growth	41.16	−27.88
Large-Cap Value	38.35	−15.52
Small-Cap Growth	51.19	−30.26
Small-Cap Value	46.03	−21.77
International	69.44	−23.45
Bonds	22.10	−2.92
Real Estate Investment Trusts	37.04	−23.44

However, during the 2008 financial crisis, the various asset and subasset classes generally marched together. When they moved in unison, the benefits of diversification virtually disappeared. Only bonds backed by the U.S. government provided a safe haven for investors. No one knows whether the recent behavior of a diversified portfolio represents a temporary or permanent trend reversal. Therefore, I plan to stick with a broadly diversified portfolio and a sufficiently high percentage of my portfolio allocated to bonds backed by the U.S. government that I can safely sail in any direction the market winds tend to blow. Mindful of the uncertainty surrounding the future performance of diversification, I discuss more fully the ways in which asset allocation and diversification can be used to construct a retirement portfolio in the next chapter.

TIP!

When you invest in bonds, bear in mind that their total returns are influenced primarily by credit rating, type (short-, medium- or long-term), and costs. Once you have decided on the credit rating and type, look for bond funds with the lowest costs or expense ratios. If you include short-term bonds in your portfolio, investment-grade bonds produce higher returns than U.S. Treasury bonds without any additional volatility risk. However, U.S. Treasury bonds provide the greatest protection in the event another financial crisis develops. If you purchase intermediate bonds, U.S. Treasury bonds and investment-grade bonds produce nearly identical returns (Swedroe & Hempen, 2006).

Worksheet: Evaluating Your Investment Portfolio

To evaluate your investment portfolio, you will need the following information available for each of your holdings (stocks and mutual funds):

Ticker symbol

Number of shares

Value of holding

Also, have available the total you are holding in cash.

Log on to the Morningstar.com website, click on “Tools,” and click on “Instant X Ray.” After you enter the ticker symbol and the value of each of your holdings (use Cash$ as ticker symbol for Cash), you will be provided with the following information about your portfolio:

Operating expenses

Asset allocation (U.S. stocks, international stocks, bonds, and cash)

Diversification

Stocks (valuation by size)

Bonds (interest rate sensitivity and credit quality)

Sector (information, service, and manufacturing)

Log on to www.riskgrades.com, register if you haven't, and create a portfolio using the following information about each of your holdings (stocks and mutual funds):

Ticker symbol

Number of shares

You will be provided with information about the risk and return of your investment portfolio, including, but not limited to:

A risk grade—the higher the grade, the higher the risk

Type of investment strategy you are using (e.g., conservative/aggressive)

Volatility of your portfolio relative to the S&P (Standard & Poor's) 500 Index

Whether you are being adequately compensated for the risk you are taking (click on "RA" on the risk grade chart)

How risky your portfolio is relative to a sample of portfolios (click on "RR" on the risk grade chart)

With the information you have gathered, you will be able to judge if your portfolio needs to be modified.

CHAPTER SEVEN

What Investing Principles Would Serve Me Well?

Now that you understand the role that costs, allocation, and diversification play in selecting investment vehicles, you are ready to take a brief quiz on your current investment approach. Answer each of the following questions with a simple yes or no:

1. Do you own more than 10 mutual funds?
2. Do you own funds that do not fit an overall strategy?
3. Do you chase hot-performing stocks or mutual funds?
4. Do you sell when the stock market drops 15%–20%
5. Do you ignore investment costs?
6. Do you purchase stocks or mutual funds on tips?
7. Do you invest in initial public offerings (IPOs)?
8. Do you try to outsmart the market?
9. Do you invest too conservatively?
10. Do you fail to rebalance your investments annually?
11. Do you lack an investment plan?

Well, if you answered yes to the majority of these questions, you are in good company. Most investors have committed these common investment mistakes. Through my reading I have discovered that a way to avoid these errors is to use a set of proven principles when making investment decisions. I know because during my lifetime I made my decisions without such principles in mind and committed most of these mistakes. Perhaps, the most important lesson I have learned during the last few years is the importance of following these basic principles.

In this chapter, I would like to share with you the investment principles that I have gleaned from my study. In the following chapter, I will illustrate how you might implement these principles to reduce the risk of going broke if you are fortunate enough to beat the odds and live longer than you expect.

Investment Principles

As you read these investment principles, bear in mind that they assume you have established your savings goal and translated them into investment objectives.

Principle 1: *Decide on your asset allocation.* Perhaps, the most important investment decision you will make is how much of your investment portfolio you will invest in stocks, bonds, and cash. Bonds and cash lower your volatility risk and stocks combat inflation. Following the rule of 100 – age = % invested in stocks (110 – age = % invested in stocks for those who are comfortable with more risk) appears to be a sensible rule these days given the increase in life expectancy. This means if you are 35, you can invest 65% of your portfolio in stocks; if you are 70, the percentage in stocks drops to 30%. By adhering to this simple rule of thumb, 100 – age = % invested in stocks, younger persons enjoy higher returns and have sufficient time to recover from major declines in the market. Older persons have shorter time horizons and less time to recover from severe market declines; therefore, they need to limit their volatility risk in exchange for somewhat lower returns.

Principle 2: *Spread it around.* Diversify your investments in terms of investment style (growth and value), size (large cap, mid cap and small cap), and geographical location (domestic and international). Different types of investments move in and out of favor. Some years value stocks are in vogue; other times investors favor growth stocks. Sometimes domestic stocks lead the way while international stocks lag, and later the pattern reverses itself. Because no one has consistently predicted which segment of the market will flourish or flag, wise investors hedge their bets and spread their money around. In this way, investors lower their risk and increase their returns. As for bonds, investing in short and/or intermediate bonds makes sense because the main function of bonds is to lower the volatility risk of your portfolio. Lower your risk even more and protect yourself against financial crises by investing in bonds backed by the U.S. government. If you concentrate your investments in a red-hot sector of the market, you likely will regret it in the end. Those who loaded up on tech stocks in the mid- to late 1990s lost their shirts when the tech bubble burst. Diversification is one of the keys to *preserving* your wealth.

Principle 3: *Be cost conscious.* When choosing your mutual funds, select ones with below average cost and turnover of their holdings—the lower the better. Costs matter. Investors don't receive the market returns; they pocket what's left over after costs. When you shop for cars, groceries, or clothes, you look for bargains—good value at the lowest cost. Use that same mentality when shopping for investments. Costs are predictable; returns aren't.

Principle 4: *Choose funds with stable investment policies.* You can't really build a diversified investment portfolio representing various segments of the market if you can't count on the funds maintaining their investment approach. By diversifying your investments, you acknowledge that at any given point in time some segments of the market will be outperforming others. For example, you invest some of your money in a value fund, and it decides to bet heavily on growth stocks. Value stocks climb while growth stocks fall. Your value fund will lag because the fund diluted its investment strategy.

Principle 5: *Look for funds with consistent performance.* Generally, these funds will be run by managers with long tenure in their position. Moreover, these funds have finished in the top half of their category most of the time and rarely, if ever, spent time in the bottom quarter. You can find this information on the Morningstar website. Bogle encourages investors to invest in actively managed funds that have finished in the top half of their category at least 50% of the time over the past 10 years and rarely (less than three times) in the bottom quartile.

Principle 6: *Be tax efficient*. The biggest drain on your returns in a taxable account is taxes. To increase the tax efficiency of your investment portfolio, there are several steps one can take—purchase index or tax-managed funds and municipal bonds if the tax-equivalent yield is lower and place real estate investment trusts (REITs) in a tax-deferred account if you decide to invest in them. Every dollar you save in taxes guarantees an extra dollar in your pocket with no additional risk or luck involved. Look for funds with *tax-adjusted returns* that are consistently in the top half of their category (see "Tax Analysis" on Morningstar website).

Principle 7: *Rebalance*. Once you have decided on your asset allocation (mix of stocks, bonds, and cash) during the accumulation stage, you should rebalance your portfolio annually to maintain your asset allocation (see appendixes A and D). By rebalancing, over time you will lower your risk and increase your returns. Despite the ease and sensibility of this technique, most people don't do it. Swensen (2005) studied the behavior of professors investing in Teachers Insurance and Annuity Association-College Retirement Equities Fund (TIAA-CREF) and discovered that the vast majority of them didn't rebalance their portfolio. As a result, their returns suffered; by rebalancing they would have earned 8.6% annually instead of 8.2%. Though the difference seems small, over time it is significant (see Table 7.1). We learned during the 2008 meltdown in the stock market that this

TABLE 7.1
Effect of rebalancing on $100,000 investment

Annual Yield (%)	Balance: 20 Years	Balance: 30 Years
8.2—Without Rebalancing	$483,666	$1,063,697
8.6—With Rebalancing	$520,711*	$1,188,214**

*7.6% greater
**11.8% greater

failure to rebalance proved costly for those investors who had 70% or more of their portfolio in stocks.

Principle 8: *Stay the course.* Your resolve to follow the first seven principles will be tested. You can count on it. Friends or colleagues may boast about how much money they are making in ________ (fill in the blank). Some financial "guru" touts the next hot-performing stock or sector of the market on television. A segment of the market heats up and tempts you to pour money into it. The market drops a lot, and you sense your resolve ebbing. If you don't resist the powerful, emotional tugs to act, you are likely to regret it. The more volatile your portfolio, the greater the likelihood that you will abandon the course you have set so limit the volatility and stay the course.

When you follow these investment principles, they may not look good in the short run, but they will serve you well in the long run. Those who invest for the long term are called winners, particularly if they stay the course with a portfolio built on these eight investment principles.

Worksheet: Investment Principles

Through my study of investing, I have gleaned these investment principles. Which of these do you use?

__1. *Asset allocation*: I have approximately 100 − age = % in stocks. Others may be uncomfortable using this rule of thumb and prefer the "Asset Allocation Questionnaire" on www.smartestinvestmentbook.com. It takes about 10–15 minutes to complete. When I used it, the results were similar to what I allocated based on the rule of thumb.

__2. *Diversification*: I spread my investments around; they cover investment style (growth and value), size (large cap, mid cap and small cap), and geographical location (domestic and international).

__3. *Cost conscious:* My mutual funds have below average operating expenses and turnover of their holdings.

__4. *Stable investment policies:* I have chosen mutual funds that stick with their investment policies over time.

__5. *Consistent performance:* My funds have finished in the top half of their category at least 50% of the time over the past 10 years and less than three times in the bottom quartile.

__6. *Tax efficiency:* In my taxable accounts, I own funds that are consistently in the top half of their category in terms of *tax-adjusted returns* according to Morningstar. Usually, but not always, these are index funds, tax-managed funds, and municipal bond funds. If I own REITs, they are in my tax-deferred account.

__7. *Rebalancing:* Every year I rebalance my investment portfolio to its original asset allocation.

__8. *Staying the course:* When the market drops, I hang on and don't sell. I resist the temptation to chase the hot performers.

CHAPTER EIGHT

How Do I Build an Investment Portfolio?

Keep it simple.

—John Bogle

With an understanding of the role played by costs, allocation, and diversification in mind, along with the investment principles discussed in the previous chapter, we are ready to tackle the task of building an investment portfolio. There are countless ways to implement what we have learned in the previous chapters. You can do it with only one mutual fund or several funds using indexed or actively managed. As I indicated in chapter 4, actively managed funds, unlike index funds, rely on market timing and/or stock-picking prowess. Most index funds have substantially lower investment costs than actively managed funds and on average produce higher total returns as well. Retirees, as well as other investors, can be reasonably sure of matching or closely matching the returns of the market by investing in inexpensive index funds as long as they stay the course.

If you have the itch to try your luck at outperforming the market, you should scratch it with an actively managed fund that has rather consistently beaten its comparable index and mirrors the characteristics of index funds—low expenses, low turnover, and adherence to a particular investment style (e.g., large-cap value stocks). In addition, you want an actively managed fund with a long-term manager in the driver's seat who has produced consistent results. Be forewarned; even successful investors like Warren Buffett have bad years.

In the remainder of this chapter, I will illustrate a number of approaches you might implement with index funds, actively managed funds, or both.

Low Maintenance

With only one fund you can satisfy all eight of the investment principles. Investors who choose this approach have three options:

1. *Target-date retirement funds.* This type of fund represents the ultimate buy-and-forget-it approach to investing. You select a fund, actually a fund of funds, which most closely approximates your date of retirement. Over time the percentage of your investment portfolio invested in stocks declines while the percentage allocated to bonds and cash increases. You don't need to rebalance, calculate your minimum distribution requirement, or adjust your asset allocation. The fund manager handles all of these tasks for you. Investors in target-date retirement funds stay the course and receive stronger returns than investors in other types of mutual funds (Charlson, 2010).

   According to a recent study of target-date retirement funds (Lutton, 2009), Vanguard's funds ranked at the top of its class. The average annual expense ratio for its funds is 0.19%, one-fourth of the industry average; moreover, the Vanguard Target Retirement Funds have treated their shareholders to good, risk-adjusted returns.

2. *Life-cycle funds.* Like target-date retirement funds, life-cycle funds consist of a fund of funds. However, life-cycle funds tend to use a static asset allocation that does not change over time. Investors who want greater control over the risk level of their portfolio may gravitate toward a life-cycle fund. Vanguard offers four different life-cycle funds with allocations

to stocks ranging from 20%–80%. An investor, for example, might be comfortable with a stock allocation of 60% until age 80 at which time (s)he switches to a life-cycle fund with a 40% allocation to stocks. Once investors choose a life-cycle fund matching their preferred allocation to stocks, the fund manager manages the portfolio while investors savor their retirement (e.g., Vanguard LifeStrategy series of funds).

3. *Conservative to moderate allocation funds*. These funds split their holdings among stocks, bonds, and cash (in small amounts). Conservative allocation funds typically have 40% invested in stocks while moderate allocation funds have 50%–65% invested in stocks. Conservative and moderate allocation funds generally, but not always, invest in individual stocks and bonds rather than several different funds as life-cycle and target-date retirement funds do (e.g., Vanguard STAR Fund, Pan American Fund, Fidelity Asset Manager, and CREF Social Choice).

If you choose to use one of these low-maintenance funds, bear in mind that they are not all created equal. They vary in the following respects:

- Costs (operating expense ratios)
- Type of investments (index or actively managed funds)
- Quality of the underlying funds if a fund of funds
- Nature of the asset allocation (risk and level of diversification)
- Tax efficiency (if in a taxable account)

Core/Satellite

Investors who follow this approach choose core funds that consist of stocks, bonds, or a combination of stocks and bonds. These core funds should produce consistent returns relative to their peers for 10 or more years. Moreover, they should be inexpensive relative to their peers. This core generally consists of large cap or total market funds, large cap or total international funds, and short- or intermediate-term bond funds or hybrid funds containing stocks and bonds. According to Sue Stevens, a financial analyst who writes for Morningstar, the core should account for 70%–90% of one's portfolio.

Investors adhering to the core/satellite strategy have a number of choices for the satellite component.

1. Real estate investment trusts (REITs) generate above average income and total returns near stocks; they also reduce the volatility of one's portfolio because they are moderately related to stocks and weakly related to bonds.
2. Large-cap value and small-cap value stocks historically have produced higher total returns than their growth counterparts; this pattern holds for domestic and international stocks.
3. High-yield bonds, though riskier in terms of credit quality, produce higher yields than short- and intermediate-term bonds.
4. Inflation-protected securities issued by the U.S. Treasury provide a measure of protection against inflation, unlike their counterparts—bonds. A portfolio that employs the core/satellite approach might consist of the following.

Core/Satellite Portfolio: An Example

Core

Total stock market index (30%) (covers the domestic market)

Total international stock index (10%) (covers European and emerging markets)

Total bond index (40%) (intermediate-term, diversified bond fund)

Satellite

REITs (5%) (generous yield and reduces volatility of one's portfolio)

High-yield bond fund (5%) (produces high yield but with greater volatility and credit risk)

Inflation-protected securities (5%) (suitable for tax-deferred accounts and a measure of protection against inflation)

Small-cap value fund (5%) (high returns)

To ensure near market returns, one could rely on index funds for the core and use actively managed funds for the satellite in an effort to increase total returns.

Slice and Dice

Because various sectors of the market fall in and out of favor at different times, some investors prefer to position themselves to take full advantage of the returns being generated by the hot performers. The investors following this approach use separate index funds to cover each of the following: short- or intermediate-term bonds and large-cap growth, large-cap value, small-cap, small-cap value, REITs, and international stocks. This approach requires investors to overweight small-cap and small-cap value stocks in expectation of higher returns. Adherents to the *Slice and Dice* approach might have a portfolio that corresponds to the ones advocated by Schultheis (2005) or Bernstein (2002). The simplest way to implement this approach is to use the Coffeehouse portfolio (see below). This portfolio uses index funds and consists of 40% in bonds with equal percentages invested in large-cap, large-cap value, small-cap, small-cap value, REITs, and international stocks. Bernstein forms his *Slice and Dice* portfolio by varying the percentage in these sectors and dividing international stocks into European, Pacific, and Emerging Markets.

Coffeehouse Portfolio

Bond funds
Intermediate-term bonds (40%)

Stock funds
(10% in each of the following index funds)
Large cap (Standard & Poor's [S&P] 500)
Large-cap value
Small cap
Small-cap value
REITs
Total international

Source: Schultheis (2005).

All-Weather

The chief investment officer for Yale University, David Swensen, has compiled an outstanding record (16.1% annual returns) over an extended period and recently discussed his investment philosophy in his book titled, *Unconventional Success: A Fundamental Approach to Personal Investment* (Swensen, 2005). His approach addresses the following concerns of investors: need for high returns and protection against inflation, deflation, and financial crises. To tackle these concerns, Swensen recommends an investment portfolio containing domestic and foreign stocks for higher expected returns, Treasury Inflation-Protected Securities (TIPS) and real estate for combating inflation, and U.S. Treasury bonds for dealing with deflation and financial crises (see below).

Swensen Portfolio

Bond funds
U.S. Treasury bonds (15%) (highest credit rating)
U.S. Treasury Inflation-Protected Securities (15%) (highest credit rating)

Stock funds
Domestic equity (30%)
Foreign developed equity (15%) (Europe and Japan)
Emerging market equity (5%) (highly volatile with potentially high returns)
Real estate (20%) (characteristics of fixed income *and* equity)
Note: Swensen acknowledges that some investors will be more comfortable with somewhat less money invested in stocks.

Swensen goes further and urges investors to purchase low-cost index funds and avoid actively managed funds. He praises two investment companies, Vanguard and Teachers Insurance and Annuity Association-College Retirement Equities Fund (TIAA-CREF), for their commitment to clients.

Asset Dedication

Like Swensen, Huxley and Burns (2005), employ a goal-driven approach. However, their approach is much more complicated and views the functions of various asset classes quite differently—cash for emergencies, bonds for income, and stocks for growth. The amount of money invested in bonds depends on the income needed for a 5-, 7-, or 10-year period. This sum is placed in a laddered (individual bonds with increasingly longer maturities) set of AA bonds or better and is used to fund living expenses for the time period chosen. The rest, minus the cash set aside for emergencies, is invested in stocks via index funds. In an effort to further clarify the *asset dedication* approach, let me lead you through it step by step:

1. Decide on the amount to place in cash for emergencies (I assumed 9%).
2. Calculate your living expenses for the next 5, 7, or 10 years taking into account inflation (I assumed a 10-year period with 3% annual increases for inflation).
3. Purchase a laddered set of AA-rated bonds or better to cover the living expenses you calculated in #2 (that amounted to 41% of my portfolio invested in bonds).
4. Invest the rest of your portfolio in stock index funds (in my case that would be 50% with 9% in cash and 41% in bonds).

Bonds

(Percentage allocated depends on living expenses needed for the time period you have chosen)

Rated AA or better by Moody or S&P, Laddered

Index funds

(Percentage determined by adding the percentage of your portfolio allocated to bonds and cash and subtracting this amount from 100)

Invest in index funds with the best historical track record for growth over the time horizon chosen

Note: At the end of the time period you have chosen, you use the money invested in stocks to purchase a set of laddered bonds to cover your living expenses for the next time period.

There are several advantages to using the *asset dedication* approach: (a) it provides a rational way of determining how much to allocate to stocks and bonds; (b) it enables investors to reinvest their stock dividends; (c) it reduces the risk associated with a bear market at the outset of one's retirement; and (d) it reduces the potentially negative consequences of volatility during retirement. However, creating the laddered bond portfolio can be quite complex and requires the investor to use Huxley and Burns's website (http://www.assetdedication.com) to construct this portfolio. In my opinion, most investors should use a financial planner familiar with this approach to create their investment portfolio.

Safe Assets Approach

Bodie and Clowes (2003) maintain that investors should *take little or no risk with their retirement savings* at any stage of life, especially after retirement, by investing in *safe assets*. In line with this view of risk management, young investors put roughly two-thirds of their retirement savings account into low-cost index funds and the balance in TIPS. Around age 45, the entire retirement savings account is invested in TIPS and stable-value funds. If you adhered to this view of risk management, you would craft your investment portfolio as follows:

Under age 45: Total stock market index, total international index, inflation-linked bonds, and a stable-value fund like TIAA Traditional, with roughly one-third in inflation-linked bonds and a stable-value fund, and two-thirds in the stock index funds.

Over age 45: Inflation-linked bonds and a stable-value fund with the former providing more protection against inflation than the latter.

After age 45, this portfolio lacks diversification, namely in stocks which Bodie and Clowes (2003) regard as more risky and a less safe asset class.

Easy Allocator

If you still are a bit confused about building your retirement portfolio or have retirement money invested in taxable, as well as tax-deferred accounts, let me recommend that you use the following website: www.easyallocator.com. This free site draws on academic research to build investment portfolios. Moreover, it provides answers to frequently asked questions about the Easy Allocator. I suggest that you begin by reading two sections under "Frequently Asked Questions"—"How do I use Easy Allocator?" and "Core Inputs." In my judgment, Easy Allocator is especially useful for people with money invested in taxable and tax-deferred accounts and who prefer to use low-cost exchange-traded funds or index funds. Using your risk tolerance, the value of your taxable and tax-deferred retirement accounts, annual savings to retirement, and other retirement income, Easy Allocator recommends an investment portfolio, along with its investment costs, and forecasts the following:

- Returns
- Loss in year 1 and the year you retire if it occurs during a bear market
- The value of your portfolio in today's dollars the year you retire
- Your pretax and after-tax retirement income in today's dollars with an initial 4% withdrawal rate

You can use this service free of charge—a real bargain.

Conclusion

As I thought about the eight investment principles, possible ways of implementing them, and the investment mistakes mentioned in the previous chapter, it seemed to me that retirees with less than $1,000,000 dollars in their retirement accounts would be better off with an immediate fixed-income annuity (subject to the considerations discussed in chapter 12) and a moderate or conservative allocation mutual fund. With 50% in an immediate fixed-income annuity and 50% in a moderate allocation fund or a life-cycle fund, the retiree should be able to withdraw 4% in the first year, increase it thereafter by the rate of inflation, devote little time to maintenance of the portfolio, breathe easily when the stock market nosedives, and not fret about outliving one's retirement account.

Others may for sensible reasons avoid a fixed-income annuity. These individuals would be well advised to choose a low-cost, low-maintenance fund (Target Retirement, life-cycle, conservative or moderate allocation). Most people lack the self-discipline to maintain and stick with a multiple-fund portfolio containing highly volatile funds. Rick Ferri, an author and money manager, claims that in his experience only 5% of the investors who have an asset allocation plan actually implement and maintain it. Other money managers have echoed these same sentiments. My own personal experience with investing is consistent with Ferri's claim. I suspect my difficulties stemmed from my failure to establish habits of sound investing early in my adult life.

If you want to improve your investment results, you might invest in low-cost balanced funds (roughly 60% stocks, 40% bonds). The allocation to bonds lowers volatility while the low costs exert a large impact on the relative performance of the fund. Recent research by Morningstar clearly shows that investors who use funds with preset portfolio mixes do less switching and receive higher returns than other types of investors. Hewitt Associates found that people who invested in target-date retirement, life-cycle and conservative/moderate allocation funds had higher returns from 2001 to 2003 than those who developed their own portfolios. Clements (2006) reports similar results for balanced fund investors over the past decade. By investing in low-cost balanced funds during or approaching retirement, retirees increase the likelihood that they will not switch during turbulent market conditions, and, therefore, reap higher returns on their investments.

A low-maintenance approach to investing makes sense for other reasons as well. We never know if or when we will become incapacitated, and someone else will be saddled with the responsibility of managing our investment portfolio. By keeping our investment approach relatively simple, we ease the burden on our spouse and/or the trustee of our estate.

Before you choose a low-maintenance fund, I suggest that you subscribe to the premium service of Morningstar and do your research. The cost for one year will be less than the fee charged by a financial planner. It will save you time and money in the long run. Once you have chosen the one that suits you, cash your monthly checks and fish, hunt, read books, travel, or play chess. By all means, skip television channels dispensing investment advice and cancel your investment newsletters. Enjoy what life remains.

When you retire, you should consider adding a bond fund to your moderate allocation or all-in-one fund. This addition may serve two purposes. First, it enables you to reduce your risk in retirement. Take, for example, a retiree who has been investing in the Vanguard STAR Fund (62.5% in stocks and 37.5% in bonds) and wants a less risky portfolio containing 50% each in stocks and bonds. By moving to 80% in STAR and 20% in a bond fund, the retiree has achieved a diversified portfolio containing a 50/50 split between stocks and bonds. Second, during a bear market you can sell shares in the bond fund and avoid selling shares in the STAR

Fund, which has a higher potential for growth. When the market turns positive, you can sell shares in the STAR Fund to cover living expenses and rebalance your portfolio.

If you are *absolutely* convinced that you can create an asset allocation plan, implement it, and stay the course, you may decide to use one of the other approaches I discussed or cherry-pick the investment ideas that I discussed in the previous section. As long as you build your portfolio with the seven investment principles in mind that I discussed in the previous chapter, I believe that you will enjoy many happy returns.

In closing, let me emphasize that *it is impossible to forecast the optimal investment portfolio by any technique* (Bernstein, 2001), and there is no guarantee of a certain rate of return on your stock or bond investments. However, the investment principles I identified in chapter 7 will serve you well if you stick with them through the inevitable gyrations of the market and resist the numerous temptations to deviate from whatever investment strategy you choose. That may prove to be your greatest challenge.

CAVEAT

The percentage of investment plans put into action and maintained for three years is about the same as weight loss programs put into action and maintained for the same period. Nice dreams, but that's where most end.

—Rick Ferri

Worksheet: Designing a Portfolio

Factors to consider (Check the items of prime importance to you.)

__1. Ease burden on my spouse and/or trustee in case I am incapacitated.

__2. Devote as little time as possible to managing my investments.

__3. Ensure I don't go broke.

__4. Minimize my investment costs.

__5. Be well diversified.

__6. Match or nearly match the returns of the market.

__7. Obtain adequate returns for risk I am taking.

__8. Protect myself against inflation, deflation, and financial crisis.

__9. Increase the odds of my staying the course.

Options

Bear in mind the numbers of the factors you have checked above as you think about your options.

Simple portfolios (three examples)

1. Target Retirement	2. With annuity	3. Core
Vanguard Target Retirement Fund	Fixed Income Annuity	Total Stock Market
	VSMGX (Vanguard LifeStrategy Moderate Growth Fund) (Moderate Allocation)	Total Bond

Complex portfolios (two examples)

Coffeehouse	All-Weather
Total Bond Index	U.S. Treasury Bonds
Large-Cap Growth	U.S. Treasury Inflation-Protected Securities
Large-Cap Value	Domestic Equity
Small-Cap Blend	Foreign-Developed Equity
Small-Cap Value	Emerging Market Equity
REIT	REIT
Total international	

Note: All of the examples use low-cost index funds, reflect sound investment principles, and provide sufficient returns for the level of risk.

CHAPTER NINE

What Role Should TIAA-CREF Retirement Annuities Play in My Investment Portfolio?

Investing is like dieting—simple, but not easy.

—Warren Buffett

Like so many professors working in private universities in the 1960s, I had no choice but to invest in Teachers Insurance and Annuity Association-College Retirement Equities Fund (TIAA-CREF). In light of what we have learned about investment costs, asset allocation, diversification, and portfolio design, did TIAA-CREF (TC) represent a viable choice for us then and, more importantly, does it remain one now? However, as a gateway to answering this latter question, let me foreshadow for you the types of investment vehicles offered by TC, the second largest source of pension income for retirees. Only Social Security provides more retirement income.

Participants in TC, depending on the plan offered by their employer, may have access to one or more of the following types of investments: retirement annuities, retirement class mutual funds, and life-cycle funds. In this chapter, we will focus on retirement annuities as a vehicle for accumulating wealth. You will learn about the strengths and limitations of the available options and how you might build a diversified investment portfolio. In the chapter that follows, we shift our attention to the retirement class mutual funds and life-cycle funds.

Retirement Annuity Options

When I joined the Stanford University faculty, I had only two investment options: TIAA Traditional and CREF Stock. In 1988, the situation changed due in part to the activism of professors at my institution and elsewhere. TC changed slowly; it initially added a Money Market Account, followed in the 1990s by Social Choice, Global Equities, Growth Equity, Equity Index, Bond Market, Inflation-Linked Bond, and Real Estate. All of these options are annuities; although they resemble mutual funds, they are not mutual funds. As you will discover later in this chapter, this distinction is significant. Shortly after the turn of the century, TC added retirement class mutual funds. Stanford University elected not to offer any of these funds; instead, it chose mutual funds provided by Vanguard and Fidelity.

TIAA Traditional

The TIAA Traditional Annuity is popular with TC participants; two-thirds of them have invested in this product. Moreover, they allocate more dollars to this account than any of its other products. TIAA Traditional exemplifies an investment vehicle referred to as stable-value funds. Swedroe and Kizer (2008) in their recent book on alternative investments give high marks to stable-value funds and cite TIAA Traditional as an example. Two-thirds of all defined contribution plans offer this type of fund; roughly one-third of the assets in these plans are invested in stable-value funds (Babbel & Herce, 2007). Like other stable-value funds, TIAA Traditional serves as an excellent diversification tool for an investment portfolio (Swedroe & Hempen, 2006). Babbel and Herce (2007) have shown in their in-depth study of stable-value funds that they have outperformed money market and intermediate government bonds; moreover, these stable-value funds when combined with stocks and long-term bonds occupy a prominent role in optimal portfolios. (See "TIAA Traditional Annuity Safety and Stability to

Retirement Portfolios," August 2008, for an informative discussion of this account.)

During the accumulation stage, TIAA Traditional's returns consist of two components: a guaranteed interest rate and dividends or additional amounts. Therefore, your contributions earn different crediting rates at different times due to the additional amounts. Prior to retirement, the guaranteed rate is 3%. The Traditional Account has distributed a dividend every year since 1948 based on the performance of investments in the General Account. From 1980 through 2007, the crediting rate for TIAA Traditional "averaged 8.16% and ranged from a high of 10.8% in 1985 to a low of 5.12% in 2006" ("TIAA Traditional Annuity: Adding Safety and Stability to Retirement Portfolios," Winter 2009).

This account invests most of its 176 billion dollars in a wide array of corporate and government bonds and preferred stocks, and structured financial products (mortgage-backed securities, asset-backed securities, and commercial mortgage-backed assets). It invests smaller amounts in conventional mortgages, equities, commercial real estate, cash, and others. Because the New York State insurance regulations govern TIAA, they limit TIAA's exposure to higher risk assets and require higher levels of capital for riskier investments, thereby increasing the overall safety of its investment portfolio.

During the subprime credit and liquidity crisis, many financial firms and their clients lost huge amounts of money by investing in subprime mortgages, collateralized debt obligations, auction rate securities, commercial mortgage-backed securities, and Structured Investment Vehicle-issued commercial paper. According to a TC memo posted online on August 1, 2008, TC's fixed-income and guaranteed accounts had low exposures to these highly risky investments. In fact, the Inflation-Linked Bond and Money Market accounts had no exposure. According to Brett Hammond, chief investment strategist and fund manager for TC, TC has "an *independent* risk management function that works hand in hand with our investment professionals to measure and monitor investment risk and to control, mitigate, or hedge those risks."

Despite its laudable efforts to control risk, two rating agencies—Fitch and Standard & Poor's (S&P)—changed their financial outlooks from stable to negative reflecting TIAA's "significant exposure to structured securities, particularly commercial mortgage backed securities . . . [which] together with a large commercial mortgage portfolio, exposes the company to potential weakness in the commercial mortgage sector in the ongoing difficult economic environment" (TIAA statement on "Triple-A" financial strength ratings from Fitch and S&P, 2010). At the time of this posting, both rating agencies affirmed their highest ratings for TIAA's financial strength, a comfort to holders of lifetime income annuities like myself.

The most frequently asked question by holders of the Traditional Account is, "How are the earnings calculated?" Until I read TC's booklet, "Calculating TIAA Traditional Annuity Earnings," I considered the answer to be a "riddle wrapped in a mystery inside an enigma" (Winston Churchill). After reading the booklet, I now view the answer as understandable but complicated. Moreover, I pity the programmers who built the program to track each investor's returns on this account. If you happen to be among the curious ones and are not intimidated by mathematical formulas, I urge you to download a copy of the booklet from the TC website and read it. After logging onto the TC website, click on "Publications" and scroll down the page until you reach "Calculating TIAA Traditional Annuity Earnings."

If you invest in this annuity, you need to understand it has three major limitations.

1. In exchange for a diversified, low-risk investment that has produced fine returns while preserving the principal, you cannot easily maintain the percentage of money you desire to have in this investment. For example, if you desire to allocate 30% of your total accumulation to TIAA Traditional and it eventually drops to 15%, you should earmark your future contributions to TIAA Traditional until it nears 30% of your total accumulation. Investment experts recommend that you maintain your desired allocation in order to limit your risk and increase returns.

2. Before you retire, you can only make withdrawals from TIAA Traditional in 10 equal payments over a period of 9 years and 1 day. Those who have elected to invest a portion of their retirement money in TIAA Traditional and have not bothered to read beforehand about the restrictions on withdrawals may complain bitterly when they later learn of this limitation.

3. After you retire, you can withdraw money from TIAA Traditional; however, you have limited control over the amount of money you wish to withdraw. TC limits your withdrawal options to four: a Transfer Payout Annuity over 10 years and one of three income options (lifetime annuity, interest-only, and minimum distribution). If you elect a lifetime income annuity, you expose yourself to some potential hazards that I discuss in chapter 23.

Juxtaposed with these limitations of TIAA Traditional are several noteworthy advantages, namely,

1. Investment performance characteristic of, even slightly superior to, intermediate-term bonds
2. Money market–like stability
3. Little or no correlation to stocks and bonds
4. Superior returns per unit of risk
5. Reasonably predictable income in retirement
6. Cushioning your retirement nest egg against huge losses during a severe bear market and
7. Guaranteed principal

TIAA does not report the operating expenses for this account. Because TIAA Traditional is an insurance product, it is not required to follow federal securities laws. The performance of TIAA's General Account supports the returns of TIAA Traditional. My inquiries to TIAA regarding the operating expenses for this account prompted the following statement from a senior individual consultant with the Individual Client Services: "Strictly speaking, there are none." In actuality, there are operating expenses because the dividends declared for TIAA Traditional are net of expenses.

For purposes of full disclosure, nearly 60% of my retirement funds currently are invested in TIAA Traditional. I faced a number of aggravations while withdrawing funds from this account (more about these later). Moreover, I agonized over whether to purchase lifetime income annuities with the money I had invested in TIAA Traditional. The decision became less straightforward as I learned about the possible pitfalls. You will discover the basis for my mixed feelings in chapter 23. The decision was a tough one for me, as it may be for you. To be forewarned is to be forearmed.

TIAA Real Estate

Although TIAA launched the Real Estate Variable Annuity in 1995, I, and other California investors in 403(b) pension accounts, was unable to invest in it. Despite my efforts to understand the reasons behind this prohibition, I remain unenlightened. In 2006, the California State Legislature enacted legislation permitting TC participants to invest in the TIAA Real Estate Account. Stanford University allowed its employees to invest in this account but only through an Individual Retirement Account (IRA), not the 403(b) plan. When I learned of this opportunity from my wealth management advisor, I immediately opened an IRA with TC and invested in this annuity.

TIAA Real Estate, like the Traditional Annuity, represents a unique investment opportunity. By purchasing this variable annuity, I directly owned a small, admittedly very small, share of commercial real estate in this country and abroad. I especially like its diversification by type of property (office, retail, industrial, and apartments) and region (West, South, East, Midwest, and Foreign). In addition, this annuity holds roughly 20% in short-term investments and real estate investment trusts (REITs).

Besides directly owning a share of well-diversified property, I like the role it plays in an investment portfolio. This annuity has an extremely low correlation to stocks and bonds and has been much less volatile than stocks. Thus, it reduces the volatility risk of a portfolio while producing stock-like returns over time and providing a reasonably good hedge against inflation. For 11 years, this annuity never experienced a quarter with negative returns. When the financial crisis struck in 2008, it suffered its first yearly loss of 14.15%. Given the woeful state of the economy, the outlook for commercial real estate looks bleak. Because TIAA Real Estate relies much less on leverage than REITs, it has weathered this downturn better than they have. For example, TIAA Real Estate outperformed the Vanguard REIT Index Fund for four of the past five years, most noticeably in 2007 and 2008 (see Figure 9.1).

Over the past five years, TIAA Real Estate gained 2.52% while the Vanguard REIT Index Fund lost 4.59%.

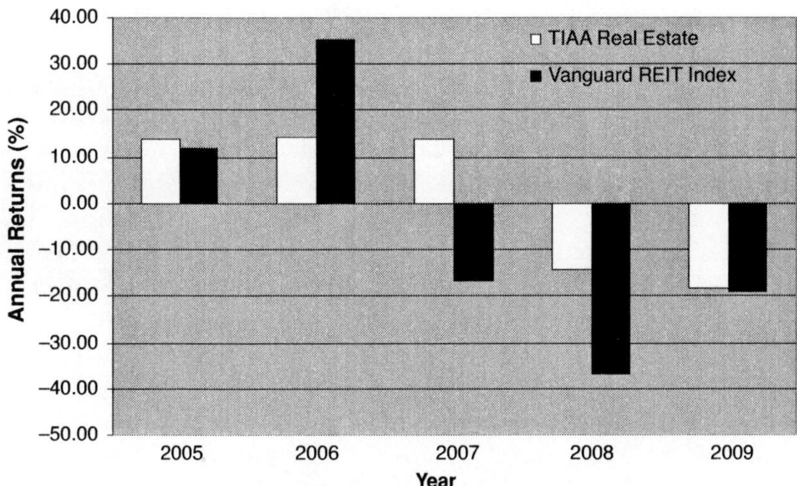

FIGURE 9.1

Annual returns for TIAA Real Estate and Vanguard REIT Index Fund, 2005–2009.

TIAA Real Estate's total returns consist of income from rents, sales, and capital appreciation. The daily price of this variable annuity remains somewhat of a mystery to me and others. It rises some days and falls other times, most often by extremely small amounts. Typically, shares move less than 50 cents daily even though each share currently sells for more than $200. These daily changes do not represent what buyers are willing to pay for it or sellers are willing to sell it for on any given day as in the case of stocks, REITs, and bonds. Rather, the net asset values fluctuate due to changes in the appraised value of properties, income flows, capital expenditures, and purchases and sales of properties (TIAA-CREF Asset Management, 2008). The largest changes in net asset value generally occur during the fourth quarter of each year.

As a retiree, I don't like two features of the TIAA Real Estate Annuity. First, its annual operating expenses have been rising and now reach 1.01%. Second, TIAA includes the income portion of the total returns in the price of the Real Estate Annuity. To live off the income generated by this annuity, I need to sell shares. An investor in REITs, on the other hand, has the option of taking the dividend income in cash.

Roger Gibson (2007), a recognized authority on asset allocation, expresses several additional concerns about such investments as TIAA Real Estate—its lack of transparency, the low volatility of real estate values due to the lagged appraisal process, its questionable role as a portfolio diversifier, and its low correlation with REITs, supposedly a member of the same asset class. He favors REITs plus fixed income, especially Treasury Inflation-Protected Securities (TIPS), over funds like TIAA Real Estate.

If you desire additional information about TIAA Real Estate, check the "Fund Facts" for this account on the TC website. The discussion answers the questions that investors commonly ask.

CREF Variable Annuity Accounts

CREF currently has eight variable annuity accounts (Equity Index, Stock, Global Equities, Growth, Social Choice, Inflation-Linked Bond, Bond, and Money Market). In appraising them as potential investments for my TC portfolio, I employed the same criteria that I use in evaluating mutual funds, namely, costs, assessments by independent financial experts, performance relative to similar mutual funds, risk relative to members of the investment category, and contribution to diversification. When I have completed the selection of my investments, I analyze my portfolio using the Morningstar X Ray tool.

Costs. As we discussed in chapter 3, operating expenses or investment costs matter. By a wide margin, costs are the single best predictor of a fund's future performance. The trend of operating expenses for CREF variable annuity accounts can be summarized in one word—Up. In Table 9.1, you can see for yourself the magnitude of the increase for CREF Stock, the most popular account. (See Appendix H for the operating expenses of all variable accounts.)

TABLE 9.1
Operating expenses for the CREF Stock variable annuity, 1997–2008

Variable Annuity	1997 Operating Expenses	2008 Operating Expenses
Stock	0.31%	0.56%

Because I don't want to exaggerate the extent of the increase, I report the actual operating expenses instead of the percentage increase. Part of the increase is due to the imposition of a 12b-1 fee (0.085%) for distribution and marketing costs. In effect, "current TIAA-CREF investors give up a portion of their returns to fund the firm's asset growth" (Davis, 2005). According to Jason Zweig (2009), a highly respected financial journalist, "Reports by SEC (Security Exchange Commission) economists in 1990 and again in 2004 found no evidence that 12b-1s were worth what they cost investors." Other firms like Vanguard bring in additional assets without imposing a 12b-1 fee and lower, not raise, overall operating expenses as they increase assets to provide better economies of scale. The increase in CREF Stock operating expenses is especially troubling to me.

Subsequently, CREF Stock raised the expense charge to 0.59%, meaning that this account now generates more than one-half billion dollars annually in fees. This hefty amount places CREF Stock seventh on the list of mutual funds that bring in the highest fees in absolute dollars (Dolan, 2009). CREF boasts that it provides "financial services for the greater good" and certainly in my opinion could charge lower, not higher, fees for those investing in this fund, instead of transforming it into a cash cow for the firm.

Operating expenses do not reveal the entire costs incurred by investors. These expense ratios fail to include the transaction costs associated with the buying and selling of stocks in the portfolio. To estimate the transaction costs of each equity account, you should identify the turnover rate and multiply it by 1% (Bogle, 2007, p. 115). You derive the total investment costs for an account by adding the transaction costs to the operating expenses. Using this approach, I discovered that the total costs for all of the equity accounts with the exception of Equity Index increased substantially (see table in Appendix I). For example, the total costs for the popular Stock Account jumped from 0.56% to 1.05% when the estimated transaction costs were taken into account. The estimated total costs for the various equity variable annuity accounts place them in the second cost quartile according to data reported by Bogle (2007, p. 117). Equity Index showed the smallest increase, ending with 0.59% total investment costs.

TC's transaction costs may be less, even much less, than I have estimated using Bogle's informed rule of thumb. According to Greenenough (1990), TC initiated an experimental trading program to reduce its transaction costs, along with discounts it receives from using corporate dividend reinvestment programs. As investors become more aware of the hidden costs with buying and selling stocks, TC, in the spirit of transparency, should disclose its transaction costs and how it has sought to reduce them.

To explore the impact of total investment costs on how much I could safely withdraw from an initial principal of $100,000 without going broke, I ran an analysis using two different mutual funds (CREF Stock Account and a comparable composite fund consisting of the Vanguard Total International Stock Index Fund and the Total Stock Market Index Fund). In this analysis, I varied the total investment costs (CREF Stock Account, 1.05% and Vanguard composite fund, 0.22%) and assumed an average return of 8%, a standard deviation of 16%, an inflation rate of 3%, and a probability of 90% that my retirement account would last 30 years.

The safe withdrawal rate for the Vanguard composite fund was 13.3% higher than the CREF Stock Account. If I had used the Global Equities Account with its 1.70% total investment costs, the difference would have been much greater—25.4% versus 13.3%. Costs matter!

Assessments from knowledgeable, independent sources. I enjoy reading about financial matters, something I had no time for during my career. In addition, I am curious about my investments, what their holdings are, and how they stack up against other options. My quest for information and appraisals by independent sources has been frustrating. Morningstar does not cover variable annuities, and I have been unable to locate any source that does. The few books that focus on TC have not been particularly helpful in answering the many questions that have arisen since I retired.

The picture for mutual funds is quite different. Morningstar provides me with an array of tools, valuable information about most mutual funds, and frank evaluations by its analysts. When I've finished my homework, I have a clear idea of a mutual fund's investment objectives, strategy, performance in bull and bear markets, strengths, and weaknesses. I also know if the portfolio manager has any skin in the game; I prefer managers with a million or more dollars invested in the funds they manage. That way I know whether their interests are aligned with mine.

Performance relative to similar funds. CREF supplies information about the performance of its variable annuities and a composite index that reflects the returns of a similar investment portfolio. In all cases with one exception, the composite index shows slightly higher returns than the comparable variable annuity. This general pattern of higher returns for the composite index that serves as a benchmark for judging the performance of an investment is not unexpected. As you may recall, in my discussion of costs, I noted that total returns = market returns – costs; therefore, beating the average market returns is virtually impossible on a consistent basis.

Risk relative to its category. Return and risk go together—the higher the return, the higher the risk. Given the coupling of risk and return, I consistently look at risk, as well as returns, to rule out the possibility that the performance of a mutual fund relative to its peers is due to its assuming greater risk. When making this assessment, I compare apples with apples, not apples with oranges. While searching the Internet recently, I observed on a college website that TIAA Traditional's performance had been downgraded as an investment because it had returned less than a stock fund. Needless to say, I was surprised to see this inappropriate comparison, a classic case of apples and oranges.

To judge the risk of comparable investments in stocks, I generally examine the volatility risk as measured by the standard deviation of returns. I find it relatively easy to judge the volatility risk of a mutual fund relative to its peers or category by using Yahoo! Finance. Yahoo reports this information for each mutual fund contained in its database. To judge the volatility risk of a CREF variable annuity account, I have to follow this four-step procedure:

1. Compute the standard deviation for each account.
2. Make a decision about what mutual fund category it most resembles.
3. Obtain the standard deviation for the appropriate mutual fund category on the Yahoo! Finance website.
4. Compare the two.

When I used this somewhat elaborate procedure to judge the relative risk of Social Choice, I chose to compare it with the Vanguard Balanced Index Fund. During the past 10 years, both funds held

60% in domestic stocks and 40% in bonds. Over this period, the Vanguard fund showed slightly higher returns with slightly lower risk than the Social Choice Account. Even this comparison is not completely comparable; Social Choice screens for stocks of companies that match its socially responsible criteria while the Vanguard Balanced Index Fund does not. Despite this limitation, my example demonstrates the difficulty one faces when trying to judge the volatility risk of a CREF variable account relative to its peers.

When judging the relative risk of a fund's bond portfolio, I focus on *credit rating* and *duration*. Lower quality bonds have higher yields because they are more likely to default than higher quality bonds. In other words, junk bond investors run a greater risk of losing their interest payments, their investment, or both. Duration of the bond signals how much the value of the bond will rise or fall with moves in interest rates. For example, a bond fund with an average duration of five years will move 5% for every 1% movement in interest rates. Put another way, the higher the average duration of a bond fund, the greater the volatility risk. CREF provides both sets of information on the "Fund Fact" sheets for the Bond Fund Account and the Inflation-Linked Bond Account. Both bond funds carry high-quality bonds while the Inflation-Linked Bond Account has a higher duration (8.23 years) than the CREF Bond Fund Account (4.25 years). Thus, the former bond account is subject to much more volatility risk than the latter.

If you spot a bond fund that looks more attractive than the CREF Bond and Inflation-Linked Bond accounts, check out the credit rating and the duration of the portfolio. Higher returns may well be due to longer durations, lower credit ratings, or both. For example, Fidelity's Inflation-Protected Bond Fund suffered losses by taking some "stand-alone positions in subprime-related securities" (Herbert, 2007). The CREF Inflation-Linked Bond Account adopted a more cautious stance and limited its holdings to TIPS. Look under the hood before investing your hard-earned money in a bond fund. I find it reassuring to know that CREF Bond accounts follow a conservative investment philosophy.

Diversification. When investing, I try not to put all of my eggs in one basket. To improve returns and lower volatility risk, I prefer to diversify my investments by using ones that have low to moderate correlations with one another. Naturally, I am sensitive to the level and type of diversification that I can achieve using

CREF variable accounts. Unfortunately, all of the equity-oriented accounts (Equity Index, Stock, Global Equities, Growth, and Social Choice) are heavily weighted with large-cap stocks (i.e., stocks of companies with more than 10 billion dollars capitalization). When I examined the top holdings of these accounts, I observed great similarities. This observation led me to examine the correlations among these five accounts for the 11-year period, 1997–2007. Not surprisingly, only one correlation did not exceed 0.90—the one between Global Equities and Social Choice (0.83). Strikingly, the correlation between the Equity Index, a domestic stock fund, and Global Equities, a hybrid fund of international and domestic stocks, was 0.92. Because of these high correlations, one should not expect any one of these accounts to provide a cushion when the market is falling. When one of these accounts moves up, all of them rise; when one declines, all fall. If TC had a more diverse set of variable annuities, you could, perhaps, create a portfolio using Modern Portfolio Theory (Armstrong, 2004) that usually, but not always, exhibits less volatility and higher returns.

In closing my discussion of these CREF variable accounts, let me note two additional limitations of these offerings. None of these accounts enable investors to tilt their portfolio toward two segments of the market that historically have produced the highest returns (Fama & French, 1993): small-cap stocks (i.e., stocks of companies with less than two billion dollars capitalization) and value stocks (i.e., stocks of companies trading at a low price relative to their dividends, earnings, and sales). The CREF variable accounts also lack an equity-income account that concentrates on dividend paying stocks. As a retiree interested in income and preservation of my wealth, I would have welcomed such an account.

To TC's credit, it recently decreased the weighting of large-cap stocks in most of its CREF Stock accounts. Mid-cap and small-cap stocks now have larger weightings.

Portfolio analysis. When I have finished selecting investments using the criteria described above, I perform an overall analysis of my portfolio. The Morningstar X Ray tool enables me to answer the following questions about my investment portfolio:

1. What is my asset allocation (mix of domestic stocks, international stocks, bonds, and cash)? According to research,

asset allocation is the overwhelming determinant of the variability of the returns in your portfolio (Brinson, Singer, & Beebower, 1986).

2. How diversified are my stocks in terms of valuation (value, blend, and growth) and size (large, medium, and small)? Research has also shown that value and small capitalization stocks have generated the highest returns over time (Fama & French, 1993). This pattern holds for domestic and international stocks.

3. What are the interest sensitivity (short, intermediate, and long) and credit quality (high, medium, and low) of my bond holdings? Short- and intermediate-term bonds are less sensitive to changes in interest rates while high- and medium-quality bonds are less likely to default than low-quality or junk bonds.

4. What are the average mutual expense fees and expenses for my portfolio relative to a similarly weighted portfolio? You don't have to be a professor of rocket science to understand that costs matter—a lot.

With my mutual funds, I can easily answer these four questions with the Morningstar X Ray tool. However, I have been unable to locate any comparable tool for analyzing a portfolio designed around the CREF variable annuities.

A Diversified, Low Volatility TC Portfolio

Based on my analysis of the correlations among all of the CREF and TIAA variable accounts, I have concluded that investors who can't stomach high levels of volatility risk and want to cushion their falls during most bear markets can do so by using the following accounts:

- TIAA Traditional
- TIAA Real Estate
- CREF Stock (75% domestic and 25% international)
- CREF Inflation-Linked Bond

TABLE 9.2
Correlations among the Stock, Real Estate, Inflation-Linked Bond, and TIAA Traditional Accounts, 1997–2007

Accounts	Real Estate	Inflation-Linked Bond	TIAA Traditional
Stock	+0.33	−0.67	−0.41
Real Estate	—	−0.43	−0.55
Inflation-Linked Bond	—	—	+0.28

Note: $n = 11$ for all accounts with the exception of Inflation-Linked Bond; the first full year for this account was 1998.

The low correlation among these four accounts is evident in Table 9.2.

The only positive correlations among these four accounts are between Stock and Real Estate, and Inflation-Linked Bond and TIAA Traditional; neither correlation exceeds +0.33, representing a low to moderate correlation. Correlations do fluctuate, especially over short time periods and different market conditions; however, I do not expect the pattern of correlations among these four accounts to change markedly because each account represents a different asset class.

Before you decide to lower your volatility risk, you should consider if your expected returns with this portfolio will enable you to reach your long-range financial goals. You have to balance your comfort quotient against your need for higher returns. During the wealth-building stage bear markets do provide you with an opportunity to purchase shares at a lower price and offset the higher prices you pay during bull markets.

The Bottom Line

The TC retirement annuities provide a reasonable set of investments for those individuals seeking to build a retirement nest egg. Most of these annuities have sported below average operating expense ratios, the single best predictor of future returns, generated reasonable returns, and offered participants the possibility of creating a diversified portfolio.

At the same time, these annuities suffer from a number of limitations. If you are like me and want to obtain independent analyses of these options, they aren't available. Because these annuities resemble mutual funds but are not, you can't perform fine-grained analyses of your portfolio using tools like Morningstar's X Ray. Moreover, the CREF retirement annuities lack the two investment options that have produced the highest returns in the past—small-cap stocks and value stocks (Fama & French, 1993). The increased weighting of mid- and small-cap stocks in the stock-oriented accounts compensates somewhat for this limitation. Finally, TIAA Traditional presents investors with a set of restrictions that limit rebalancing and may pose other problems for them during the wealth-building and spending stages.

IRA Version of TIAA Traditional

TIAA also offers TIAA Traditional, without withdrawal restrictions, as an investment option in an IRA. I use it instead of the money market fund. During 2010, a period of low interest rates, this version of TIAA Traditional earned me 4.1% and solidified my belief that it represents an excellent investment option.

CHAPTER TEN

What Role Should TIAA-CREF Retirement Class Mutual Funds Play in My Investment Portfolio?

> *October, this is one of the particularly dangerous months to speculate in stocks. The others are July, January, September, April, November, May, March, June, December, August, and February.*
>
> —Mark Twain

In the previous chapter, we focused on Teachers Insurance and Annuity Association-College Retirement Equities Fund's (TIAA-CREF) retirement annuities and discovered that these investment vehicles, despite some limitations, have represented reasonable choices for those who have invested in them. We now turn our attention to TIAA-CREF's (TC) retirement class mutual funds. Our discussion, like the one for retirement annuities, will center on the strengths and limitations of TC's mutual fund offerings and suggest a diversified portfolio that might be used during the wealth-building stage.

TC, several years ago, decided to offer three sets of mutual funds: actively managed, index, and life-cycle. Most of these mutual funds were actively managed, so called because managers of these funds seek to beat the stock market via stock selection and market timing. The remainder of the retirement class mutual funds is passively managed, so called because their managers try to replicate the performance of a particular index that tracks a group of stocks like those in the S&P (Standard & Poor's) 500 Index. TC, as well as firms with similar offerings, labels these funds as *index funds*. In addition to the actively and passively managed mutual funds, TC offers a number of Lifecycle Funds. Investors in these funds choose one of these life-cycle funds based on their anticipated retirement date. Each of these funds is designed to become more conservatively invested over time, that is, to increase its proportion of bonds and decrease its proportion of stocks. Until late 2009, these life-cycle funds consisted of many actively managed mutual funds. Responding to criticisms of target-date retirement funds, TC and several other mutual fund companies instituted changes in their offerings. Laudably, TC began to offer Lifecycle Index Funds with lower operating expense ratios than its earlier life-cycle funds that consisted of actively managed funds.

All three sets of these retirement class mutual funds have several distinct advantages over the retirement annuities discussed in the preceding chapter.

1. A concerned investor can obtain independent analyses of the mutual funds, if not now, certainly in the near future. These mutual funds are relatively new arrivals on the investment scene, and a time lag usually exists between their creation and coverage by analysts. Morningstar already covers a few of TC's funds and, in all likelihood, will cover more as they become more popular.

2. The mutual fund offerings include a broader range of investment options than the retirement annuities. Noteworthy additions include funds dedicated solely to the international stock market, value stock funds (large-cap), small-cap stocks (but not small-cap value), mid-cap (growth and value), and REITs (real estate investment trusts).

3. A portfolio consisting of these mutual funds can be analyzed using the Morningstar X Ray tool. As we discussed in the

preceding chapter, this tool can be used to provide valuable information about your asset allocation, level of diversification, investment costs compared with similar portfolios, and the credit quality and interest sensitivity of your bonds. If you become a subscriber to Morningstar, the X Ray tool will also supply you with an analysis of the strengths and weaknesses of your portfolio.

4. Investors in these funds can easily rebalance and maintain their desired allocation to the major asset classes and diversification within subasset classes.

Actively Managed Funds

In my judgment, the actively managed funds represent a less than optimal choice for the wealth builder. The basis for my lukewarm opinion about this class of mutual funds rests on the following:

1. *Costs.* We have entered an era of low returns for stocks and bonds. Bonds, in particular, have provided investors with relatively strong returns over the past 20 or so years primarily because of the high interest rates in the 1980s. As the interest rates from that earlier period have fallen, investors have benefited from the increases in the value of their bonds. Currently, interest rates are low, and as they begin to rise, the value of the bonds will fall. When that happens, the total returns from bonds will be substantially lower than in the past. As for stocks, they too have benefited from a long run of high returns until the turn of the century. The long-range outlook for growth in the U.S. economy is bleak; with lower growth comes lower earnings and lower stock prices. In this investment climate, investors need to capture as much of the market returns as they can. To do this, they need to invest in mutual funds with low operating expenses and transaction costs. TC's actively managed mutual funds have higher transaction costs and operating expenses than the passively managed or index funds. Over an extended period of time, one can expect the index funds to outperform most, if not all, of the passively managed funds. To repeat, in the words of John Bogle, "You get what you don't pay for."

2. *Skin in the game.* I am not inclined to consider investing in an actively managed fund if the managers don't have any skin in the game. If they don't invest much, if any, of their own money in the fund, why should I? Russell Kinnel, in one of his Morningstar columns, had this to say about TC's actively managed funds:

   > The biggest shocker, though, was TIAA-CREF, where managers have just $10,000 invested in their own funds on average.

3. *New funds.* I make it a rule never to invest in a new, actively managed fund unless the managers have proven themselves elsewhere. The track record of a manager matters. When I require an operation, I check out the past performance of the surgeons I am considering. When it comes to my money, as well as my life, I want to know if my money and my well-being are in the hands of an exceptional professional. My efforts to learn about the experience of TC's active managers proved fruitless.
4. *Expected performance.* The evidence is overwhelming that actively managed mutual funds underperform index funds over time (Bogle, 2007). Lower fees and lower transaction costs give the edge to index funds. Higher costs limit the ability of active managers to beat a comparable index fund consistently (Bogle, 2007). We expect the same pattern to prevail over the lifetime of wealth builders. If TC narrows the operating expenses and transaction costs between its actively managed and index funds, they might be worth considering.

Index Funds

TC's index funds provide investors with the opportunity to construct a portfolio that is more likely to match the returns of the market than the actively managed funds. The lower operating expenses and transaction costs of index funds give them the edge over the actively managed funds. Moreover, index funds, unlike actively managed funds, assure investors that the fund managers will maintain a stable investment policy.

Before TC dropped its small-cap value index fund, I would have suggested that investors create the Coffeehouse portfolio (Schultheis, 2005) because it has a fine track record over the past 20 years. This portfolio would have included the following funds:

S&P 500 Index

Large-Cap Value Index

Small-Cap Blend Index

Small-Cap Value Index

International Equity Index

Real Estate Securities (actively managed because no REIT index offered)

Bond Index

This approach capitalizes on the two segments of the stock market that have rewarded investors handsomely over time—value and small size.

With this investment option foreclosed, I believe that investors can adopt a relatively simple portfolio consisting of the following funds:

Equity Index

International Equity Index

Small-Cap Blend Index

Bond Index

This four-fund portfolio covers much of the world's stock market and U.S. bond market at a reasonable cost. "While such an index-driven strategy may not be the best investment strategy ever devised, the number of investment strategies that are worse is infinite" (Bogle, 2007). If you want to play the winner's game and be content with whatever the market delivers, this simple portfolio will enable you to do it. Rest assured that there will be times when some actively managed funds beat your index funds. However, over the long haul, you will do fine as long as you resist the temptation to time the market or to chase the hot-performing sectors of the market. If you don't resist, you surely will convert the winner's game into a loser's game (Ellis, 1998).

Life-Cycle Funds

Perhaps you prefer a simpler approach. If so, TC now offers a series of life-cycle funds. "While the TIAA-CREF Lifecycle Funds aren't truly exceptional, the series is devoid of serious flaws, making the entire package a better-than-average target-date option." (Morningstar, 2009) You simply invest in one fund designated by the year that corresponds to your expected retirement date. The managers do the heavy lifting for you; they choose the mutual funds, they determine the asset allocation, they rebalance annually, and they reduce over time the money allocated to equities.

According to a recent report on target-date funds by Morningstar (Charlson et al., 2009), TC's average expense ratio for its Lifecycle Funds is 0.69%, slightly below the average of 34 families in the target-date universe. However, the expense ratio for its Lifecycle Funds is 0.50% higher than Vanguard's (0.19%). This difference mounts up over time; according to Charlson (2009), an investor at the end of 25 years would have $69,000 less in the life-cycle funds than in Vanguard's given the same contributions and returns. Moreover, TC's Lifecycle Funds have temporary fee waivers. The expense ratios of these funds are scheduled to rise in the future. With the addition of Lifecycle Index Funds in late 2009, the large discrepancy between the fees of Vanguard and TC will narrow but not disappear.

Before investing in one of these life-cycle funds, let me offer two additional caveats. First, target-date retirement funds like TC's Lifecycle Funds disappointed investors during the recent bear market. As a result, the Department of Labor is currently reviewing its decision to make these funds the default investment in retirement accounts. Second, these life-cycle funds don't guarantee a return or an amount of income when you retire. They carry risks, and the risk/possible returns depend on their allocations to stocks and bonds. For example, Morningstar reports that the equity allocation for 2010 target-date funds ranged from 27% to 70%.

TC's equity allocation for its 2010 Lifecycle Fund was 52%; its total returns in 2008 were −23.47%, the fifth best performance among 21 target-date funds. Although Vanguard had a slightly higher equity allocation (55%); its returns ranked first in performance with a decline of 20.58%. When you examine a TC Lifecycle Fund that corresponds to your anticipated retirement date, you may discover that it has a higher allocation to stock than you desire. In this event, look for an earlier retirement date with a stock allocation that better fits your risk tolerance.

Conclusion

Several years ago, TC began to offer retirement class mutual funds. This class of mutual funds consisted of 32 options distributed among actively managed funds, index funds, and life-cycle funds. My review of these mutual funds highlighted a number of advantages over the annuities discussed in the preceding chapter. To assist my readers in sorting through these options, I examined the strengths and limitations of these mutual funds. Based on this analysis, I favored the index funds and suggested a relatively simple portfolio consisting of only four funds—Equity Index, International Equity Index, Small-Cap Blend Index, and Bond Index. John Bogle offers a useful rule of thumb for deciding your allocation between stocks and bonds—your age in bonds; others use 100 − age in stocks. A 40-year-old investor who followed either of these decision rules would allocate 40% to bonds and 60% to stocks. As this investor neared retirement, the percentage invested in bonds would exceed the percentage allocated to stocks. To further simplify your decision making, you might follow the lead of the coffeehouse investor and allocate equal amounts to each of the three stock index funds.

At the end of each year, reset your allocations to the four funds. Allocate your age in bonds and then equalize the amount of money you have in each of the three stock index funds. Investment specialists refer to this technique as *rebalancing*; it reduces your risk and increases your returns by roughly one-half of 1% over time. During the financial crisis of 2008, those who rebalanced regularly fared much better than those who did not.

If you prefer to lead a simple life and have a professional do the heavy lifting for you, you could opt to invest in the Lifecycle Index Funds that TC introduced near the end of 2009.

In the final analysis, you must decide for yourself whether to follow my suggestions or travel another route. Hopefully, my discussion enables you to sort through TC's mixed bag of investments, design an investment portfolio based on solid investment principles, and estimate the historical returns of your portfolio.

PART TWO

Preretirement Considerations

As you near retirement, you will confront a number of difficult decisions. I wrestled with each of them and share with you what I learned that was of value to me and perhaps will be of value to you. These decisions centered on important questions with far-reaching consequences, such as the following:

- Can I afford to retire?
- When should I take Social Security?
- How much do I need to set aside for health insurance?
- Should we sell our home and relocate?
- How should I use a financial planner? (As part of this discussion, I discuss my own experiences with independent financial planners and financial services companies like Teachers Insurance and Annuity Association-College Retirement Equities Fund [TIAA-CREF].)

CHAPTER ELEVEN

Can I Afford to Retire?

Thirty-one percent of pre-retirees would rather clean their bathroom or pay bills than plan for retirement. Eighteen percent have spent no time planning.

—National telephone survey conducted
by Ipsos Public Affairs in 2005

Several years before I decided to retire, I phoned a financial planner to request an appointment. The first question she asked me was "What's on your mind?" I replied, "I am thinking about retiring and need to know if I can afford to retire." She then instructed me to bring the following information to our first meeting:

- Current living expenses
- Projected retirement expenses
- The total money in my 403(b) account
- The total amount of other investments
- Other income

Assembling this information proved easier than I initially imagined. Fortunately, I use Quicken to track my expenditures, so estimating my current living expenses proved easy. As I have discovered from conversations with friends and colleagues, supplying this information is not so straightforward with most people. Many had no idea of what their annual expenditures were.

When I met with my financial planner to obtain the results of her efforts to answer my question, she confronted me with a spreadsheet and the bottom line. "You can afford to retire," she said with a smile. I took her word for it and submitted a letter to my employer declaring my intention to retire.

Caveat Emptor

Looking back on this meeting, I now realize how naïve I was. Like so many who hire a financial planner to assist in retirement planning, I failed to understand that I was paying for the assumptions and projections of the software program my financial planner used, as well as her skill and judgment. Most financial planners use an off-the-shelf retirement planning program, and virtually all of these software programs have limitations. The program my financial planner used assumed *constant* rates of return and inflation. This assumption provides misleading results because rates of return and inflation vary. This variability affects how much retirees can "safely" withdraw from their Individual Retirement Accounts (IRAs) without going broke.

Take for example a couple who is considering retirement and approaches a financial planner. They pose the following question to the planner: How much can we "safely" withdraw from our retirement account over the next 25 years without going broke? To answer the question, the planner uses a software program that assumes constant rates of return and inflation. After reviewing the results, the planner announces with a smile, "You can safely withdraw $7,662 monthly depending upon the average return (6%–8%) you are willing to assume."

Being skeptical, the couple hires another financial adviser to provide a second opinion. The adviser uses the same information but uses a software program that assumes varying, not constant, rates of returns. After reviewing the results, the financial adviser states, "The maximum amount that you can 'safely' withdraw monthly is $5,617."

When we compare the markedly different conclusions of the two planners, it is clear that assuming fixed rates of returns and inflation can lead one to adopt unsafe monthly withdrawal amounts. More realistic assumptions about the variability of returns suggest a much lower withdrawal rate. If a genie granted retirees three wishes, I suspect one would be a low volatility market. Alas, there are no genies and no steady state stock markets.

My financial adviser's analysis also suffered from other limitations. It failed to take into account many of the risks I mentioned earlier in my discussion of retirement roulette, namely,

- Information about our health status and life expectancies
- Information about health insurance costs
- Information about our desire to leave money for our heirs
- How much we intended to withdraw annually from my pension fund
- The need to set aside money for future large purchases and/or unexpected financial emergencies
- The impact of possible future government actions to raise its revenues and/or reduce expenditures
- Conservative, rather than average, rates of return

Do It Yourself?

Based on this experience and what I now know, you might use one of the free retirement planning calculators I have located on the Internet. Two helpful calculators that I have found use different approaches; however, both are superior to the one my financial planner used. You are well advised to study the discussion of the assumptions underlying each of these calculators. Because these calculators use different approaches, I encourage you to compare the results generated by each—the equivalent of seeking a second opinion.

To locate Vanguard's retirement calculator follow these steps:

1. Enter "Vanguard Lifetime Spending Analyzer" into your search engine
2. Click on "Vanguard Lifetime Spending Analyzer"

You can enter the requested information in five minutes or less. The retirement calculator relies on *historical back testing*, an approach that assumes different retirement dates, for example, 1960, 1961, 1962, using subsequent market returns and inflation rates to determine the percentage of times your investment portfolio is depleted if you decide to withdraw X amount (you specify the monthly withdrawal rate) initially from your account and increase it by the actual rate of inflation in subsequent years. In addition to the estimated success rate over 20- and 25-year periods, the lifetime spending analyzer provides information about the life expectancy for you and your spouse. (See example below.)

Example: Lifetime Spending Analyzer

INPUTS

Current age of you and your spouse: 65

Marginal tax rate: 25%

Balance of tax-deferred retirement account: $1,000,000

Total after-tax spending amount from tax-deferred account: $3,200

Investment portfolio: 40% stocks/60% bonds

RESULTS

How long could my retirement portfolio last?

Estimated success rate: 93% (20 years); 73% (25 years); 59% (30 years)

Estimated survival rate for you or your spouse: 20 years (69%); 25 years (41%); 30 years (15%)

Note: Although there is a 59% probability of your money lasting 30 years, there is only a 15% probability that either you or your spouse will be living at that time.

T. Rowe Price calls its retirement planning calculator the "Retirement Income Calculator." It estimates the probability that you will outlive your retirement assets given the following conditions:

- When you plan to retire
- How long you expect to live
- The amount of money in your retirement account
- The monthly pretax income you expect in retirement
- Your allocation to stocks, bonds, and cash

If you discover that the probability of your assets lasting a lifetime is too low for comfort, you can alter one or more of the conditions listed above (e.g., delaying your retirement) and rerun the calculator. To use the Retirement Income Calculator, follow these steps:

1. Google "T. Rowe Price Retirement Income Calculator."
2. Click on "T. Rowe Price Retirement Income Calculator."
3. When you enter the T. Rowe Price website, click on "Retirement Income Calculator."

See the example below for the inputs used and the results provided by this calculator.

Example: Retirement Income Calculator

INPUTS

Current age of you and your spouse: 65

Retirement length: 25 years

Balance of tax-deferred retirement account: $1,000,000

Monthly income goal from tax-deferred account: $4,200 (pretax)

Investment portfolio: 40% stocks/40% bonds/20% cash

RESULTS

Congratulations: Your monthly income goal of $4,200 was met in our simulations! You have an 80% success rate in our simulations that your money will last throughout your Retirement Length.

Can you achieve a higher monthly income?

Click on the Portfolio tab to see the initial monthly withdrawal amount from every portfolio at your chosen simulation success rate.

Or, click on the Success tab above to see the impact of changing your portfolio composition on the level of withdrawal.

When we compare the results of the two calculators, which use slightly differently inputs, we see that the probable rate of this couple's retirement account lasting for 25 years is 73% and 80%. Because there is a 41% probability that either the retiree or the spouse may live 25 years or more, the couple may decide to delay retirement.

Bear in mind that these calculators also have several limitations. The Vanguard lifetime spending analyzer ignores investment costs. Neither calculator takes into account that retirees typically cut back on their spending when the market falls. Both calculators do not use conservative rates of return and ignore the need to set aside funds for large purchases and emergencies. Finally, both calculators estimate the probability of running out of money, but they shed no light on the magnitude of the consequences for you if it occurs (see Powell, 2009). In light of these limitations, one should view the probability estimate as a one-sided indicator of risk.

If you wish to use a retirement program that lacks most of these limitations and are willing to spend $99.99, I strongly recommend that you purchase the Otar Retirement Optimizer. I have examined a number of software programs and found Otar's the easiest to use and the most comprehensive. The software program can be downloaded from his website (www.retirementoptimizer.com) along with a well-written manual and a case study that leads you step-by-step through the program. The output of his program estimates how much you can safely withdraw from your retirement account, the probability of lasting success, your projected balance under three different scenarios (unlucky, average, and lucky), and other issues of interest to preretirees and retirees. You can even test the effects of purchasing a fixed or variable annuity on how much you can withdraw safely without fear of going broke.

Use a Financial Services Company?

A number of the well-known financial services companies offer free retirement planning to their clients. Recently, a writer for the *Wall Street Journal* reported a test drive using the services of four major firms—Fidelity, Vanguard, Nationwide, and Schwab. The author, Anne Tergesen (2009), rated Fidelity's Retirement Income Planner the highest. Even with this strong rating, she noted one major limitation—the length of time to complete the worksheets. This service, laudably, can be completed on the phone or with the assistance of an adviser; in addition, Fidelity notifies you when your portfolio plan requires rebalancing. If you plan to retire within five years and invest with Fidelity, this program suits you.

Take a Trial Run

Those who discover a shortfall and seriously consider living on less money in retirement may find it beneficial to conduct a trial run. Try to live on your projected retirement budget for a period of 6–12 months. If you do, you are likely to discover whether lowering your living expenses represents a sensible alternative.

If the trial run signals trouble ahead, you might pursue the "TIP!" below or purchase an immediate lifetime annuity, an alternative I discuss in the next chapter.

TIP!

If you decide to reduce your living expenses, read *Retire on Less Than You Think* (Brock, 2004). He does a marvelous job of showing his readers how to reduce their living expenses, a factor often overlooked by financial planners who may be pushing stocks, bonds, and other investment products instead.

Worksheet: Can I Afford to Retire?

Use this worksheet in conjunction with the Vanguard Lifetime Spending Analyzer and the T. Rowe Price Retirement Income Calculator.

To use Vanguard's Lifetime Spending Analyzer follow these steps:

1. Enter "Vanguard Lifetime Spending Analyzer" into your search engine.
2. Click on "Vanguard Lifetime Spending Analyzer."

To use the T. Rowe Price Retirement Income Calculator, follow these steps:

1. Enter "T. Rowe Price Retirement Income Calculator into your search engine."
2. Click on "T. Rowe Price Retirement Income Calculator."
3. When you enter the T. Rowe Price website, click on "Retirement Income Calculator."

Information You Will Need

1. Current age: you__, spouse__
2. Marginal tax rate: __%
3. Balance of tax-deferred retirement account(s): $________
4. Pretax monthly income goal from tax-deferred account(s): $________
5. Total after-tax spending amount from tax-deferred account(s): $________
6. Investment portfolio: __% stocks, __%bonds

Note: If you want to set aside money for emergencies and/or large purchases, reduce balance by 5%–10%.

Results

Estimated success rate: Vanguard__, T. Rowe Price__

Estimated survival rate for you and your spouse: 20 years __; 25 years__; 30 years__

Caveat: Bear in mind the limitations of these calculators. They do not use conservative rates of return, and the Vanguard lifetime spending analyzer ignores investment costs. Neither assumes that you will reduce your spending in a bear market. Treat the results as an estimate of your risk of going broke and recalculate annually using updated information for items 1–6 above. Alternatively, conduct the annual checkup described in Appendix P to see if your retirement plan is on track prior to and during retirement.

Action(s) Needed

Circle all that apply

1. Change the percentage of portfolio allocated to stocks and bonds
2. Delay retirement
3. Downsize
4. Move to a less expensive community
5. Reduce living expenses
6. Rent the basement or a room in your home
7. No changes required

Note: One way to evaluate the effects of these choices is to use the Otar Retirement Optimizer. See Appendix P.

CHAPTER TWELVE

Should I Purchase an Annuity?

Most retirees underestimate longevity risk, the risk of outliving one's retirement income. The odds are roughly 50/50 that one member of a married couple will live to age 90 and beyond. If you are a TIAA participant like me, the odds are even greater—74% that you or your spouse will live past 90.

When I reached age 69, I began to think seriously about a host of issues related to my retirement account. One of the things I considered was purchasing an immediate income annuity. It is an insurance product that you may purchase in exchange for a stream of future income payments. As I learned, this type of annuity comes in two distinct flavors—a fixed-income annuity and a variable-income annuity. Several features of these kinds of annuities appealed to me: protection against longevity risk (the risk of outliving my money), a lifetime stream of income, and an increase in my annual income. Despite these appealing features,

I was reluctant to purchase an annuity for the following reasons:

1. Once the annuity goes into effect it becomes *irreversible.*
2. When you expire, nothing remains for heirs unless you have opted for a guaranteed payout period in exchange for lower payments.
3. Annuities can be costly, up to 2.5% annually for insurance, operating expenses, and management fees.
4. I am a poor candidate for an annuity because my health status augurs a shortened life expectancy.
5. If the annuity payout is fixed, over time inflation reduces its purchasing power.

However, as I more fully understood my financial needs and resources during retirement, I concluded that I needed to purchase a lifetime fixed-income annuity with one-seventh of my 403(b) account and signed a purchase agreement. Hours before the annuity contract went into effect, my investment company, Teachers Insurance and Annuity Association-College Retirement Equities Fund (TIAA-CREF), changed its withdrawal policy. Under the old policy, I could withdraw only enough money to satisfy the minimum required distribution (3.6%). Under the new policy, I could withdraw the interest generated by TIAA Traditional. Because the interest-only option provided enough money to cover my living expenses, I canceled the annuity contract. Nonetheless, I recognize that others may be faced with a different set of circumstances, namely

1. A need for a higher income
2. No need to worry about conserving money for an inheritance
3. Good health and an expectation of living past age 80
4. Concerns about outliving their retirement income (longevity risk)

If you face one or more of these situations, you probably should consider purchasing an immediate income annuity with a portion of your retirement account. Don't expect most financial planners to provide you with impartial advice. They stand to lose commissions or fees from managing your money if you purchase an immediate income annuity. "Financial advisers have a charming term for this phenomenon—*annuicide*" (Lieber, 2010).

To assist you in thinking through this irreversible decision, let me share with you what I have learned during my study of this important decision. Where there are differences between the immediate fixed-income and variable-income annuities, I will highlight them.

How Safe Is My Principal?

After I retired and long before the current credit crisis on Wall Street, Will Rogers's famous quote became my mantra, "I am not so much concerned with the return *on* capital as I am with the return *of* capital." Insurance companies fail, and like many current investors I worry that the insurer might some day become insolvent. Four major agencies rate insurers (A.M. Best, Moody's, Fitch, and Standard & Poor's). When you shop for an immediate fixed-income annuity, you want an insurer with high ratings from these rating agencies. Bear in mind that a potential conflict of interest exists between the rating agency and the annuity issuer because the latter pays a fee to the former. We have just lived through a credit and liquidity crisis created in part by rating agencies with similar conflicts of interest.

With this rating scandal and financial crisis in mind, I set out to find an independent rating agency that does not accept compensation from the companies it rates. My search led me to the Weiss ratings.com website, recently changed to TheStreetRatings.com. This firm evaluates the financial safety of nearly 1,700 U.S. life, health, and annuity insurance companies quarterly. The financial strength ratings compiled by this company have proved to be the most accurate among the major rating agencies. TheStreet.com Ratings lists the strongest and weakest life insurers on its website. I urge you to consult this list when you consider purchasing an immediate fixed-income annuity. Moreover, request a complimentary, one-time only, copy of the complete report for the insurance company you have in mind. Weiss rates each insurance company using five major indices: capitalization, investment safety, profitability, liquidity, and stability.

A Weiss report does not apply to immediate variable-income annuities because they "offer a choice of mutual funds, known as subaccounts. These are segregated accounts which means that if the insurance company files for bankruptcy, creditors can't file claims against them" (Block, 2008).

What If My Insurer Declares Bankruptcy?

Banks and insurance companies, even supposedly strong ones, have declared insolvency. If you have done your homework, you don't expect your insurer to file for bankruptcy. Yet, the unexpected occurs, and investors must consider the personal consequences of this financially devastating possibility, no matter how improbable (Taleb, 2007). In a recent article, Peter Bernstein (2008) underscored the importance of considering what could go wrong and how serious the consequences would be for individual investors. With knowledge of the consequences, you can either hedge your bets or not place a bet in the first place.

When an insurance company fails, the state organization of the Life and Health Insurance Guaranty Association provides relief to its member companies. It assesses other insurance companies writing the same kinds of insurance to meet the contractual obligations of an insolvent company. This protection applies to holders of fixed-income annuities, but not variable-income annuities. Investors in variable annuities bear the investment risk themselves. Even if policyholders move to another state, the guaranty association of the state in which the annuity was issued continues coverage.

Most states limit the coverage to $100,000 per policy covered by the same insurer (see www.nolhga.com for the amount covered in your state). California, my state of residence, limits the coverage to 80%, not to exceed $100,000. In light of these limitations, financial experts recommend that those who purchase fixed-income annuities should limit their investment to $100,000 per strong insurer. From 1994 through 2004, customers purchasing fixed-income annuities from approximately a dozen interstate carriers received cash from the state guaranty association. Every state guaranty fund covered at least $100,000 of cash value (www.safemoneyplaces.com/guaranty.htm). By diversifying your portfolio of fixed-income annuities, you lower your risk if your insurer is covered by the state guaranty association. Let the buyer beware!

Will an Annuity Lower My Longevity Risk?

Ameriks and Warshawsky (2001) conducted a study of failure rates (depletion of the nonannuity portion of the retirement portfolio) using a 4.5% initial withdrawal rate adjusted annually for inflation. In their study, they examined five different time horizons and three types of million-dollar portfolios. Two of the portfolios placed a portion (25% and 50%, respectively) of the retirement accounts in fixed-income annuities paying a 7% fixed rate of return. The asset allocation for each portfolio appears in the following table.

Portfolio	Asset Allocation (% stocks/% bonds/% cash)
Balanced/No Annuities	40/40/20
Growth/25% Annuities	60/30/10
Aggressive/50% Annuities	85/15/0

The *Aggressive portfolio* with 50% fixed annuities had the lowest failure rates in every time horizon from 20 to 40 years. The failure rate reached 7.4% at 40 years; at 30 years it was only 2.5%. The *Balanced portfolio* with no annuities had the highest failure rate at every time horizon. By 30 years the failure rate had reached 23.7%; at 40 years it was 55.4%. The authors concluded that a fixed annuity lowered longevity risk (i.e., the risk of outliving one's retirement account and going broke) for every time horizon they examined. This study applies only to immediate fixed-income annuities.

Economists often dodge issues with the comments, "On the hand and on the other hand." When the issue centers on annuities, virtually all of the economists become one-handed. They favor using annuities as part of a retiree's portfolio. Or, as one observer noted, "If you laid all economists end-to-end, they would never reach a conclusion—except with respect to annuities."

What Will Be the Effect on My Income Stream?

In early 2008, I began to reconsider the possibility of annuitizing the money I had in one of my retirement accounts. My decision focused on how this decision might impact my income stream. My quest for answers led me to a website (http://bobsfiles.home.att.net) that contained a report prepared by a potential purchaser of an immediate fixed-income annuity. He obtained a quote from Vanguard in December 2007 for a fixed-income annuity. The annuity had an initial payout of 6.18% and increased 3% annually. This initial payout beats the 4% Consumer Price Index (CPI)-adjusted rate considered safe for a balanced retirement portfolio by 54.5% (6.18% divided by 4%). You can repeat this research for yourself by assuming an initial payout of 4% from your retirement account and obtaining a quote from a reputable provider of immediate fixed-income annuities. It's a safe bet for me to assume that the annuity will generate much more income than the relatively safe withdrawal rate of 4%. Why? The insurer can provide a higher payout over your entire lifetime because it is based on returning the money you used to purchase the annuity, the earnings generated by your principal, and the expectation that some annuitants will die early and a portion of the money they paid can be used to finance higher payments for those who live longer.

Variable-income annuities, as you might expect, can produce wide swings in income. If the stock market rises year after year, you will find your payouts rising substantially year after year. If the stock market declines, your payouts will also plummet, sometimes substantially for long periods of time. In chapter 24, I report data showing substantial variations in payouts from CREF variable-income annuities.

How Does the IRS Tax Annuities?

If you expect favorable tax treatment of the income from your TIAA annuity, forget it. The Internal Revenue Service (IRS) currently taxes your income annuity payments as regular income. If your marginal tax rate is 25%, your annuity income will be taxed at the same rate. Most, if not all, states tax income from payout annuities as regular income. Two things are certain—death and taxes. You can't escape either one by annuitizing the money you have in your tax-deferred retirement account. Moreover, any money remaining in your account may be subject to estate taxes as well.

Will My Annuity Payouts Satisfy My Minimum Distribution Requirement?

The simple answer is, "Yes." However, if your annuity payout exceeds your minimum distribution requirement, you cannot use the excess to offset any minimum distribution required on the remaining portion of your Individual Retirement Account (IRA) or 403(b). In other words, your annuity payout, regardless of its size, can be used to satisfy the minimum distribution requirement for the amount you have annuitized and nothing else.

What If I Have Significant Health Issues?

Every cloud has a silver lining. If you have health problems that may shorten your life expectancy, ask for an age rate-up. A contributor to the Diehard Forum on Morningstar reported that his age was increased from 80 to 82 years due to health problems. This age rate-up increased his annual payout because he was considered older at the time he purchased the annuity, and your age is one of the determinants of your annual payout. You will have to request the age rate-up; insurance companies won't be asking you about your health status unless you want to buy life insurance.

Should I Purchase an Annuity? If So, When?

Should you annuitize a portion of your retirement assets; if so, should you do it when you retire or delay the decision? Like most of life's important decisions, opinions vary as the following excerpts taken from Morningstar's discussion forum demonstrate:

> I know that I rejected the Wealth Management Advisor's advice to annuitize. It rubs me the wrong way to give up what I worked hard to earn to someone else because they try to instill the fear of a long

> life! Also, given up forever is the choice of building it up even more if one chooses annuitization. If I learned to make it grow in the first place, then why do I need big brother to think for me?
>
> I don't know what the future will hold and I believe this is a reasonable thing to do. I would plan the annuity in a manner to hopefully exceed the rate of inflation. But basically I would annuitize a third to add to my SS and Army pension, both of which are indexed for inflation. And I expect the day may well come when I will no longer have the intellectual ability to effectively manage my own money. So this is another reason I want to put some in a reasoned, secure investment—the annuity.

Opinions, buttressed by research, vary about annuitizing today or tomorrow. Those who focus on the negative impact of poor early returns report that purchasing an annuity at the start of retirement lessens the impact of these early downdrafts in the market. If one delays the purchase of an annuity, the retirement portfolio never recovers from a two-year bear market that occurs at the outset of retirement (http://bobsfiles.home.att.net). Annuitization today protects against a bear market during the most vulnerable period of retirees—the first few years.

Arguments in favor of delaying the annuitization decision have been advanced by the Canadians and the Brits. Milevsky and Young (2002, p. 35) maintain that any irreversible personal decision should be made only when the option value to delay has no value. By annuitizing later in retirement, one may benefit in several ways: increases in interest rates, better annuity options, favorable tax treatment of annuity payments, and lower life expectancies. I would add shortening the time the purchasing power of a fixed-income annuity can be ravaged by inflation to the list. Using a complex statistical analysis, Milevsky and Young (2002, p. 2) estimate that delaying annuitization "is quite valuable until the mid-70s or mid-80s (depending on one's gender and risk aversion), at which point fixed immediate annuities become the optimal asset class."

Boardman (2007), drawing on lessons from the United Kingdom, indicates that there is limited value from annuitization before age 76. From that age forward, he maintains that annuitization becomes essential to provide income for life. By the time one reaches age 85, the retiree's pension pot should contain all bonds and annuities, no equities.

Studies of TIAA-CREF participants reveal that retirees delay the decision to annuitize with increasing frequency. "Settlements into life annuities are occurring at older ages, and partial settlements into life annuities are becoming more common, as participants choose to keep their options open longer" (Poterba & Warshawsky, 1999).

If you remain unsure about annuitizing a portion of your retirement assets, you might consider following the strategy of Jim C. Otar, an expert on retirement (Otar, n.d.) His strategy begins with your sustainable withdrawal rate (SWR), the largest amount you can withdraw from your retirement assets without exhausting them before age 95. He shows how you can calculate your SWR to determine whether you need to purchase a lifetime income annuity, as well as how much you need to annuitize. Otar provides a lucid discussion of his strategy along with numerous examples.

What Type of Annuity Contract Should I Purchase?

Your choices depend upon the options offered by the insurance company or the charity. TIAA-CREF holds the bulk of my assets and offers a number of possibilities including the following:

1. *A single life annuity with guaranteed income for life.* If you are single with no heirs, your highest payout will come from this option.
2. *A lifetime annuity with a full or a partial benefit to the spouse.* The greater the benefit provided to the spouse, the lower the annual payout, so the benefit chosen for the spouse should depend on your needs and circumstances.
3. *A lifetime annuity with a guaranteed payout of 10, 15, or 20 years.* If you want to provide for heirs, you might consider adding a guaranteed 20-year payout. If you and your spouse die before the 20 years, the annuity will continue payments until the 20-year guaranteed term ends. If you or your spouse lives to age 105, the survivor continues to receive the full payment. The length of your guaranteed period lowers your annual payout a bit, and that may not fit your circumstances.

4. *A lifetime graduated annuity.* If you want to protect yourself against inflation and can live on a lower initial income, consider a graduated annuity that increases its payout over time. It takes approximately 18 years for a graduated annuity to catch up with the payout from a fixed-income annuity; after 18 years, the payout from the graduated annuity exceeds what you receive from the fixed-income annuity. You can also mix your choices of annuities. For example, you may split the amount you place in annuities between a fixed and a graduated annuity.

Investigate the available options, weigh them in light of your needs and goals, and make your choice. If you decide to purchase an immediate fixed-income annuity with a portion of your IRA or 403(b), you need to take this into account when deciding on your asset allocation (see chapter 5).

Should I Purchase an Equity-Indexed Annuity?

Never underestimate the financial industry; it is always looking for ways to transfer money from investors to the investment community. One of the newest ways to fleece investors is equity-indexed annuities. They are great deals for the sellers and lousy deals for the investors. Agents who sell these investment products typically receive from 9% to 15% of the principal. Surrender fees may amount to 25%, and if you withdraw up to 10% of the principal each year, you lose the income every year you withdraw some of the principal (Kristof, 2006). If you consider signing a contract to purchase one of these annuities, remember the warning of National Association of Securities Dealers (NASD) and state regulators, "Don't."

The Choices You Make

Although I am reasonably comfortable with the decision we eventually made to purchase immediate fixed-income annuities using funds in my 403(b) retirement account, I understand how you might be reluctant to lock up a substantial chunk of your savings at one time. You may decide to test the waters by annuitizing a small amount when you retire to provide a measure of protection against a bear market in the early years of your retirement. A few years later you may decide to annuitize another portion of your retirement nest egg, say around age 70, then again at ages 75 and 80. On each occasion, you will have more information about your health status, interest rates, your financial situation, and a somewhat more accurate estimate of your longevity risk. If you are married and your spouse has passed away, you can choose a one-life annuity and receive a larger payout.

If you prefer a variable-income annuity, there appears to be little reason to delay your decision (Milevsky & Young, 2002).

TIP!

Women beware. If you purchase a commercial annuity, you will receive less income than if you purchase an annuity under a "qualified pension plan" like a 401(k) or a 403(b) plan. Women live longer than men, and commercial annuities, unlike annuities under a qualified pension plan, are not required to be gender neutral.

The sales charges are lower if you purchase an immediate fixed-income annuity with a qualified account [retirement account like a 403(b) than with after-tax money (nonqualified)].

Worksheet: Should I Purchase a Fixed-Income Annuity?

Worth Considering If You Have

__A need for higher income

__No need to worry about conserving money for an inheritance

__Good health and an expectation of living past age 80

__Concerns about outliving your retirement income (longevity risk)

Caveats

1. Irreversible decision
2. Nothing remains for heirs when guaranteed term expires
3. May be costly, up to 2.5% annually for insurance, operating expenses, and management fees
4. Inflation reduces its purchasing power over time
5. People with poor health unlikely to benefit from an annuity
6. Women who purchase a commercial annuity will receive less income than they would under a qualified pension plan

Options

1. Allocation of retirement savings to annuity (25%–50%)
2. Annuity provider (insurance company)
3. Type of contract (single life with guaranteed income for life; lifetime with full or partial benefit to spouse; lifetime with guaranteed payout of 10, 15, or 20 years; graduated annuity with payouts increasing each year)
4. Age (single or multiple if expect interest rates to increase)

CHAPTER THIRTEEN

When Should I Start Taking Social Security?

Social Security is the Rolls Royce of annuities—a guaranteed income that increases annually to cover the rate of inflation. "It would cost you well over $700,000 to buy a benefit to match what Social Security pays a married couple with one high lifetime earner and a stay-at-home spouse. That's some serious jack."

—Allan Sloan (2006)

Sixty percent of Social Security recipients depend on its benefit payments for more than half of their retirement income (Gaffney, 2008), whereas only 3% of faculty members expect it to be their largest source of income (McDonnell, 2006).

With Social Security, you can breathe easier when it comes to two of the biggest risks facing retirees—inflation risk and longevity risk. You don't have to worry about safe withdrawal rates, managing your investment portfolio, market returns, or the possibility of your "insurer" declaring bankruptcy. Despite these major benefits, some troubling signs appear on the horizon. Unless the government takes preventive action, the so-called Social Security Trust Fund may eventually run out of funds. Given the popularity of Social Security, the government is unlikely to let this happen; more than likely, the government will make one or more of the following changes in this program: raise the retirement age, reduce benefits, means-test the benefits, or raise the taxes on Social Security. I expect the government to spread the pain around and do all four. Even if these changes occur, Social Security remains a great deal.

When my wife reached age 62, she became eligible for Social Security. Although it meant a reduced benefit, she wanted to begin at this early age. With this extra monthly income plus the money she received from a small state pension and a part-time job, she could spend more time traveling. Knowing that she loved to travel, I thought her decision to retire early was reasonable and sensible. Nonetheless, I thought it wise to examine the implications of her decision before finalizing it.

As I researched this decision, I learned a few things about Social Security that may interest you. By taking her benefits early, my wife reduced her annual income by 20%; moreover, her future increases for inflation would be based on this lower amount. On the plus side of the ledger, if I die before her as expected, her annual income from Social Security will be stepped up to equal what I, as the higher wage earner, received. For example, assume that she received $700 per month, and I received $1,800. Upon my death she would no longer be paid $700 per month; instead, she would be paid $1,800. Future increases due to inflation would be based on the larger amount.

Because she planned to begin her Social Security payments at age 62, what is the optimal time for me, the higher wage earner, to begin mine? Research on this question suggested that I should wait until age 70. By delaying, I could increase my earnings by more than one-third. Forever more, my increases for inflation would be based on this higher figure. Upon my death, my wife would receive this higher amount as long as she lived. In the end, I elected to begin Social Security at age 66, when I retired. With the early retirement bonus from Stanford and income from rentals and Social Security, I could postpone withdrawing funds from my Teachers Insurance and Annuity Association-College Retirement Equities Fund (TIAA-CREF) retirement account. This decision enabled me to increase my future withdrawals from TIAA-CREF by several thousand dollars a year.

Before deciding to delay taking your Social Security benefits, you should be aware of a little known regulation governing Medicare. Delaying your Social Security benefits may cost you money in a stagnant economy. Medicare expects premiums to cover 25% of the average costs of Part B. Because Social Security recipients will receive no cost of living in 2010, Medicare by law cannot raise their premiums. However, those Medicare beneficiaries who are not receiving Social Security benefits must make up the difference by paying higher premiums (Greene & Tergesen, 2010).

As for me, I now question my decision to begin Social Security benefits at age 66, despite the increases in my future TIAA-CREF income. If I had delayed taking my Social Security benefits until age 70, I would have increased my payments by 36%. Moreover, my wife's monthly benefits would have been higher, because her current benefits were based on one-half of mine, minus the penalty she incurred by beginning Social Security payments at age 62. Over time, the increases in our Social Security income due to inflation would surpass the money I withdrew from my TIAA-CREF account. Based on my experience, I urge readers to hire a financial planner to assist in making this consequential decision. Each person must take his or her own situation into account when deciding the advantageous time to begin payments from Social Security. Alternatively, you might use the calculator on the Social Security website, http://www.socialsecurity.gov/OACT/quickcalc/when2retire.html.

Currently, the full retirement age (FRA) depends on your date of birth (e.g., 66 for those born between 1943 and 1954, and 67 for those born in 1960 and later). Once you reach your FRA and are married, the Senior Citizens' Freedom to Work Act of 2000 grants you several unusual options. (Center for Retirement Research, 2008.) For example, you may file for your Social Security benefit at your FRA and simultaneously *ask for a "voluntary suspension"* of payments. By using this strategy, your spouse can claim a (half) benefit while you continue to work and, thereby, increase the value of your future benefits. This strategy seems especially beneficial for professors who often work past their FRA.

You are certainly a plausible candidate to begin your benefits at FRA or later if you have good health, a family history of living past 80, and don't need Social Security to get by before reaching the age of entitlement. Bear in mind, if you contemplate retiring before your FRA and remain working, you will lose $1 for every $2 you earn above $14,160 until you reach your FRA.

Think of Social Security as your inflation fighter and first line of defense against going broke in retirement. I am grateful to have it in my retirement arsenal as an important risk management tool. To replace Social Security with a stock and bond account to be managed by the recipients strips them of this tool and places them at greater total risk of living in poverty during retirement. In my opinion, Social Security represents a welcome addition to my retirement investments and the investment portfolio of any retiree.

DID YOU KNOW?

Spouse's benefits: If you are eligible for your own retirement benefits and for benefits as a spouse, you will receive a combination of benefits equaling the higher spouse benefit provided you have been married for at least 10 years. If you choose to retire early, you will receive a reduced spouse's benefit upon reaching FRA. You cannot receive spousal benefits until your spouse files for retirement.

Worksheet: When Should I Take Social Security?

Calculate Your Benefits

Go to www.socialsecurity.gov to calculate your retirement benefits.

Factors to Consider

- Health
- Family history of living past 80 years
- Money from Social Security not needed for living expenses*
- Under age 65 and earning more than $12,000
- Spouse's benefits
- Fear of going broke in retirement

* Even if you don't need the money, consider taking Social Security earlier and investing it.

When?

- Early (age 62)
- Age of entitlement (age 67)
- Delay (age 70)

See "When is the Right Time to Draw Social Security?" on Vanguard.com.

CHAPTER FOURTEEN

Do I Need Long-Term Care Insurance?

Along with inflation, the need for long-term care is retirement's wrecking ball. Long-term care is a must for most. (Stevens, 2000)

When my wife and I reached age 60, her employer offered an attractive long-term care (LTC) plan. After a lengthy discussion, we decided to purchase it. During the past 15 years, we have paid roughly $30,000 in premiums. If one of us became eligible for benefits tomorrow, we would recover the premiums that we both have paid in only 209 days. Stays in nursing homes are expensive, and the costs are rising every year. Roughly 60% of 65-year-olds will need LTC with 40% entering a nursing home, typically after age 85 (Vanguard.com, 2005).

Coverage

Initially, we chose a plan with lifetime coverage; however, as our premiums rose we reduced the duration of our plan to six years. That duration should be sufficient unless one or both of us develops Alzheimer's disease; this condition often extends nursing care to eight years or more. Our current coverage costs us $250 per month,

Feature	Benefit
Duration	6 years
Nursing Home Daily Maximum (payable when cannot perform two or more of the *activities of daily living* without substantial assistance)	100% of covered expenses up to $166 per day
Assisted Living Facility Daily Maximum	100% of covered expenses up to $116 per day
Home and Community Care Monthly Maximum	100% of covered expenses up to $3,486 per month
Hospice Care Benefit	Included with no waiting period
Care Advisory Services	100% of covered expenses
Total Benefit Amount	$363,540
Nontaxable Benefits	Included
Deductible Period	90 days; met once per lifetime
Waiver of Premium	Included
Benefit Increase Option	Included
Return of Premium Death Benefit	Included
Coverage Guaranteed Renewable	Included

but the issuer of the policy recently announced rate changes ranging from 15% to 25%. Surprisingly, 40% of the policyholders who are receiving benefits are between the ages of 18 and 64.

California Public Employees' Retirement System (CalPERS) offers this self-funded, not-for-profit plan to current and former state employees. Because this plan would cost much more from a commercial insurance company, you should request bids from multiple insurers for whatever coverage you prefer. The principal features of our plan appear in the table on this page.

We become eligible to receive these benefits if we require aid of another person in performing two *activities of daily living* (e.g., bathing, dressing, eating), if we suffer from a cognitive impairment like Alzheimer's, and/or if we have a *complex yet stable medical condition* (medical necessity to receive 24-hour-a-day nursing observation or intervention).

Regrets

Knowing what I do now, I would have done two things differently. First, I would have opted for inflation coverage, rather than the opportunity to increase our benefits every three years or so. I never anticipated that nursing home costs would skyrocket and show no signs of flaming out.

Second, I would have hired a financial planner who charged by the hour to evaluate the following options in terms of their effects on my retirement accounts (namely, sustainability or success rate and ending balance at age 95):

1. Carry no coverage and never have a need for it.
2. Carry enough to cover one-half of current costs adjusted annually for inflation.
3. Carry enough to cover all of current costs adjusted annually for inflation.
4. Carry my current coverage with the option to increase benefits every three years.

With this assessment, I might have made a more informed decision and one that was different from the one I initially chose. (See Vanguard.com, 2005, for an interesting case study of two professors who wanted to know how long-term care costs could affect their portfolios.) In any event, the eventual outcome depends upon the croupier's spin of the roulette wheel. None of the options carries a guarantee.

Duration

In choosing the duration of your coverage (e.g., three years to lifetime), you probably will take into account your financial resources and your family history. Most people writing about LTC cite average stays in a nursing home lasting from two to three years. However, if your family history includes a history of diabetes and you become afflicted with this disease, your average stay jumps to four years. If Alzheimer's disease runs in your family and it strikes you, your need for LTC leaps to eight years on the average. Because diabetes and Alzheimer's are becoming more common and life expectancies are increasing, a more prudent, but more expensive, course of action is to choose lifetime coverage if one can afford it. Because we have no history of Alzheimer's on either side of our family, we reluctantly reduced our lifetime coverage to six years for financial reasons.

Insurers

My wife and I purchased a self-funded plan from CalPERS, as the State of California was her former employer. Those who purchase their plan from a private insurer should consider one of the major insurance companies that are highly regarded by major insurance rating agencies like A.M. Best. As a final check, obtain a report from Weiss Ratings, a truly independent rating agency.

Medicare/Medicaid

If you think that you don't need LTC insurance because you have qualified for Medicare, think again. Under certain conditions, Medicare pays for up to 90 days in a skilled nursing facility. After that, you are on your own. If you have exhausted all, or nearly all, of your financial resources, you may qualify for Medicaid, a program for people with low incomes who fit into an eligibility group recognized by federal and state law. However, and it is a big however, the funds in Medicaid may be insufficient to cover nursing home costs. The national debt has soared in recent years while an aging population that requires more and more care also soars. The combination of these two forces may transform the silver ball in the retirement roulette wheel into a giant wrecking ball for uninsured retirees.

TIP!

Purchasers of LTC insurance policies face a bewildering array of choices and will find few sources of independent help to assist them in making a choice. To obtain insight into the issues inherent in comparing policies, go to the AARP Public Policy Institute and read Enid Kassner's *In Brief: Comparing Long-Term Care Insurance Policies: Bewildering Choices for Consumers* (2006).

Worksheet: Should I Buy LTC Insurance?

LTC Calculators

You may find it helpful to use the following two calculators on the website Smartmoney.com LTC Insurance Evaluators:

1. Should you buy LTC?
2. Evaluate a specific policy.

Coverage

You can use the chart on this page to record the features/benefits of the policy that you prefer and/or are provided by the carrier.

Additional Considerations

Financial strength of carrier

Rating by insurance rating agencies (e.g., A.M. Best and Weiss Ratings)

Claims process and payment history

Feature	Benefit
Duration	
Nursing Home Daily Maximum	
Residential Care Daily Maximum	
Home and Community Care Daily Maximum	
Care Advisory Services	
Deductible Period	
Waiver of Premium	
Benefit Increase Option	
Inflation Coverage	
Return of Premium Death Benefit	
Tax Qualified (Benefits & Premiums)	
Monthly Premiums (Stable?)	
Nontaxable Benefits	

Options to Be Evaluated by Fee-Only Financial Planner*

1. No coverage and never a need for it
2. Enough to cover one-half current costs adjusted annually for inflation
3. Enough to cover all of current costs adjusted annually for inflation
4. Other (specify): ______________________________

* After you have priced the policy you are considering.

CHAPTER FIFTEEN

How Much Should I Set Aside for Health Insurance?

From January 1, 2000, to January 1, 2009, Medicare Part B premiums more than doubled while the Consumers Price Index, a measure of inflation, increased 25%. Clearly, Medicare premiums are rising much faster than the rate of inflation and Social Security benefits.

Learning that I was writing a book about saving and planning for retirement, a colleague of mine asked me a question that worried him as he contemplated retirement, "Ed, I am thinking seriously about retiring this year and need some idea of what the health insurance costs will be for me and my wife over the next 20–25 years. Can you help me?" Hearing that question prompted me to examine Stanford University's new health-care benefits program as well as Medicare. I decided to narrow my analysis to the current and projected costs of Medicare premiums, supplementary insurance premiums, and dental plan premiums. Even though I recognized that he and his wife would have additional health-care costs for deductibles and co-pays, I chose to exclude them from my analysis because they depend on so many different factors such as eating a healthy diet, exercising regularly, smoking, and inheriting good genes. The results of my analysis shocked me, as they will you.

Medicare

Congress enacted Medicare in 1965, and the first enrollees paid only three dollars a month in 1966 for Medicare Part B medical insurance (Davis & Burner, 1995). Thirty-four years later, the monthly premium had grown to $45.40; it now stands at $96.40 for current retirees and $110.50 for new enrollees. (More affluent retirees will pay even higher premiums—$154.70 to $353.60 each month.) Since Medicare's inception 44 years ago, the premium increases have averaged 8.4% per year. In 8 of those years, there were no increases whereas in 2 of those 44 years the premiums actually declined (Hahn, 2008). During the last 20 years, Medicare Part B annual premiums have nearly quadrupled the rate of inflation as measured by the Consumers Price Index (CPI).

With these results in mind, I obtained ballpark estimates of the annual Medicare Part B premiums for single retirees and retirees with spouses over two different time periods—20 and 25 years. To make these estimates, I used the average annual increase (8.4%) for Medicare Part B premiums since its inception.

- Single retirees will see their Medicare premiums increase from $1,326 per year in 2010 to $6,139 in 20 years and $9,189 in 25 years.
- Single retirees who live 20 years will pay out $63,437 in premiums; if they live 5 years longer, the figure jumps to $102,790.

As a result, these costs will cut into their potential asset base for retirement in two ways. To cover these costs, retirees will need to increase the amount of money they withdraw from their retirement accounts and forego the interest and dividends that would have been produced by this money.

For couples on Medicare, the premiums double. They face total premium outlays of $126,874 over 20 years and $205,580 over 25 years.

Because Medicare premiums are rising much, much faster than the increases in Social Security, retirees will suffer a steady loss in purchasing power and inevitably a lower standard of living unless they set aside more money to cover the increases in Medicare costs. If you expect to finance your Medicare premiums solely from your Social Security benefits, over time you will experience a substantial decline, as much as 50% over time, in what you receive after the government deducts your Part B premiums. My colleague won't welcome this news; I certainly didn't as a current retiree.

Supplementary Insurance

Medicare, as you may know, does not begin to cover all of your medical costs. To protect yourself, you need a supplementary health insurance plan to fill your shortfall. Stanford University, like most institutions in higher education, provides retirees with several supplementary insurance options and offsets some of the premium costs. In years past, Stanford switched from a uniform offset for all retirees and their spouses to one based on years of service and family status (single, married, or married with dependents).

To obtain a clearer picture of my colleague's current and projected costs, I requested a booklet about retiree health benefits from the Human Resources department. When I began to peruse the booklet, I looked for the cheapest supplementary insurance plan and eventually selected a *Medicare Advantage Plan*. This particular plan requires retirees to assign their Medicare benefits to a Health Management Organization or HMO. Retirees who prefer a supplementary insurance plan that allows a much greater choice of physicians, specialists, and hospitals will pay roughly 65% more in premiums if they are married and 225% more if they are single.

Because my colleague estimates that he will have logged 25 years of service at Stanford if he retires this year, the initial annual premium for him and his wife will be $2,261.

- If I assume an annual increase of 8.2%, the average increase from 1999 to 2008 (Schoen et al., 2009), he needs to set aside $92,691 to finance his supplementary insurance over 20 years.
- If he and his wife survive 25 years, the figure jumps to $143,006.
- Corresponding figures for single retirees are $23,982 and $37,000.

When I finished my analysis of the Medicare and supplementary insurance costs, I shared it with a close friend of mine who lives in Vancouver, British Columbia, one of the two Canadian provinces that mandate a health insurance premium. After hearing my current costs and future projections, he said, "Ed, you and Margie should move to Canada. My wife and I only pay $1,224 this year for health insurance; that represents a 6% increase over what we paid eight years ago."

Dental Insurance

When I completed the supplementary insurance analysis, I turned my attention to dental insurance. Stanford's contribution to the dental plan is modest ($72 a year), the same for all retirees regardless of family status. The initial annual premium for him and his wife is $874.20; single retirees pay $377.40.

To estimate the future dental plan premiums and total costs for single retirees and couples, I assumed an annual premium increase of 5%. (My search for data on historical trends in dental plan premium increases proved fruitless.)

- Single retirees, according to my projections, will experience a 55% increase in 10 years, a 255% increase in 20 years, and 322% in 25 years.
- If single retirees live the full 25 years, they will need to set aside approximately $18,000 to cover their dental premium costs.
- The dental insurance premiums for married couples increase at roughly the same rate as the ones for single retirees. However, the married couples need to set aside roughly $29,000 for 20 years and $42,000 for 25 years.

The Bottom Line

Even though my colleague and I are fortunate to work in a private university with a substantial endowment, the premium costs we face, along with other retirees, over our lifetimes seem beyond the reach of many retirees. Let's total them up for single retirees and retirees with spouses (see Figures 15.1 and 15.2).

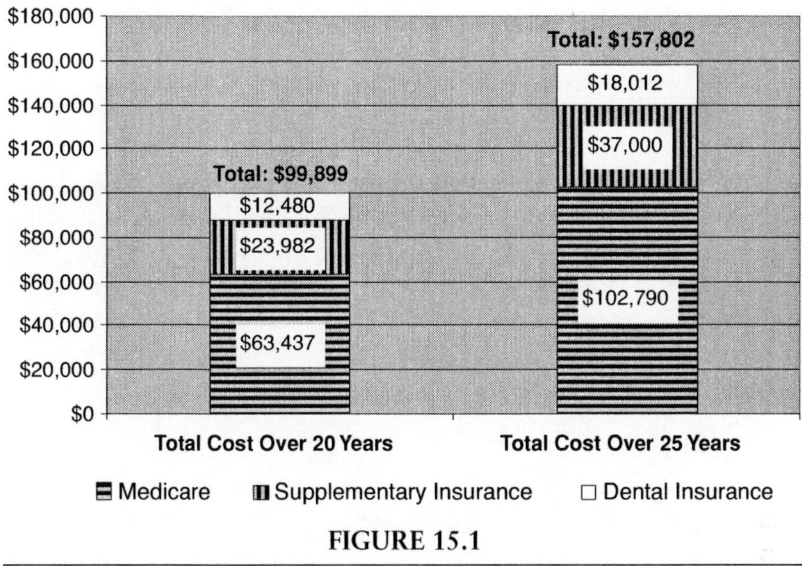

FIGURE 15.1

Health plan premium costs for single retiree over 20 and 25 years.

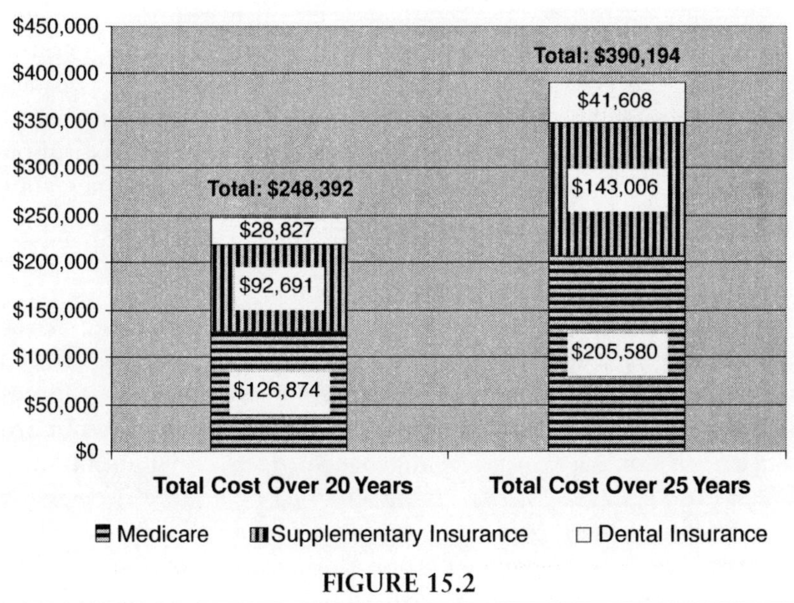

FIGURE 15.2

Health plan premium costs for retiree with spouse over 20 and 25 years.

By studying these two figures, it is clear that when it comes to health plans two cannot live cheaper than one. A married couple will spend over two and one-half times as much as a single retiree over 20 and 25 years. Most of the difference stems from doubling the costs of the Medicare premiums and the nearly fourfold increase in the total costs of supplementary insurance.

Even these substantial costs for health insurance do not fully cover all of one's expenses for health care. For example, this past year, my wife needed a crown replaced; our share of the cost was $850. Between us we paid nearly $800 for prescriptions and $500 for eyeglasses. Finally, there were multiple visits to the doctor that totaled about $200 in co-pays. Fortunately, my outpatient surgery to repair a hernia was fully covered.

Conclusion

When I shared the ballpark estimates of total health premium costs over the next 20–25 years with my colleague, he said, "It looks like I may have to delay my retirement several years." The health-care costs facing retirees from a relatively well-off institution of higher education with a reasonably attractive benefit plan stagger the imagination. If you intend to live a worry-free retirement, you will need to set aside a substantial sum of money to cover your various health-care costs unless the health-care plans at your institution surpass the one I have just analyzed. If you intend to finance your Medicare Part B premiums solely through Social Security, be prepared to suffer major declines in your Social Security payouts due to the expected increases in these premiums.

If you can't envision yourself saving enough money to cover your health-care costs, you might explore other options such as moving to Canada, Thailand, or Mexico where American retirees are fleeing in increasing numbers. In case that option does not appeal to you, consider the novel approach proposed by Lunquist and Golub (2004) in the *Journal of the American Geriatrics Society*. If you are like my wife and enjoy travel and have good or excellent cognitive function, look into cruise ship travel care. Cruise ships offer "many amenities, such as three meals a day with escorts to meals, physicians on site, and housekeeping/laundry services" and are roughly equivalent to assisted daily living facilities (Lunquist & Golub, 2004).

A Cautionary Note

Government-run programs tend to have complex rules; Medicare is no exception.

- You become eligible for Medicare when you reach age 65.
- If you are receiving Social Security benefits, you are enrolled automatically in Parts A (hospital insurance) and B (medical insurance).
- If you continue working past age 65 and are covered by insurance from your employer, you may delay signing up for Medicare.
- However, when you stop working, you have only eight months to sign up for Medicare Part B (medical insurance).
- If you fail to sign up during this period, you must wait until the general enrollment period, January 1st to March 31st.
- Moreover, your coverage will not begin until the following July.
- To avoid late-enrollment penalties of 10%, as well as an extended period without coverage, you must apply for Medicare benefits within the eight-month window following cessation of employment.

CHAPTER SIXTEEN

How Do I Put My Financial House in Order?

Prepare for the worst, but expect the best.

May the odds be with you, and you and your loved one don't need to use long-term care insurance. If the odds aren't with you, it is imperative that you have your financial house in order. Someone will need to manage your financial affairs, and that someone will be a relative, conservator, fiduciary, or attorney. Unless you have laid the groundwork, your stand-in will face a formidable task in putting your financial house in order. I know firsthand how formidable this task can be because I manage our finances and have created a road map that my wife can follow if I become incapacitated or die prematurely.

The road map that I created included the following components:

- Family records
- Financial commitments
- Investment policy
- Authorization to access account information
- Trial run to identify what I may have overlooked

In the remainder of this chapter, I intend to discuss each of these components more fully and provide a worksheet that may prove useful to those who decide to lay the groundwork for the person(s) who may be called upon to manage their financial affairs.

Family Records

If you are like us, you undoubtedly have several different kinds of insurance policies. We have life insurance, earthquake insurance, auto insurance, health insurance, long-term care insurance, household insurance, accident insurance, and umbrella insurance. No one can accuse us of being insurance poor except when it comes to paying the monthly premiums. For each of these policies, I have recorded in a Family Records Organizer the insurer, the policy number, and contact information. Moreover, I have placed all of these policies in folders in one drawer of a filing cabinet.

Of course, we also have numerous accounts—banks, credit unions, retirement, brokerage, and credit cards. To assist the person who has been granted the power of attorney for these accounts, I have recorded the account number, the institution carrying the account, and the contact information. As I had done with our insurance policies, I have placed a copy of the account information in folders in the same filing cabinet.

We have a safety deposit box so I have recorded information in the Family Records Organizer about the contents of the box, its location, and where we keep the key. If you have a safety deposit box, I am confident that your stand-in would appreciate having this information.

No list of financial records would be complete unless it included information about real estate, wills, trusts, and Social Security—location of documents and contact information.

Although I have tried to assemble all of our pertinent financial records, I suspect that I may have missed one or more.

Financial Commitments

In most households, one person manages the finances. During the early years of our marriage, my wife managed our financial affairs; years later, I took over these chores. If something should happen to me, my wife or one of our children will assume this responsibility. In preparation for this day, I prepared a list of payees, mode of payment (check, BillPayer, or monthly deduction from our checking account), amount of payment (fixed or variable), and passwords for electronic access to our accounts and our computer. The office manager of a local nonprofit organization my wife is affiliated with failed to record the password for the office computer. When he died, no one could access the client records in the computer. It was a disaster, which now that you are forewarned you can avoid.

Investment Policy

I am not interested in controlling our money beyond the grave or if I become incapacitated. Nonetheless, I have spent considerable time in choosing my asset allocation and selecting investments. I have my retirement accounts at Teachers Insurance and Annuity Association-College Retirement Equities Fund (TIAA-CREF) and Vanguard. Under these circumstances, it makes sense to let my wife (or the person with my power of attorney) know why I chose these investments. In addition, if my wife decides to sell our house after my death, I offer some options for investing the money from the sale. If she decides to disclaim some or all of the assets in my retirement accounts, I alerted her to the requirements of the federal government and the pitfalls to be avoided. Finally, I offered suggestions for liquidating and rebalancing my investments.

Authorization to Access Accounts

Heaven forbid, the time may come when you can no longer manage your own financial affairs. If that happens, your stand-in needs to obtain access to your various accounts. Unless you have signed the necessary forms authorizing your designee to access these accounts, (s)he will be unable to secure information about these accounts or to perform any transactions. With this unwelcome possibility in mind, I proceeded to identify those accounts that are solely in my name (e.g., retirement accounts and long-term care insurance) and arrange for my wife to access them. She, in turn, has made similar arrangements for me.

Trial Run

It is a mistake to assume that your financial road map is complete or that your designee will be able to implement it. I discovered the inadequacies of what I thought was a well-thought-out plan when I shared it with my wife. She identified items that I had overlooked while assembling the Family Records Organizer. Moreover, when she completed a trial run of managing our financial commitments, she encountered problems, and I was able to answer her questions as they arose. To ensure a smooth transition, a trial run is essential.

Conclusion

Few of my friends and colleagues have created a road map for those who may be called upon in the future to manage their financial affairs. After completing mine, I have a deeper understanding of why they haven't bothered to create such a road map. It is time-consuming grunt work, and there are countless other things I would prefer doing. At the same time, I don't want to leave my wife a mess. At a time when she deals with a heavy emotional burden, she doesn't need to spend time piecing together the road map of our financial lives. If you feel the same way, my approach may prove helpful to you as you begin to put your financial house in order.

Worksheet: Putting Your Financial House in Order

Family Records

Insurance policies (check those that apply)

__Life

__Earthquake

__Auto

__Health

__Long-term care

__Household

__Accident

__Umbrella

__Other: ______________

Note: Record the name of the insurer, the policy number, contact information, and location of the policy.

Accounts (check those that apply)

__Banks

__Credit union

__Retirement

__Brokerage

__Credit cards

Note: Record account number, name of institution, contact information, and location of account documents.

Safety deposit box

__Location of key

__Contents of box

__Location of box

Miscellaneous (check those that apply)

__Real estate (deed, title, loan)

__Wills

__Trusts

__Social Security number

Note: Record the location of the documents and contact information.

Financial Commitments

Payees

__List of payees

__Mode of payment (check, BillPayer, or automatic deduction from checking account)

__Amount of payment (fixed or variable)

Note: Record password information for accounts and institutions used.

Investment Policy

__Share the thinking and philosophy behind your investments and any thoughts you may have about managing these investments (e.g., liquidating, rebalancing, pitfalls to avoid, and deadlines that must be met).

Authorizing Access to Accounts

__Secure the forms authorizing access to each of your solely owned accounts (e.g., retirement and long-term care insurance).

Trial Run

__Have spouse or partner review the records you have compiled and identify any records that you may have overlooked.

__Have spouse or partner manage your financial affairs for a month or more to identify the limitations of your instructions and to answer questions that arise.

CHAPTER SEVENTEEN

Should We Sell Our Home and Relocate?

Shortly after I retired, my wife and I seriously considered selling our home and relocating. By using www.bestplaces.com we knew that we could reduce our living expenses by 40%–50% if we sold our home and moved to a less expensive community. We considered Columbia, Missouri, where we met, and retirement communities in Palm Springs, Sacramento, and Santa Barbara. Eventually, we decided against moving. Our decision became evident when we each prepared a list of what we liked about our current living situation and what we would gain and lose if we sold and relocated. We had nearly identical lists, and the decision boiled down to a choice between having a few more dollars to spend and sacrificing aspects of our lives that meant a great deal to us. In the end, we chose not to sacrifice our current living arrangements. *Even if we had been inclined to move, we would have rented an apartment in the community where we planned to live and spent a year there before making the final decision.*

As you consider this possibility, you may wish to follow the process that we used. To facilitate your deliberations, let me provide you with the list of things that we liked and didn't like about our current living arrangements:

Health care: We live less than 10 minutes away from a first-rate hospital and health clinic. Moreover, we have a great deal of confidence in our health-care providers.

Living costs: This is definitely a negative as we live in an area that is one of the most expensive in the United States. Our total living expenses would decline if we moved—as much as 50% depending on where we moved.

Climate: The Bay Area of California has a moderate climate year round. There are few places on earth that surpass it. I can take daily walks and keep physically fit and enjoy the scenery throughout the year.

Family: We have four children and four grandchildren whom we dearly love. All live within 45 minutes of our home. Moving would mean no more family gatherings on birthdays and holidays.

Friends: We have friends whom we cherish and we would not look forward to leaving them behind.

Safety net: If money becomes a problem, we can always rent one or two of our upstairs bedrooms to college students. The rear wing of our home is separate from the rest of the house and affords us a great deal of privacy.

Physical safety: Thus far, we haven't had to worry about our physical safety, day or night. Our crime rate is quite low with violent crimes virtually nonexistent. The police department is within walking distance, as is our fire department.

Taxes: California has relatively high state income taxes, but thanks to Proposition 13, the property taxes on our home are so low that I am embarrassed to tell others what they are. If we moved to any of the places that we were considering, our property taxes would rise substantially. If we sold our home, we would pay a truckload of federal and California taxes, thus, lowering the value of our estate.

Proximity to international airport: My wife loves to travel. Several times a year she boards a plane and heads for India, Grecian Islands, Kenya, England, Ireland, Scotland, China, Hong Kong, Indonesia, Russia, Australia, or New Zealand. Her travel itinerary is a long one. Other times she flies the friendly skies to pursue her interest in genealogy. Being near an international airport is a necessity for her.

Access to public transportation: At some point in our lives, my wife, I, or both will be unable to drive our car. To maintain our independence we need access to public transportation. Fortunately, we live less than 5 minutes from free public transportation that runs every 15 minutes to shopping and our medical care provider. This access provides us with the independence that we have enjoyed and valued throughout our lives.

Access to the Internet: My wife and I spend considerable time on the Internet communicating with friends and colleagues and doing research. We wouldn't feel whole without high-speed access to the World Wide Web.

Downsizing: When we thought about living in smaller quarters with little or no storage space, we realized that our current home was filled with things that we had collected throughout our 56 years of marriage. Parting with these objects and the associated memories would be extremely difficult, if not impossible. Moreover, the prospects of moving and the disruption in our lives didn't appeal to us. A friend of mine who moved to a smaller place in the same community described his experience as "moving Hell." He and his wife both became ill during the move, more than likely from the stress they experienced.

Floor plan of our home: We own a two-story home. We recently remodeled the rear wing of our home to accommodate us in the event one or both of us develop serious health problems and become incapacitated.

Consequences for our heirs: If we sold our home, we would owe a tidy sum of taxes to the Internal Revenue Service (IRS) and the State of California. We prefer that this money go to our heirs, not the tax collectors.

Cultural resources: Because we live on the Stanford University campus and near San Francisco, the opportunities to attend lectures, plays, musical events, and sporting events are limitless. None of the communities we considered could match what we have.

Others may compile a different list. For example, my father-in-law retired and moved to Florida so that he could play golf every day and enjoy the companionship of his best friend. The following year, his friend moved out of state, and not long after, his wife died. His golf days were cut short by macular degeneration. He somehow managed with the help of neighbors, but his life in retirement didn't meet his expectations.

A local resident decided to move into an assisted living facility—one of the nicest in the area. Shortly after he paid the entrance fee (over a quarter of a million dollars), he learned that he could not bring his beloved dog. Because there is a long waiting list, he decided to keep the apartment in the assisted living community but not move in until his dog died. Ten years later, the dog's owner passed away, and his dog, still alive, mourned his dead master. I learned from these two examples that the best laid plans do not always work as expected. Retirement is filled with uncertainty, and we never know where the ball will land on the next spin of the roulette wheel.

Like the man with his beloved pet, my wife and I considered selling our home and moving to an assisted living community. Unlike the dog owner, neither of us warmed to an institutional living situation, even the one in our community that offered an attractive set of services. We have become attached to our historic home and decided to remodel the rear wing of our home and move downstairs. The newly remodeled bedroom has a wet bar, large built-in closet, entrance to our deck, a bathroom that accommodates the handicapped, a fireplace, built-in bookcases, and a lovely view of the garden. We intend to spend the last years of our lives at home until, and if, we can no longer be cared for at home. At that point it won't make much difference whether we are in a nursing home or a place in an assisted living facility that cares for the infirm.

Each person or couple will need to consider their own situation and preferences when making the decision to sell their home and relocate. Perhaps our approach may be helpful as you grapple with this difficult decision.

Worksheet: Should We Sell Our Home and Relocate?

After you have rated each item, compare your responses to your spouse's.

If we move to ______________, we will be:

+ = better off

o = about the same

− = worse off

? = unsure

__Health care

__Living costs

__Climate

__Proximity to family

__Proximity to friends

__Our financial safety net

__Physical safety

__Taxes

__Proximity to international airport

__Access to public transportation

__Access to the Internet

__Living quarters

__Consequences for our heirs

__Cultural resources

__Other (specify):______________

__Other (specify):______________

__Other (specify):______________

__Other (specify):______________

__Quality of life

__Reducing our living expenses (in our case this would have little or no effect on our quality of life; however, we recognize that some people will be able to improve their quality of life by reducing their living expenses)

Note: Place an asterisk next to the factors of greatest importance to you.

CHAPTER EIGHTEEN

Is a Reverse Mortgage Right for Me?

To sleep soundly in retirement, I follow a belt-and-suspenders investment philosophy. Consistent with this conservative stance, I am a firm believer in contingency plans in case spins of the roulette wheel deal me a worse fate than I have incorporated into my retirement planning. My backup plan involves my home, but not a reverse mortgage as you might surmise. In my judgment, the latter rightfully belongs in the court of last resort.

My wife and I are fortunate enough to own a large home that includes seven bedrooms and four and one-half baths. Moreover, our home resides within two blocks of a major university campus. If we fall on hard times, we plan to rent one or two of the bedrooms to students or postdoctoral fellows. Based on our experience in renting two cottages on our property, this contingency plan seems reasonable and feasible.

Other retirees may lack our option and are considering a reverse mortgage if rain clouds appear on the financial horizon. (For additional information, go to the AARP website and type "reverse mortgages" into the search window.) With reverse mortgages, the lender pays the borrower, and the payments represent *tax-free income*. The borrower may receive this income in one of the following ways: a lump sum payment, a monthly payment, a line of credit, or some combination of these. However, the income comes with a few strings attached—closing costs amounting to 4%–5% of the mortgage amount, servicing fees, and in many cases, insurance premiums to protect the lender against the possibility that the loan balance exceeds the value of the home. On a $200,000 loan, that could cost you $10,000—not chump change. When the borrower no longer occupies the home, the loan must be paid off with interest. The interest rate is adjustable (the rate of a one-year Treasury bill plus 3.1% plus 0.5 points for insurance) and tax deductible when paid. As with conventional home loans, the borrower remains responsible for the home's taxes, insurance, repairs, and maintenance costs.

To be eligible for a reverse mortgage, the property must be occupied by the owner. Moreover, the owner must be 62 or older, own the home outright, or have a mortgage balance that can be paid off with the proceeds from the reverse mortgage. The amount that can be borrowed depends on the value of the home, the age of the owner, current interest rates, and the location. (For an estimate of how much you can borrow, go to www.reversevision.com.)

If you opt for a reverse mortgage, your heirs, if you have any, lose the amount of money you have been paid plus the interest that has accrued. In addition, you run the risk of having any income from Medicaid or Supplemental Security Income (SSI) reduced if you don't spend the entire reverse mortgage income each month.

Before opting for a reverse mortgage, you may want to investigate the possibility of taking a home equity line of credit. The closing costs are much lower, and you only need to pay it back if you tap the line.

CHAPTER NINETEEN

How Should I Use a Financial Planner?

Nearly two-thirds of 55- to 59-year-olds and almost half of 60- to 70-year-olds wish they had done better financial planning.

—Marilyn Gardner (2006)

People are likely to be more cautious about car dealers and real-estate brokers than investment professionals.

—Jonathan Burton

Now that you have some sense of what's involved in answering some of the questions you will face when contemplating retirement, you may prefer to rely on a financial planner. If you make this decision, I believe that you will be well served by considering five questions that I failed to take into account when I consulted my first planner, namely,

- What is the nature of a financial planner's business?
- How do I evaluate potential advisers or planners?
- How do I use the adviser effectively?
- How do I assess the adviser's advice?
- How do I know if my adviser is doing me any good?

Nature of the Business

The planner has self-interests, and you have your interests. These interests may overlap or they may not. To ensure that your interests are served, you need to understand that financial planners make their most money from the following services and products:

1. Selling clients load funds with sales charges hovering around 5%. Let's say that you have $100,000 to invest, and you decide to follow the adviser's advice to invest in load funds, that is, funds with a sales charge. Your adviser invests $95,000 in your Individual Retirement Account (IRA) and $5,000, the sales charge, in his/her IRA. As a result, you are now playing catch-up and need to earn 5.26% ($100,000/$95,000 = 1.0526%) just to break even. Is that in your interests or the interests of your adviser?
2. Managing your investments for 1% annually. Let's return to your original investment of $100,000 that shrank to $95,000 when you agreed to purchase load funds. By agreeing to pay the adviser 1% annually on your investment, your break-even point has risen from 5.26% to 6.3% ($100,000/$94,050 = 1.063%). Moreover, as your account increases in value, you will continue to pay a 1% annual fee to the adviser who spends 10–20 hours per year servicing your account (Evanson Asset Management). This is a good deal for the financial adviser who devotes about the same amount of time servicing a $100,000 account as a $1,000,000 account. It may be a good deal for you if you can't resist chasing performance (buying high) or selling when the market nosedives (selling low). It may also be adding value if you are like some of my colleagues who don't want to be bothered with managing their own accounts. In any event, it is important to remember that the market produces returns, and investors and financial advisers alike try to capture as much of these returns as they can.
3. Selling you a variable annuity. These are generally expensive products, and some of the expense derives from commissions paid to financial advisers. As I pointed out in chapter 12,

the National Association of Security Dealers questioned the suitability of this product for retirees, and you should too.

4. Selling you insurance. There is money to be made from commissions on life insurance and long-term insurance, and these commissions can be substantial. According to Frey (www.insure.com), commissions for life insurance agents range from 35% to 100% of the first-year policy premium. In subsequent years, the agent receives 5%–12% of your annual premiums. Because these commissions vary from one company to another, there is the possibility that your adviser may direct you to policies with the highest premiums, highest commissions, most attractive incentives, or all three. That is in the adviser's best interest, not yours.
5. Appealing to your desire for higher returns. Performance chasing seems to be the favorite past time of investors, and financial advisers know that. If you succumb to these appeals, you may wind up buying IPOs (initial public offerings of stocks), hedge funds, and/or stock options. Remember the iron law of investing—the higher the returns, the higher the risk of volatility and/or losing your money. There are no free lunches except at the soup kitchens; that's where you may be eating if you fall for these sales pitches.

Financial advisers tend to make less money on other services, and it is these services that can provide value for those contemplating retirement. Here's a list of possibilities:

1. Answering questions related to retirement
2. Recommending an investment plan
3. Providing guidance or a second opinion on financial matters
4. Doing research on financial matters
5. Evaluating your need for insurance and recommending policies (and companies) that meet your needs
6. Educating you about investing and managing your investments

Choosing a Financial Adviser or Planner

If you search for advice about shopping for a financial adviser or planner, most likely the advice will focus on fee-only advisers with credentials that read like an alphabet soup: Certified Financial Planner (CFP), Certified Public Accountant (CPA), Certified Financial Analyst (CFA), Registered Investment Adviser (RIA)—see Vanguard's discussion, *Evaluate Credentials*, on its website). In my judgment, you need to dig deeper, much deeper, to determine the likelihood that the planner's self-interests will not undermine yours. Credentials and fee-only won't shed light on that determination. In addition, you are well advised to examine the websites and brochures of potential advisers to determine the products, services, and approach they offer and emphasize. If any of these advisers seem appealing, talk with them to determine how likely they are to balance their self-interests against yours. Here's a set of questions you might ask a prospective financial adviser:

1. I am thinking about retiring in the next few years and want someone to look at my investment portfolio. If you decide that I would be better off with a different set of investments, what fund family or families do you ordinarily use? Are these load or no-load funds? What are their typical operating expenses? Can I purchase these directly, or do I have to purchase them through you? (*Note:* Costs matter, especially in a period of low expected returns. Make sure your investment dollars are compounding in your IRA, not your adviser's.)

2. One of the things I am considering is whether I should put a portion of my IRA into a variable or a fixed annuity. What do you think of variable annuities and fixed annuities? (*Note:* Variable annuities can be costly to you and a profit center for the adviser. Most experts agree that few people benefit from buying a variable annuity.)

3. I'm really not sure if I have enough money saved to retire. From what I have read, there are a number of approaches to answering this question. What approach do you use? Would you explain that to me? (*Note:* If the explanation doesn't indicate whether the adviser uses fixed or variable rates of

return and inflation, probe to find out the approach. Fixed rates are of limited use at best. Unfortunately, the rates of returns from stock and bond markets vary, and retirees need to take this into account when making projections about how long their money will last.)

4. If I decide to have someone manage my money, do you provide this service? What is the minimum balance you require? How much do you charge for this service? (*Note:* You want your money working for you, not for your adviser. If you don't feel comfortable managing your own money or don't want to be bothered, negotiate. Yes, I said, "negotiate." Remember it only takes 10–20 hours per year to manage your account, and that's true whether your account is $100,000 or $2,000,000. If push comes to shove, tactfully remind the adviser of this.)
5. If I enter into a relationship with you, it's important for me to know every way in which you make money besides giving advice and managing my portfolio including commissions on stocks, annuities, insurance, and other products, as well as referral fees. (*Note:* Should you encounter resistance, insist. Ask if the adviser has a fee schedule that discloses how he or she is paid.)
6. I am fairly cautious and sometimes seek second opinions for medical diagnoses. How would you feel if I sought a second opinion from another financial adviser? (*Note:* An adviser with your interests in mind should welcome this suggestion. Bear in mind that perfectly honest and capable financial advisers can disagree because they operate from different assumptions or investment philosophies.)
7. Who holds my assets and provides a quarterly statement—you, an independent brokerage, or other third party? (*Note:* You need to know how well you did and how it compares with an appropriate benchmark. Your adviser should provide this information plus a separate brokerage statement so you can check your portfolio.)

As you converse with financial advisers, you also need to consider their interpersonal relations and communication skills.

Listening Skills

How good a listener does the adviser seem to be? Is the adviser paying attention to what you are saying by paraphrasing what you have said or asking for clarification? Does the adviser answer your questions, sidestep them, or ignore them? Does the adviser pick up on any feelings you might have and respond to them? Does the adviser interrupt you? Does the adviser seem impatient? Does the adviser talk much more than he/she listens? Does the adviser encourage you to talk?

Communication Skills

As you talk with potential advisers, check out their communication skills. Are their explanations clear and understandable? Do they ever check to see if you understand their explanation, or do they assume that you understand and move on to another topic? Do they provide examples to clarify concepts or professional jargon?

If you use the approach that I have outlined, I believe that you will be in a better position to judge whether the planner is likely to have your financial interests uppermost in his/her mind. Moreover, you will have some idea of whether the adviser has the listening and communication skills that will enable you to work effectively with him/her. If the adviser passes these tests, one remains—the personal chemistry test. It is important that you feel comfortable with your financial adviser.

Using Your Financial Adviser Effectively

Now that you have chosen your financial planner, you need to do some homework, something I didn't do before consulting one. Before meeting with your adviser, I think it would be beneficial for you to clarify your goals, decide on your asset allocation, make a list of the questions which you want answered, estimate your living expenses in retirement, and decide on the services and/or products which you want, as well as those which you won't consider. If you don't do your homework, you may wind up with an inappropriate and costly set of services and/or products.

Goals

If you are married or have a partner, it makes sense to set your goals together. Think of the future results that are most important to you; by doing this you may be able to clarify your goals. What are some of the possibilities? Those that occur to me include enough money to last a lifetime, money left over for family members or favorite charities, money to cover travel, gifts to charity, or family members from time to time, tax savings, and money to cover large purchases, increases in health-care costs, and requests from children. It makes sense to rank order these goals in terms of their importance to you.

Asset Allocation

As you may recall, how much you allocate to stocks, bonds, and cash determines to a large extent the performance of your investment portfolio. Two of the biggest risks facing us retirees are volatility and inflation. Historically, stocks have been the inflation fighters while bonds and cash have lowered volatility risk. Assuming this pattern persists, we retirees face a dilemma: the more we invest in stocks, the more we reduce inflation risk but increase volatility risk. How do we deal with this dilemma? That depends on one's time horizon (how long we expect to live), tolerance for risk, and need for income. Generally, if you or your spouse or your partner expects to live 20–30 years after retirement, you should consider allocating your age in bonds. Shorter life spans suggest a lower allocation to equities. Because preservation of wealth plays an important role in retirement, take no more risk than necessary.

Complexity of Portfolio

In my experience, financial planners are inclined to provide you with a complex portfolio consisting of seven or more funds. If you intend to manage your own portfolio and prefer a simple portfolio with only one to three mutual funds, communicate your preference up front to your adviser.

List of Questions

To assist those contemplating retirement, I have provided a list of potential questions in Appendix B subsumed under the following categories: readiness to retire, investment advice, taxes, managing your portfolio, contingency plans, and assessing your adviser's recommendations. I urge you to study this list, and select those for which you want answers. If you happen to be a do-it-yourselfer, I have indicated after each question where you might find an answer in this book or a planning tool (calculator) to obtain an answer.

Based on my study of retirement and retirement planning, I believe that everyone considering retirement would be well advised to include the following questions in their list if it seems appropriate:

1. Have I saved enough to retire? If not, how much do I need to save in order to retire?
2. How much can I safely withdraw from my 403(b) or IRA in the first year?
3. How much can I increase my subsequent yearly withdrawals?
4. What is the length of time my 403(b) or IRA is likely to last?
5. What is the probability that my money will last that long?
6. If it appears that I have insufficient funds to cover my retirement needs, what are my options?

Living Expenses in Retirement

When you estimate your living expenses in retirement, it's important to distinguish between the *nondiscretionary* expenses (e.g., food, shelter, transportation, and taxes) and the *discretionary* expenses (e.g., gifts, travel, and entertainment). I would also identify which of the nondiscretionary expenses are *fixed*, as these won't be subject to inflation (e.g., fixed mortgage payments or life insurance premiums). You may find it helpful to use the *Retirement Expense and Income* worksheets on the Vanguard website (available to anyone regardless of whether they are a Vanguard client).

Services and Products

To guard yourself against potential sales pitches, you need to identify the services and/or products that are of no interest to you, as well as those that you want or need. I suggest you review my earlier discussion in this chapter of the products and services that represent profit centers for the adviser and the services that are likely to add value to you. During a meeting with your financial adviser, you may sense that a product or service not on your list of preferences seems attractive. If this occurs, postpone a decision until you have had a chance to reread this chapter and do additional research.

How Do I Assess My Adviser's Advice?

In my experience, a financial planner will provide you with a report bound and printed on slick paper, with colored graphs and charts, along with a written text. These reports vary in length—20–40 pages or more. In working with a client, planners may use one of the following approaches:

1. Hand you and your spouse or partner a copy of the report and proceed to review its contents section by section, pausing occasionally to answer any questions you might raise. When the meeting ends, you retain the copy for whatever use you may make of it in the future.
2. You will receive a copy of the report several days in advance of your meeting. Prior to the meeting, you study the report and subsequently use the time with your financial adviser to obtain clarification and raise any questions you may have.
3. You meet with the planner who gives you a memo (one to three pages) that briefly summarizes the answers to the questions that are of greatest importance to you. The ensuing

discussion centers on the contents of this memo. At the conclusion of the meeting, the adviser will offer you a copy of the complete report. If the report recommends that you commit to additional services or products, the adviser will probe your interest in them and move to close the sale if any seem attractive to you.

Because you are the client, you may have a preference for one of the three approaches that I have discussed above. If you do, you shouldn't hesitate to inform the adviser of your preference. As for me, I prefer either the second or third approach. Obtaining a copy of the report in advance provides me with an opportunity to read the report several times, think about its contents, and mull over the questions that I want to ask. The brief memo shines a laser beam on my most important questions and spares me from having to spend time on contents of the report that are of marginal interest to me.

Once you have the report, answers to your questions, and a set of recommendations, you would be well advised to assess what you have. When it comes to projections of market returns, inflation, whether you have enough money to last a lifetime, and the probability your money will last that long, you should view these projections as merely estimates subject to error. Don't let these numbers inspire more confidence than they warrant! These projections aren't chiseled in stone, and they certainly weren't delivered in front of a burning bush on Mount Sinai. You need to revisit these projections annually and incorporate new information about inflation, returns, volatility, withdrawals, and account balances into these projections.

Is My Adviser Doing Me Any Good?

When you hire an adviser, you need to consider what you are purchasing. Are you paying for the adviser's *time*? Are you paying for the adviser's *expert advice*? Are you paying the adviser to achieve *better investment returns* than you could achieve on your own? Or, are you paying the adviser for *some combination* of the three? To judge whether your adviser is doing you any good, you need to be clear about what you expect to receive from your adviser in exchange for what you are paying.

If you decide to use a financial adviser to manage your investment portfolio and want some idea of how much this service is really costing you, here's a simple, but crude, way to estimate the cost.

Ask your adviser to provide the following information about your investment portfolio: the percentage of the portfolio allocated to stocks and bonds, the total returns at the end of the year, and the adviser's fees. Subtract the fees from the total returns. Example: returns = 10%; fees = 1%; returns after fees = 9%.

Select a well-diversified Vanguard fund with a similar allocation to stocks and bonds, and look at the annual returns. Example: using Vanguard LifeStrategy Moderate Growth Fund, returns = 8.5%.

In this example, you hit a triple. Even though you paid the adviser 1% of the amount you have invested, you received three benefits—the adviser's time spent on your behalf, the adviser's expertise, and higher returns. In effect, your adviser paid you one-half of 1% in the form of higher returns for using his/her time and expertise.* Clearly you are better off using the adviser if this situation prevails in most years.

If you observe that you consistently earn more using a simpler, do-it-yourself investment approach, you will need to decide whether the amount you are sacrificing is worth the time you save and the expertise you relied upon in constructing and managing your investment portfolio.

*Bear in mind that the adviser may be achieving higher returns by investing in riskier investments than are reflected in the Vanguard fund, a risk you may prefer not to take.

Not everyone has an interest in learning whether their adviser is providing a valuable service at a reasonable price. Usually, these people have been relying on the advice of someone whom they like, and they are unwilling to face the possibility that they have misplaced their trust. A recent conversation with a former colleague of mine illustrates this point. When he shared with me that he was using an adviser to assemble and manage a municipal bond portfolio for him, I asked him what he was paying for this service. He answered, "Thirty-five hundred dollars a year." I replied, "Have you ever calculated what percentage of your return is going to your adviser?" My former colleague responded, "No." Let's assume that he invested $500,000 and the return is 5% or $25,000.

The adviser is pocketing 14% of the return annually. Before paying this seemingly high percentage of my returns to an adviser, I would explore simple alternatives like investing in a low-cost municipal bond fund offered by Vanguard. I would seek to answer two questions. First, what are the returns after expenses for each option? Second, are the credit risks of these two options similar? I wouldn't be surprised to learn that my former colleague would be at least $10,000 better off over the past five years with the Vanguard option.

It is important for you to ask whether your adviser is doing you any good. I have tried to provide you with a way of thinking about and answering this question. Perhaps my comments may stimulate you to consider other possibilities that haven't yet occurred to me.

CHAPTER TWENTY

Can I Count on TIAA-CREF's Financial Services?

Past performance is not necessarily predictive of future results.

Perhaps you prefer to rely on a major financial services company, instead of an independent financial planner. Because I have done both, let me provide you with a sense of what I have experienced and learned. In this chapter, I intend to focus on the strengths and challenges of Teachers Insurance and Annuity Association-College Retirement Equities Fund (TIAA-CREF) as a financial services organization. (See Appendix C for a discussion of my experiences with Vanguard.) Using a wide-angle lens, I cover a range of TC's (TIAA-CREF) services including record keeping and transactions, brokerage services, website, personal assistance, and publications. In the end, you can judge for yourself whether TC has lived up to its mantra, "Financial services for the greater good."

Then and Now

In 1998, Jason Zweig, a leading financial columnist wrote a piece praising TC for its customer service. An excerpt from this article appears below:

> A little-known outfit nicknamed "The Teachers" is indisputably the biggest and, I think, the best pension fund in the country . . . The Teachers is a throwback to the days when a money-management firm was expected to *focus more on serving its existing customers than on the profits to be had by attracting new ones* . . . TIAA-CREF reaches out to its customers in a way that puts most of the fund industry to shame. [italic for emphasis]

I fear that times may have changed. Recently, TC and Fidelity ran ads that have been characterized by Senator Herb Kohl (Wisconsin) as "misleading" (Levitz, 2008). TC targeted its ads at government employees. It ran the following print ad in the Washington area:

> Do you know when your TSP (Thrift Savings Plan) retires? Your TSP won't last forever . . . make sure your assets continue to work for you throughout your retirement. So roll over your TSP to a TIAA-CREF IRA.

Because TSP offers index funds with much lower costs than TC's and allows retired federal employees to keep their assets invested in its plan, the ad renders a disservice to federal employees and military personnel, according to Senator Kohl. In my opinion, TC's behavior seems contrary to its motto, "Financial services for the greater good." To TC's credit, it agreed to pull the ad.

Record Keeping and Transactions: Errors, Delays, and Frustration

I first noticed service problems in 2006. One of my sons converted his Individual Retirement Account (IRA) to a Roth IRA over a two-year period, 2005–2006. TC delayed posting the conversion amounts; several phone calls later, he learned that the posting had been delayed due to switching from one software platform to another. To further complicate matters, TC recorded the Roth conversion in 2006 instead of 2005. My son requested a corrected 1099–R form for 2005. Although my son's situation eventually was resolved, nearly one year elapsed between the date of the initial transaction and its resolution.

I too experienced problems with delays and transactions. Months sometimes elapsed between the time I made a transaction and the time it was posted on my account. The explanation had a familiar ring to it; TC was switching to a new software platform. On another occasion, I had completed the forms to purchase TIAA Real Estate, but TC transferred my Transfer Payout Annuity (TPA) payment to the Money Market Account instead. Two weeks passed, the Real Estate Account shares rose in price, and I learned of TC's mistake. Frustrated, I sought the help of my wealth management advisor (WMA). A week or so later, he notified me that the error had been corrected and the transaction backdated. As a result, I merely lost my temper and not my money. Late in 2006, I began to wonder if my family's problems were unique and turned to my favorite search engine, Google. When I typed in "problems with TIAA-CREF service," *Problems With TIAA-CREF—Consumerism Commentary: A Personal Finance Blog* appeared. Sure enough, others had experienced similar problems.

TC later acknowledged its service problems by posting "An Update for Clients From TIAA-CREF" on its website. This memo identified its problems and responses to them. Closing on a high note, TC highlighted its various recognitions for service to its clients. Excerpts from this memo appear below.

We are a mission-driven organization and care greatly about our clients, so it is troubling to us when we fall short of the high standards we have set for ourselves . . . We continue to address problems as quickly as possible.

Reducing transaction delays.

Ensuring Accuracy.

Reducing telephone wait times.

Displaying transactions online.

. . .

Our industry-award-winning personalized, objective investment advice offering continues its success, with 93% of general participants expressing satisfaction with it. TIAA-CREF was selected 2005 Advice Provider of the Year by *Defined Contribution & Savings Plans Alert*, a publication of Institutional Investor.

TC's acknowledgement and declared commitment to improve service may have been prompted by the University of Minnesota's announcement on March 8, 2007.

> Effective July 1, 2007, the University of Minnesota will no longer accept retirement plan contributions for investment at TIAA-CREF. This decision was made after years of feedback from participants about record keeping and customer service problems. Although problems continued to be reported on the aforementioned blog through 2008, there were isolated signs that service was improving.

TC Brokerage Services: Problems With Transfers

On August 8, 2008, I initiated a request to transfer investments from my IRA account with TC Brokerage Services to Vanguard Brokerage Services. Two weeks later, I received a phone call from a Vanguard associate telling me that TC Brokerage Services had rejected my request because I held the funds in a "margin restricted account since 2006." The associate advised me to phone the TC Brokerage Services and ask them what I needed to do to lift the restriction. Here's what transpired:

I spoke with a TC Brokerage Services representative and recounted what I had been told by the Vanguard associate. I further noted that there were three problems with the stated reason for TC rejecting my request, namely,

1. I opened the account in 2008, not 2006.
2. I never held these funds in a margin account, a type of account that enables one to borrow money from the broker to buy stocks.
3. It is illegal to have a margin account in an IRA. (Why on earth would retirees want to risk their life savings by buying shares on margin? That puts one on the fast track to the poor house.)

The TC rep put me on hold and a few minutes later returned on line and said, "We have no record of your submitting such a request. I suspect that either you or Vanguard recorded the wrong account number. You should check to see if that happened."

I then phoned Vanguard and double-checked the account number. We had not made a mistake. The Vanguard associate then tried to arrange a three-party conversation—she, I, and a TC Brokerage Services rep. Her attempt failed, and she indicated that she would try to unravel the mystery. The next day I spoke with her and learned that TC had used an account number that had also been used for an annuity held in my 403(b) account. To transfer the funds in my TC Brokerage account, an IRA, I had to request a partial transfer and list each of the mutual funds I wanted to transfer. I muttered to myself, "It makes no sense to use the same account number for investments held in an IRA and a 403(b). Moreover, why wasn't I informed that TC had used the same number?"

My mutual funds eventually reached Vanguard. Three months later, I received a letter of apology and a check for $100 from TIAA-CREF.

Needless to say, the letter and a check for $100 surprised me and reassured me that TC valued my business.

Website: Improving But Still Imperfect

In this section, we deal with two important concerns for those planning for retirement: website security and retirement planning tools.

Security

In 2008, TC enhanced the security of its site by asking users to select one of five personal questions and provide an answer to the question they selected. This selection figures prominently after users enter their User ID. TC could further improve security for its customers by having users select an image that appears on the screen before they enter any identifying information.

Tools

Retirement illustration. TC offers a number of tools on its website. I have examined most of these tools and found them relatively easy to use. The retirement illustrations tool has enabled me to obtain a preliminary assessment of my monthly income from a graded or "fixed" annuity under different retirement scenarios. Before TC made this tool available on its website, I had to speak with a counselor over the phone and stipulate the assumptions to be incorporated into the retirement illustration. Usually, 8–10 days elapsed between my request and its arrival by mail. Now I can obtain this information in a few minutes.

Minimum distribution calculator. When I reached age 70.5, Uncle Sam required me to withdraw a minimum amount from my retirement account. Once a year, I searched for the IRS's (Internal Revenue Service) minimum distribution schedule and calculated the result manually. TC's calculator greatly simplifies this task and takes into account the portion of your accumulation that is grandfathered (i.e., pre-December 31, 1986, contributions are not subject to the minimum distribution requirement until you reach age 75). Although the calculator projects annual minimum distribution requirements for future years, users must calculate the minimum distribution annually because the actual year-end portfolio balances unlikely match the projections.

If you own an IRA in addition to your TC 403(b), you *must* compute the minimum distribution requirement separately for each account even if you hold them with the same financial institution. Failure to satisfy these minimum distribution requirements exacts a hefty penalty by the IRS. Ignorant of these regulations, I failed to satisfy the minimum distribution requirement for my 403(b) and IRA accounts at TC. My WMA bailed me out by instructing me to switch my TPAs to the minimum distribution option (MDO). By switching to MDO for one year, I had to make an extra withdrawal but avoided the penalty.

Target value. As a young man, I could have used this tool to establish how much I needed to save in order to replace all or part of my salary. Without the target value tool, I plucked a figure out of the air that seemed more than enough and used it to measure my progress. Knowing what I do now about retirement planning, I would have relied on this tool to modify my target as circumstances changed and to increase my savings rate accordingly. Although TC suggests a rate of return on investments (6%) and an inflation rate (3%), users can establish their own rates. Once these rates have been set, the target value tool makes calculations treating the rates as fixed. Unfortunately, rates of return and inflation rates vary from one year to the next; thus, the calculations may provide misleading projections. If you use this tool, bear this limitation in mind. The closer one comes to retirement, the more accurate the projections become.

Asset allocator evaluator. Research, as I have pointed out, underscores the importance of asset allocation in your investment portfolio. In fact, mutual fund or stock selection pale in significance compared to asset allocation. The asset allocation evaluator tool uses your tolerance for risk and suggests how much you should allocate to five different asset classes: equities, real estate, money market, fixed income, and guaranteed. To assess your tolerance for risk, TC has you answer six questions to determine your preferences for portfolios with potentially different gains and losses and how you might behave if the stock market declined 7%–28% in a year. I remain skeptical of risk assessment instruments like this one, and TC fails to allay my skepticism. It does not supply any evidence of the risk assessment tool's reliability and validity; neither do any of the other risk assessment instruments in widespread use. In my experience, most people, including myself, overestimate their ability to weather extended declines in the market and their portfolio.

Given the numerous investment options TC now offers, this tool has several strengths. Besides suggesting an allocation among the aforementioned five asset classes, the tool directs you to a list of the funds that are available to you under your retirement plan. TC lists the funds for each asset class and provides useful information about each asset class.

Retirement goal evaluator. Upon developing health problems in my early 60s, I began to consider retirement seriously. My employer, Stanford University, provided me with a financial planner to answer my basic question: Can I afford to retire? If the retirement goal evaluator had been available at the time, I might have answered that question myself or used it to obtain a second opinion, an important step for any major decision one faces. This tool on TC's website poses a slightly different question: How much of your salary might you be able to replace with Social Security, income from a defined benefit plan, and a lifetime income annuity purchased with a portion of your TC accumulation?

The major limitation of this tool is the assumption that participants desire to annuitize some or all of their accumulation; the portion is unclear (see chapters 12, 22, 23, and 24 for a fuller discussion of this topic). According to TC's own research, the percentage of retirees in its pension plan who begin a life annuity immediately is declining steadily (Ameriks, 1999). Many retirees tend to delay this irrevocable decision until after the age of 70. That is what I have done.

Personal Assistance: It Varies

TC offers three kinds of personal assistance and designates the providers as in-house consultants, consultants who make site visits, and wealth management advisors (WMAs). During the wealth building or savings stage, TC participants may take advantage of consultants via the telephone or one-on-one appointments on the employer's site. Those nearing retirement with a substantial accumulation are assigned a WMA. Thus far, I have relied on consultants at the Telephone Counseling Center and two WMAs.

Based on my reading of various blogs and forums on the Internet, it seems that TC participants are confused about the qualifications and services provided by consultants and WMAs. In discussing the role of consultants and WMAs, I focus on the issues and questions that I have read in these blogs and forums.

Individual Consultant

The qualifications for the two types of consultants became apparent when I examined the job openings for these positions.

Consultants

- Bachelor's degree or some college with related professional designations preferred
- NASD Series 6 (or 7) and 63 registrations
- State life insurance license preferred or must be obtained by end of 3-month training program
- Must successfully complete a rigorous 3-month training program

Telephone consultants are responsible for communicating details of TC retirement plans, payment flexibility, investment choices, and overall retirement and financial issues (taken from job description). Over the years, I have been impressed with some consultants and underwhelmed by others. In a few instances, I have received the wrong information and advice. As a result, I began to double-check the responses with another consultant if I had any doubts about the answers to my questions. From what I have read, others report similar experiences. More often than not, I obtained the correct information and was satisfied with the assistance I received.

To obtain one-on-one counseling, participants must schedule an appointment with consultants prior to their campus visits. According to the information provided on one employer's website, these one-on-one sessions meet for approximately 45 minutes. The consulting sessions focus on saving for retirement and retirement planning. Topics may include debt management, investments, advantages of tax-deferred savings and compounding, asset allocation, protecting assets against inflation, and income options.

TC states in its booklet titled *Building Your Retirement Portfolio*, "Our consultants receive no sales commissions as part of their total compensation. They are compensated through a salary plus incentive program that rewards client service excellence rather than product promotion."

Wealth Management Advisor

When you examine the following qualifications listed in job openings for WMAs, you will discover that TC demands higher qualifications for its advisors than its consultants.

Wealth Management Advisor

- Bachelors degree preferred
- NASD Series 7 and 66 (or combination of 63 and 65) and appropriate state insurance licenses
- Certified Financial Planner (CFP), Chartered Financial Consultant (ChFC), Chartered Mutual Fund Consultant (CMFC), preferred

- Minimum of 5 years of experience in financial sales capacity providing financial planning services to high net worth clients
- Proven track record in generating sales and managing relationships with high net worth clients, including broad technical skills in retirement products, general investment matters and applicable tax and estate planning issues

The WMAs provide three services: a retirement review, an annual review, and an investment review. My WMA has provided me with the first two services—a retirement review and a number of annual reviews. I am not interested in having an investment review. It generally focuses on investments held outside the employer-sponsored retirement plans offered by TC. The investment review analyzes your holdings by asset class (stocks, bonds, cash), investment style (value, growth), regional exposure (domestic, international), performance history, and risk. TC offers this service free of charge. I perform a similar review myself using the Morningstar X Ray tool.

Shortly after I retired, my wife and I met our WMA to discuss our retirement review. At this meeting, he obtained information about our total assets, current asset allocation, projected living expenses, and risk tolerance. He submitted this information to Ibbotson Associates, a leader in the field of stock market statistics and asset allocation. This firm prepared a slick report entitled "Retirement Review." Four weeks later, we met with our WMA who went over the report and answered our questions. In retrospect, I would like to have received a copy of the report beforehand, studied it, and identified the questions I wanted to ask. My description and assessment of the report follow:

The "Retirement Review" document was designed to answer three questions:

- Are we on track to reach our retirement goals?
- How should we allocate our retirement assets?
- What is the best way for us to take our retirement income?

The review also contained an overview of our current financial situation, a model portfolio that may better match our tolerance for risk, and a distribution plan that optimizes our use of pre-tax and after-tax retirement assets. During the meeting with our adviser, he elaborated on the contents of the report and answered our questions. The investment philosophy underlying the recommendations emphasizes asset diversification, and the asset allocation reflects our retirement needs.

The review indicated that we had sufficient assets to fund our retirement goals and suggested that we increase our asset allocation to 60% in equities. It recommended the following portfolio:

Guaranteed: 30%

Large-cap growth stocks: 19%

Large-cap value stocks: 15%

Mid-cap stocks: 5%

Small-cap stocks: 3%

International stocks: 8%

Direct Real Estate: 10%

Inflation-Protected Bonds: 10%

Given the substantial investment we had in Guaranteed (TIAA Traditional) and the limitations on withdrawing money from this account, it would take us many years to implement this recommended portfolio. Yet, the Review document offered no suggestions for implementing the recommendations. Although the retirement analysis relied on a fixed rather than a variable rate of return, it used a conservative rate of return that compensated somewhat for this shortcoming.

TC now offers participants several options in connection with the retirement review:

- Evaluate the adequacy of assets you have allocated to an emergency savings fund.
- Evaluate the adequacy of assets and life insurance to cover the cash flow needs of surviving beneficiaries.
- Request a list of the general factors to consider in estate planning.
- Evaluate the adequacy of any assets allocated toward saving for college.

The client assumes responsibility for implementing the guidance provided in the written "Retirement Review."

My annual reviews, like most, focused on changes in my financial situation with implications for my asset allocation and financial plan. In addition, I had the opportunity to discuss issues and concerns that had arisen since I retired. My WMA has solved numerous problems for me during the distribution stage, some, but not all, of them created by TC. He also has provided me with advice about the pros and cons of lifetime income annuities. Following each annual review, he sends me a letter summarizing the topics we discussed and what each of us is responsible for in relation to these topics. If I need assistance or questions arise between annual reviews, I either phone or e-mail him. He usually responds promptly. We appreciate his responsiveness, advice, and resolution to the problems that have arisen as we withdrew money from our TC account.

Clients with WMAs often ask, "Do the Wealth Management Advisors have a *fiduciary responsibility* to their clients?" According to Lori A. Richards (2006), Director, Office of Compliance Inspections and Examinations, U.S. Securities and Exchange Commission,

> All advisory firms, whatever their size, type or history in the business, owe their clients a fiduciary duty ... Understanding "fiduciary duty" ... is at the core of being a good investment adviser ... A fiduciary must act for the benefit of the person to whom he owes fiduciary duties, to the exclusion of any contrary interest ... In whatever factual scenario, *the adviser will act in the best interests of his clients*. This is a simple statement to make, but one that is more difficult to apply.

The difficulty arises for TC WMAs because of potential conflicts of interest. In the "Uniform Application for Investment Adviser Registration," the following statement appears:

> To be eligible for a full bonus (with TC), an advisor must meet mandatory prerequisites regarding the objectivity and integrity of his or her services to clients as measured by survey results ... and in part by the advisor's performance as measured against peers relative to a number of metrics. Such metrics include overall client satisfaction, *growth and retention of client assets*, and the provision of a range of client solutions, *including fee-based products and services.*

A registered investment adviser has a duty to disclose these potential conflicts of interest, but in practice few actually do. According to Richards (2006), "Inadequate disclosure has been on the 'top five' list of most frequent deficiencies for some time." When you deal with WMAs, I suggest that you be aware of their potential conflicts of interest whether they disclose them or not.

Publications: Easy Reads, Well-organized, and Informative

To locate the publications, simply log on to the TC website, click on "Education & Support" followed by "Publications." You will discover a list of publications; if you click on a publication, you will be able to read a brief description of its contents and print or order a copy. Your initial selection would be easier if TC placed these publications in categories. In Appendix J, I have grouped some relevant booklets into two categories that correspond to saving for retirement and withdrawing income from your retirement account.

Conclusion

In my experience and that of others noted in this chapter, TIAA-CREF's financial services have been uneven. TC's transition to a new software platform has been slow and tortuous, especially for those investors depending on its record keeping and transactions. To TC's credit, it has acknowledged these problems and made some progress in solving them. However, the less than speedy progress has generated some customer dissatisfaction and the decision by at least one institution to cease offering TC as an investment option.

The brokerage service and the personal assistance provided by counselors and wealth managers have also been spotty. Some of the service problems, based on the limited evidence I have found, stem from personnel turnover and poor communication, especially when wealth managers go on leave. Those who obtain a retirement review may encounter difficulty in implementing the recommendations because the review relies on a software program that does not align fully with TC's investment offerings. The asset allocation in this review reflects the investor's responses to a highly suspect risk tolerance inventory.

Over the years, TC has improved the quality of its website. The website is more secure and user-friendly. It provides much more information to investors than was the case a decade ago. The publications that can be downloaded from the website are generally well-written and informative.

Despite the shortcomings in some of TC's customer service during its transition, readers should not lose sight of its strengths. It continues to be one of the low-cost providers in the investment industry and boasts some fine investment opportunities for its investors as I note elsewhere in this book.

PART THREE

Creating a Pension Plan

Preretirees have accumulated money in their defined-contribution plans and face the task of transforming a number (dollars saved) into a pension plan. In this section of the book, you will learn about five components of a plan designed to maximize your retirement income and financial security. A key component of this plan identifies five major income sources (fixed-income annuity, inflation-protected annuity, variable-income annuity, systematic withdrawal, and minimum distribution) and the extent to which each of these income sources provides protection against six major threats to sustaining one's standard of living over a lifetime. These six threats include inflation, longevity, order of market returns, volatility of returns, unsafe initial withdrawal rate, and emotions (fear and greed). You will learn about the income sources available through Teachers Insurance and Annuity Association-College Retirement Equities Fund (TIAA-CREF) and whether its offerings are suitable for inclusion in your pension plan. Caveat emptor: TIAA-CREF's (TC) complexity and lack of transparency sometimes led me to commit planning and implementation errors.

CHAPTER TWENTY-ONE

How Do I Maximize My Retirement Income and Financial Security?

The strategy you employ will be more important than the size of that nest egg.

—Moshe A. Milevsky (2009)

Once you have decided that you can afford to retire, you are ready to craft a strategy designed to maximize your retirement income and financial strategy. If you are at all like me, you want to live comfortably for the rest of your life, free of financial worries. To ensure that you can thrive and prosper for the remaining years of your life, you may find it beneficial to keep in mind several key ideas discussed in part one (compounding, asset allocation, diversification, and low management fees) as you design your strategy around these five key elements:

1. Adopt realistic planning assumptions
2. Contain your investment costs
3. Delay taking Social Security benefits

4. Spend the assets in your taxable accounts first
5. Transform your tax-deferred assets into a pension plan

Knowing what I do now, I would have adopted these five elements when I retired on December 31, 1999. Alas, I entered retirement with little understanding of the risks that lay ahead or what I might do to maximize my retirement income and financial security. May you encounter a different fate!

Adopt Realistic Planning Assumptions

Experts like John Bogle have forecast below average returns for stocks and bonds over the next decade or two. Thus far, they have been right; in the past 10 years, the returns of stocks and bonds have disappointed investors, consistent with the predictions. Accordingly, when planning for your retirement, use conservative estimates of your future returns, roughly 6% for a balanced portfolio of stocks and bonds. Bill Gross, the acknowledged bond guru, describes this investment outlook as one characteristic of the "New Normal." In addition, incorporate reserves for large purchases and unexpected financial emergencies into your planning.

Contain Your Investment Costs

Adopt "costs matter" as your investment mantra. To find your investment costs for a particular fund or account, look for the *expense ratios* and *turnover rates* in the prospectus. The latter are important because high turnover means high transaction costs; these transaction costs are not included in the expense ratios.

To estimate the transaction costs, use Bogle's rule of thumb: "turnover costs equal 1% of the turnover rate" (Bogle, 2007, p. 115). For example, the turnover rate for the CREF (College Retirement Equities Fund) Global Equities Account in 2007 was 108%; 1% of 108% equals 1.08%. When you add 1.08% to the expense ratio of 0.62%, the total costs rise to 1.70%, hefty annual expenses that reduce the investor's returns. The CREF Stock Account has a lower turnover rate (49%) and expense ratio (0.56%)

for total annual expenses of 1.05%. Vanguard's indexed stock mutual funds typically have expense ratios of 0.20% and turnover rates of 10% or less for total annual expenses of 0.21%, a fraction of the expenses embedded in the Stock and Global Equity accounts. Although CREF account expenses appear reasonable when compared with those of the average mutual fund, they do not compare favorably with Vanguard's low-priced index funds. Remember the rules of humble arithmetic (Bogle, 2007): total market returns − total investment costs = your returns. In his timeless words, "you get what you **don't** pay for."

Delay Taking Social Security Benefits

The family member with the highest income can benefit a great deal from delaying Social Security. Retiring before your full retirement age, 66 or 67 depending on your date of birth, is costly. If you retire at age 66 instead of 62, you receive 33% more in Social Security benefits. Delay your retirement until age 70, and you will receive 76% more in benefits than at age 62 (http://www.ssa.gov/pubs/10147.html). Moreover, Social Security increases these benefits every year by the rate of inflation. If you die first, Social Security steps up your spouse's benefits to the level of benefits you have been receiving.

Unlike the income from annuities and your nonannuitized assets, Social Security benefits qualify for tax relief. The Internal Revenue Service taxes none of the income from Social Security if your total income is less than $34,000 for an individual or $44,000 for a couple. Even those with high incomes pay no taxes on 15% of the income from Social Security. Moreover, only 15 of the 41 states with broad-based personal income taxes tax Social Security benefits. (For an excellent discussion of starting Social Security benefits, see Kaplan, 2008.)

Social Security, unlike annuities that you may purchase from an insurance company, offers maximum safety. With Social Security you also obtain inflation protection and lifetime income. In my judgment, you can't find a better deal. The longer you wait to draw Social Security, the better your deal. Too bad, I did not appreciate these features when I made the decision to begin Social Security payments when I reached 66 years of age.

Spend the Assets in Your Taxable Accounts First

Like many whom I know, most of my money was tied up in my retirement accounts and my home. A day before my 66th birthday, I retired and received an early retirement bonus from my employer worth two years salary. Anticipating this windfall, I pondered several alternatives: Should I invest the money and begin withdrawing money from my retirement account, pay down my mortgage and begin to live off my retirement funds, or use the money for living expenses and postpone withdrawals from my retirement account? As I wrestled with this vexing question, I sought the advice of several colleagues. Most were like me; they did not have the vaguest notion of what to do with the bonus. One, however, encouraged me to live off the bonus and allow my tax-deferred investments to continue growing. His suggestion appealed to me, and I followed it. As a result, my retirement account increased by nearly 20% and now generates about $10,000 additional income annually. Years later, I learned that *retirement assets last from 6.4% to 13.7% longer if retirees draw on taxable assets before tax-deferred assets depending on their pretax returns and tax rates.*

Transform Your Tax-Deferred Assets Into a Pension Plan

Your 403(b) or 401(k) accumulation represents "a number, not a pension plan" (Milevsky, 2009). At or near retirement, you face the task of transforming this number into a pension plan. As you think about this task, you may find it helpful to consider the potential of various income sources in meeting eight major threats to your maintaining a satisfactory standard of living over your lifetime and that of your spouse's, if you have one in relation to your income sources. The eight major threats to your financial security are the following:

1. inflation (loss of purchasing power)
2. longevity (outliving your retirement savings)
3. order of returns (bear market during the first five years of retirement)
4. volatility of returns (wild swings in the stock market)

5. unsafe withdrawal rates (exceeding the generally accepted initial withdrawal rate of 4%)
6. behavioral (fear leads to panic selling at or near the stocks market bottom while greed leads to buying when the market is high and chasing the hot-performing funds)
7. lower returns from the stock market (forecast by most experts due to lower stock dividends which have accounted for nearly 40% of stock market returns and historically high price/earnings ratios)
8. lower total returns from the bond market (experts forecast higher yields for bonds due to inflation, which means the net asset value of bonds will drop, thus, lowering total returns from bonds)

The five sources of income that figure in most discussions include fixed-income annuity, inflation-protected annuity, variable-income annuity, systematic withdrawal, and minimum distribution.

When I considered the eight threats in relation to the five income sources, I evaluated the potential of each income source to protect retirees against each of the eight threats. In conducting my evaluation, I found it beneficial to assign the highest priority to minimizing these eight threats. I assigned less importance to objectives like leaving an estate and having liquid assets to meet emergencies; they pose less of a threat to your running out of money during your lifetime.

Using a five-point scale, I estimated how much protection each income source provided relative to each threat. My admittedly crude measurements led me to conclude the following:

- Fixed-income annuities when combined with inflation-protected annuities provided the best overall protection against these eight major threats.
- Systematic withdrawal provided the least protection.

The income source that had the greatest potential to meet the two secondary objectives (leaving an estate and having liquid assets for emergencies) was the minimum distribution option. Systematic withdrawal finished closely behind.

By combining the following three sources of income,

1. fixed-income annuity, e.g., a TIAA (Teachers Insurance and Annuity Association) Traditional Payout Annuity under the standard plan,
2. inflation-protected income annuity, e.g., a Traditional Payout Annuity under the graded plan, and
3. the minimum distribution option from nonannuitized assets,

you can maximize the income from your 403(b) and IRA (Individual Retirement Account) accounts, ensure your financial security and your spouse's, and lay the groundwork to meet unexpected expenses.

If you adopt extended guaranteed periods for the fixed and inflation-protected life income annuities, you also *may* leave a larger financial legacy for your heirs.

The proportion of your retirement account that you allocate to the fixed-income annuity, the inflation-protected income annuity, and the minimum distribution option depends on the analysis of your annual expenses, as well as the amount of money you have invested in your retirement account.

In my case, I allocated slightly more than half of my retirement account to the two types of income annuities and the remainder to the minimum distribution option. To capitalize on lower investment expenses and lower my volatility risk, I invested the money set aside for the minimum distribution option in a highly diversified portfolio of low-correlated assets at Vanguard. This portfolio embodies the eight investment principles I discussed in chapter 7. During the recent bear market, the value of my nonannuitized assets dropped less than 15% while the overall market dropped more than 40%.

Conclusion

My father once told me, "Son, money won't bring you happiness, but if you are going to be unhappy, it might as well be with money as without it." He had a realistic outlook on the role of money in one's life. As you face uncertain prospects about your own happiness in retirement, I suspect that you would rather have money in retirement than be without it. We have shown you a way to maximize your retirement income and financial security. For any number of valid reasons, you might make choices that depart from the road map I have drawn. At a time when an ever increasing number of employers are abandoning defined-benefit retirement programs and health insurance for retirees, I deemed it important to show you one way of creating a strategy for maximizing your retirement income and financial security.

In the remaining chapters that deal with creating your own pension plan, we choose to focus our attention on TIAA-CREF (TC), because it is second only to Social Security in providing income to retirees. We will explore the income options it offers to its participants with particular focus on three of them—TIAA Traditional Payout Annuities, TC variable-income annuities, and systematic withdrawal. You may find this discussion helpful in evaluating the suitability of its options for inclusion in your own pension plan or in assessing these options from another financial services company.

TIP!

The U.S. Congress created a rose garden for you to grow your retirement assets tax-deferred. When you transfer, withdraw, or bequeath your assets, you will discover that the rose garden contains scores of thorns. Touch one and the tax man will bleed you and/or your heirs dry. Protect yourself from this possibility by consulting an IRA specialist, reading *The Retirement Savings Bomb* (Slott, 2003), or doing both.

Worksheet: Maximizing Retirement Income and Financial Security

Check the Ones You Plan to Use

I intend to adopt realistic planning assumptions, including the following:

__1. Conservative estimates of future returns on stocks and bonds

__2. Reserves for large purchases and unexpected financial emergencies

__3. Other

The highest wage earner intends to take Social Security benefits at

__1. Age 70 (to maximize income)

__2. Full retirement age

__3. Other

I intend to spend the assets in my taxable accounts before the tax-deferred assets:

__1. Draw on taxable assets before the tax-deferred assets (Generally increases the longevity of your retirement assets.)

__2. Other

I intend to transform my tax-deferred assets into a pension plan by purchasing a fixed-income annuity and an inflation-protected income annuity with a portion of my tax-deferred assets to sustain my standard of living over a lifetime. (Provides the greatest protection against major threats [inflation, longevity, order of market returns, volatility of returns, unsafe initial withdrawals, fear, greed, lower returns from the stock, and bond markets] to your financial security in retirement and maximizes your retirement income.)

__1. Using the minimum distribution from nonannuitized assets to achieve such secondary objectives as liquidity to meet emergencies and to leave an estate

__2. Other

CHAPTER TWENTY-TWO

What Are My Income Options With TIAA-CREF?

TIAA-CREF provides more retirement income than any single source other than Social Security and has been doing so for nearly 100 years.

—(Franklin, 2008)

In 2008 TIAA-CREF paid 500,000 retirees $10 billion in income.

—(TIAA-CREF website, December 3, 2009)

In the previous chapter, we identified five major ways of transforming your tax-deferred retirement account into a pension plan. The Teachers Insurance and Annuity Association-College Retirement Equities Fund (TIAA-CREF) offers these five options plus additional ones. We highlight the features of these options in this chapter and delve more deeply into three of them in subsequent chapters. Be forewarned; the choices are not straightforward. TIAA-CREF (TC) links some of the options to where you have your money invested (e.g., TIAA or CREF investments). Moreover, your employer may restrict which options you can use.

Prior to 1989 TC managed the payout of funds when participants retired. With limited choices to make, participants led the simple life in retirement. How times have changed! Now, as they near retirement, TC participants commonly ask, "How should I withdraw my money during retirement?" Facing numerous choices, some with multiple variations, participants often find themselves in need of help. To be sure, TC provides booklets describing these options and guidance on how to choose among them. Despite the information provided, I found it both necessary and instructive to investigate these options using independent sources where available. In this chapter, I provide an overview of these options, discuss how one might choose which of these options to use, and conclude with several examples of how and why people might choose particular options.

The Income Options

TC now provides its participants with considerable flexibility in withdrawing the money from their retirement accounts. I summarize the major income options; if you wish to learn more about them, I suggest that you read and study, *Reviewing Your TIAA-CREF Income Choices: A Guide to Your Payment Options*. You will find a copy of this booklet on the TC website by clicking on "Publications."

Minimum Distribution

After you retire, the Internal Revenue Service requires you to begin withdrawing a minimum amount of money from your tax-deferred accounts when you turn 70.5 years old.

> If you work past age 70 1/2, you can delay withdrawing funds from your current employer's retirement plan until April 1 following the calendar year of your retirement. You can also delay required withdrawals from tax-advantaged plans of previous employers (such as 403(b), 401(k), 401(a), and IRA balances) if all your retirement savings are consolidated into a single retirement account. (Source: *Minimum Distribution: Making It Simple* (2008), a TC publication)

The procedure for calculating the minimum withdrawal amount appears in Appendix G.

Salient features

- provides some hedge against inflation
- enables accumulation to grow for first 10 years or so, depending on returns
- creates source of wealth for your heirs
- lasts even if you or your spouse live past 100 years
- creates floor, not a ceiling, for withdrawals from variable annuity accounts
- provides withdrawals that vary with the performance of your CREF investments, sometimes substantially

Participants who wish to maximize their estates may be able to delay distributions for contributions covered by the "grandfather rule."

> If you're participating in a 403(b) retirement plan, any contributions and earnings credited before 1987 are considered grandfathered and are excluded from the amount subject to the federal rules until the year you reach 75 . . . If you take any withdrawals before you are subject to the minimum distribution requirements or you make withdrawals in excess of minimum distribution amounts, *these withdrawals will reduce your grandfathered balance first.* Any retirement savings you have in IRAs, 401(a), 403(a), and 401(k) plans are not grandfathered. (Source: *Minimum Distribution: Making It Simple*, a TC publication)

Interest-Only

If you have invested money in TIAA Traditional, you can choose to withdraw the annual interest on this investment. At the point where the income generated by the interest-only option does not cover the minimum withdrawal amount required by the Internal Revenue Service, you will need to switch to another income option.

Salient features

- must elect before age 70.5
- must continue for at least one full year

- must switch to another income option when interest payment is no longer sufficient to satisfy the minimum distribution requirement
- may not be an income option authorized by your employer

Transfer Payout Annuity

If you desire to withdraw money from your TIAA Traditional Account, you can elect to use a Transfer Payout Annuity or TPA to withdraw all or a portion of the money in this account. *TIAA pays out the money in roughly 10 equal payments spread over a period of nine years and one day.* Some participants are unaware of this provision and have complained about it but to no avail.

In a period of rising interest rates, numerous experts recommend purchasing annuities over time. For example, retirees might buy an annuity with a portion of their retirement account each year for five years. In each succeeding year, they benefit from higher payouts due to higher interest rates and being older at the time of purchase. This phasing in of the annuities over time is referred to as *laddering*. Once retirees elect a TPA, TIAA prohibits laddering. TIAA requires holders of TPAs to annuitize 100% or nothing at all; in other words, it prohibits partial annuitization of the TPA contract.

Salient features

- pays out over nine years and one day in roughly 10 equal payments
- allows one to switch to minimum distribution option at any time
- prohibits changes in payout date unless you annuitize
- allows one to use the payments to cover minimum distribution requirement, invest in TIAA-CREF variable annuity accounts, transfer money to another investment company, or move money to an Individual Retirement Account (IRA)
- prohibits partial annuitization of the TPA contract

Lifetime Income Annuity

As a TC participant, you have the option to annuitize all or a portion of the money in your retirement account.

Salient features

- is an irrevocable decision
- provides income for as long as you live (or your spouse, if you choose the joint provision)
- offers three choices for taking lifetime income—the standard and graded plans for annuitizing income invested in TIAA Traditional and the variable-income plan for money invested in CREF accounts and TIAA Real Estate
- may choose to use all three plans if you decide that is appropriate
- initial income depends to a large extent on prevailing interest rates at the time you annuitize

Income under the standard and graded plans is *not fixed*. Rather, the income consists of a 2.5% guaranteed rate of interest plus any additional amounts that the TIAA Board declares. Payment of the "guaranteed rate" depends on the claims-paying ability of TIAA; therefore, *investors in TIAA Traditional assume the credit risk of the insurance company when they annuitize*. To provide you with some idea of how much the income under the standard and graded plan may vary, I analyzed data from two different data sources: a 1977 open letter to TIAA-only annuitants from John H. Biggs, TC Chairman, President, and Chief Executive Officer and a 2006 TC publication titled *Receiving Your Retirement Income From TIAA-CREF*.

In his open letter to annuitants, Biggs reports TIAA payouts under the *standard plan* from 1977 to 1996 for a 65-year-old couple who had annuitized $200,000 with 100% of the payout continuing to the survivor. During this relatively high period of inflation, my analysis showed that the annual payouts ranged from a low of $19,870 to a high of $24,432. The average annual payout was $22,849.10 with a standard deviation of $1,640.52.

Because I was unable to locate comparable data on payments under the *graded plan*, I had to rely on data published by TC for 1993–2005. During this period, a participant aged 65 who annuitized $100,000 on January 1, 1993, with a one-life annuity and a 10-year guaranteed period received $6,999.60 his first year. For the next 12 years, his income rose every year, typically by 3.8%. On two occasions, his income increased by 4.4%. By 2005, his annual income had jumped 59.3% to $11,147.28.

Income under the standard and graded plans differs in one important respect. Payouts under the graded plan start lower but increase over time because some of your current income is used to purchase future income presumably resulting in higher payments in the future. The *annual income payments* under the graded method take 8–10 years to equal the annual payouts under the standard method; afterward, the graded payments exceed the standard payments. The *total payouts* made under the graded plan take 18 years to catch up with the standard plan.

The variable annuity income depends on the performance of the variable accounts (e.g., Stock, Global Equity, Social Choice, TIAA Real Estate, and Inflation-Protected Bonds) in which you have chosen to invest. TC permits you to switch your variable annuities among these various accounts once a year.

Systematic Withdrawal

This income option for *withdrawing money from your variable annuity accounts* provides you with the most flexibility, as well as the opportunity to exhaust your money prematurely. You decide on the amount you wish to withdraw and the frequency of payment (monthly or annually). Moreover, you can change the amount, stop payments, or switch to another income option any time you choose.

You can choose to use one or more of these income options or switch among them as your objectives or needs change.

When evaluating these various income options, I found it helpful to organize them by the type of investment. In Table 22.1, you will find the income options listed separately for the TIAA accounts and the CREF accounts. *Your employer's plan may restrict the income options available to you; check its plan and/or phone TC to verify your options.*

TABLE 22.1
Income options for each type of account

Account	Income Options
TIAA Traditional	a. Interest-only b. Minimum distribution c. Transfer Payout Annuity d. Lifetime annuity (standard or graded)
TIAA Real Estate (Variable Annuity)	a. Minimum distribution b. Lifetime annuity (variable) c. Lump sum and systematic withdrawal
CREF Investments	a. Minimum distribution b. Lifetime annuity (variable) c. Lump sum and systematic withdrawal

If the plan of your employer permits, you can elect a **lump sum** payment (e.g., cash to pay off your mortgage) or a **fixed-period income** option (from 2 to 30 years or 5 to 30 years).

Choosing Among the Income Options

You may find it helpful, as I did, to identify the objectives that you wish to achieve when evaluating your income options. You may also discover, as I did, that your objectives may change over time and that you need the flexibility to make adjustments in light of these changing objectives. To assist you in identifying and/or clarifying your objectives, I have prepared a table containing objectives that you and others may have in mind when approaching retirement. Bear in mind that you may need to trade off one or more of your objectives to create the income stream you require to meet your living expenses. As you review the objectives in Table 22.2, check those that are most important to you.

To assist you in relating your objectives to the TC income options, I have prepared another table linking the seven objectives listed in Table 22.2 to each of the TC income options. Take each of the personal objectives that you have identified as most important to you and read across Table 22.3 to identify which income options are most likely to meet your objectives.

TABLE 22.2
Personal objectives

Personal Objectives	Most Important (Check Those That Apply to You)
1. Protect Against Inflation	
2. Provide Lifetime Income	
3. Preserve Legacy for Heirs	
4. Retain Flexibility and Control of CREF and TIAA Real Estate Investments	
5. Delay Decision to Annuitize	
6. Receive Reasonably Stable Income Over Time	
7. Maximize Income From Accumulation	

After using this last table, you should verify that the income options you have chosen will produce the level of income you need to maintain your standard of living. Moreover, you need to determine if you are eligible to use the income options you have chosen, given your investments, employer's retirement plan, and TC's regulations. Finally, check with your financial advisor to ensure that the income sources you have selected are consistent with your personal objectives. Retirement planning using TC has become more flexible and more complicated since 1988, the year it ended the requirement that everyone must annuitize their TC retirement account holdings. By now, I am sure that you agree.

Income Choices of Participants With Different Objectives

In the examples that follow, you should bear uppermost in mind that your objectives drive your choices. Table 22.3 can play an instrumental role in helping you to identify your objectives and the possible income options to accomplish these objectives. When you have made your choices, additional work remains. To be sure that your total anticipated income will meet your expenses for a lifetime, you should either use the Otar retirement software program discussed in chapter 11 or hire a financial planner to review your plan.

TABLE 22.3
Personal objectives and related income options

Personal Objectives	Related Income Options
1. Protect Against Inflation	TIAA Traditional lifetime income annuity—graded plan, lifetime variable-income annuity (no guarantee), systematic withdrawal (limited), minimum distribution option (limited)
2. Provide Lifetime Income	TIAA Traditional lifetime income annuity—standard or graded plan, lifetime variable-income annuity
3. Preserve Legacy for Heirs	Minimum distribution option
4. Retain Flexibility and Control of CREF and TIAA Real Estate Investments	Minimum distribution option, systematic withdrawal
5. Delay Decision to Annuitize	Minimum distribution option, interest-only, systematic withdrawal
6. Receive Reasonably Stable Income Over Time	TIAA Traditional lifetime income annuity—standard or graded plan, minimum distribution option from TIAA Traditional
7. Maximize Income From Accumulation	TIAA Traditional lifetime income annuity—standard or graded plan, lifetime variable-income annuity
8. Move Money From TIAA Traditional to CREF or Another Mutual Fund Company	Transfer Payout Annuity

Example 1: John and Mary, a married couple in good health with two grown children, have reached retirement age (65). Both of their children are financially independent and unlikely to require any financial assistance in the future. John and Mary estimate that they will have less money in retirement than they will need. They don't want to delay retirement, rent a room in their home, downsize their house, or move to a less expensive area to reduce the gap between their income and their expenses. As they review the list of personal objectives, they immediately eliminate number 3

(legacy for heirs) and circle numbers 7 (maximize income from accumulation), 1 (protect against inflation), and 2 (provide lifetime income). After reviewing the related income options in Table 22.3, they tentatively settle on three: lifetime income annuity under the standard plan, lifetime annuity under the graded plan, and systematic withdrawal. After rereading our discussion of the salient features of these three options, they request information from TC regarding their potential payouts. While awaiting this information from TC, they download the Otar software program and begin to familiarize themselves with it. When the information on payouts arrives from TC, they proceed to enter it into the Otar retirement program. The Otar program yields the information they wanted to hear—a good chance of meeting their financial needs over their lifetime.

Example 2: George (age 69) and his wife, Penny (age 64), have worked most of their lives, own their home free and clear, contributed the maximum to their TC accounts, and enjoy excellent health. George plans to continue working for a publishing company when he retires from the faculty at Elite University. One of their three children has run into financial difficulty, and it is unclear how the other two will fare in the future. George, a mathematician, uses the Vanguard calculator described in chapter 11 and announces to his wife that they appear to be in excellent financial shape when he retires. The two of them find time to examine Table 22.3 and immediately agree on objective number 3 (preserve legacy for heirs). The related income option for this objective is the minimum distribution option. They notice that this income source has an additional appealing virtue, namely, flexibility (4 in Table 22.3). George reexamines the salient features of the minimum distribution option and announces to his wife, "There is no doubt in my mind that we have made a good choice. What do you think?" Penny responds, "I agree, but I would feel more comfortable if we had an estimate of our first year's income." George turns on his computer, logs on to the TC website, clicks on "tools," and uses the minimum distributions calculator to obtain the estimate. Just as he expected, this income option would actually produce more income than they needed.

Example 3: When Paul and Mary began discussing their retirement plans, it became evident that they had some disagreements. Mary wanted the security of knowing that the two of them would never have to worry about going broke. She favored objective 2 (provide lifetime income). Paul disagreed and offered several reasons against annuitizing a portion of their TC holdings: his parents had died relatively early in life, he didn't want to lose control of the money he had worked so hard to accumulate, and he suffered from high blood pressure and high cholesterol. Not wanting to abandon her objective, Mary suggested a compromise. "Let's select an income option that postpones our decision to annuitize (5 in Table 22.3). In a few years, we will have more information about your health, our financial situation, and other issues that surface in the meantime. If we choose to postpone this decision, we can use one or more of the following options: minimum distribution, interest-only, or systematic withdrawal. We can review the salient features of each option before making our final decision." Paul agrees with her suggestion. After reviewing the features of the three income options, they decide to request estimates of their payouts for each option. When the payout information arrives from TC, they discover that they can meet their expenses by using the interest-only option for TIAA Traditional and systematic withdrawal for CREF.

Example 4: Isobel has never married; her physician rates her health as excellent for someone her age (69). Although no one else depends on her for financial support, she has some favorite charities that she would like to leave some money to, namely, the ACLU, NOW, and the boarding school she attended in the Himalayas. However, her overriding concerns center on ensuring that she has enough money to last her a lifetime and keep up with inflation. When she examines Table 22.3, she decides to prioritize three objectives: 1 (inflation) and 2 (lifetime income) are of primary importance while 3 (legacy) is secondary. As she examines the related income options for each of these objectives, she gravitates to the lifetime variable-income annuity. She has always been an aggressive investor and can tolerate the fluctuations in income because she has additional resources available. In the final analysis, she tentatively settles on minimum distribution for her TIAA Traditional, systematic withdrawal for half of her CREF account, and a lifetime variable-income annuity for the other half of CREF. She requests estimates of the payouts from TC for this retirement income plan. When they arrive, she breathes a sigh of relief; her plan apparently will generate sufficient income to meet her expenses.

Hopefully, these four examples will enable you to begin the challenging task of forging a pension plan using TC's numerous options.

CAUTIONARY NOTE

During my career in higher education, I worked at three different institutions (Washington University, University of Chicago, and Stanford University) that offered TC. Each of these institutions had rules that restricted my investment options and withdrawals. I did not realize until I retired that the *current rules of each institution always governed* the choices I could make on the money invested while working at each of these institutions, as well as the growth thereon. Fortunately, all three institutions provided plan participants with considerable latitude. If I had been less fortunate, one institution might have required me to annuitize, another might have prohibited the use of a TPA, and the third institution might have required that its contributions must remain with TC. Check your quarterly statements to see if they differentiate the sums attributable to each institution in which you have worked. When you retire, you will learn, much to your surprise, and perhaps dismay, that the plan rules of the institutions where you have accumulated your money in TC may differ and limit your choices for funding your retirement. Moreover, each institution has a contract; contracts with multiple institutions mean additional paperwork for you, as I discovered. If you move from one TC participating institution to another, you should keep abreast of the plan rules governing choices in your former institution(s), as well as your current one.

Worksheet: Choosing Among TIAA-CREF's Income Options

Step 1: Check the personal objectives of most importance to you.

Personal Objectives	Most Important (Check Those That Apply to You)
1. Protect Against Inflation	
2. Provide Lifetime Income	
3. Preserve Legacy for Heirs	
4. Retain Flexibility and Control of CREF and TIAA Real Estate Investments	
5. Delay Decision to Annuitize	
6. Receive Reasonably Stable Income Over Time	
7. Maximize Income From Accumulation	

Step 2: Using the personal objectives of greatest importance to you, you should circle the income options that appeal to you from the list of related options.

Personal Objectives	Related Income Options
1. Protect Against Inflation	TIAA Traditional lifetime income annuity—graded plan, lifetime variable-income annuity (no guarantee), systematic withdrawal (limited), minimum distribution option (limited)
2. Provide Lifetime Income	TIAA Traditional lifetime income annuity—standard or graded plan, lifetime variable-income annuity
3. Preserve Legacy for Heirs	Minimum distribution option
4. Retain Flexibility and Control of CREF and TIAA Real Estate Investments	Minimum distribution option, systematic withdrawal
5. Delay Decision to Annuitize	Minimum distribution option, interest-only, systematic withdrawal

Personal Objectives	Related Income Options
6. Receive Reasonably Stable Income Over Time	TIAA Traditional lifetime income annuity—standard or graded plan, Minimum distribution option from TIAA Traditional
7. Maximize Income From Accumulation	TIAA Traditional lifetime income annuity—standard or graded plan, lifetime variable-income annuity
8. Move Money From TIAA Traditional to CREF or Another Mutual Fund Company	Transfer Payout Annuity

Note: After reading the chapters that follow, you should revisit this table to see if the income options you circled remain appealing. If not, strike out the ones you circled and circle those that now seem more appealing.

CHAPTER TWENTY-THREE

Should I Incorporate a TIAA Traditional Payout Annuity Into My Pension Plan?

Think of annuities as long-life insurance.

Unlike the U.S. government, the British government passed a law some time ago that *required* its citizens to annuitize the money in their retirement accounts when they reached age 75. The British government feared that its elderly citizens might outlive their retirement assets and go on the dole. British citizens must shop for their annuities; from the newspaper accounts that I have read (e.g., Colman, 2008), the vendors of these insurance products frequently shortchanged buyers. A few years back, the British government, under pressure from certain religious groups, authorized the option of *alternatively secured pensions* or ASPs. These ASPs allowed retirees to leave their pension funds invested after age 75 with the option to switch to an annuity at any time thereafter.

Prior to 1989, Teachers Insurance and Annuity Association-College Retirement Equities Fund (TIAA-CREF) also required its participants to annuitize their retirement accounts (Wolf, 2001). Unlike their British counterparts, TIAA-CREF (TC) participants did not need to shop for their annuities; moreover, TC offered them annuities with no sales commissions and extremely low annual operating expenses. When TC dropped the requirement to annuitize, I suspect payments to annuitants also declined. With a less diverse risk pool due to unhealthy participants choosing not to annuitize, TIAA probably lowered payouts due to the higher life expectancies of annuitants, a phenomenon called *adverse selection*. Studies on the impact of adverse selection have found that it reduces annuity income from 2 to 10 cents per dollar of premium paid (Mitchell et al., 1999; Webb, 2006).

When I approached my 74th birthday, I seriously began to consider purchasing a lifetime income annuity from TC using money in my TIAA Traditional Account. Much to my surprise, I learned that the decision to "annuitize" was *irrevocable*, a decision not to be taken lightly. Forevermore, TC would take control of my money; moreover, TC would limit my flexibility in investing and withdrawing the money. A second surprise awaited me. A TIAA Traditional lifetime income annuity does not provide fixed-income payments as other insurance companies do. A TIAA Traditional Payout Annuity contract stipulates that a payout includes two parts: a guaranteed payment plus additional amounts, formerly referred to as dividends. When I purchased my first TIAA Traditional Payout Annuity, effective on my 74th birthday, 59.25% of my payment was guaranteed; the remaining 40.75% represented additional amounts.

With these two surprises uppermost in mind, I set out to learn more about TC's Traditional Payout Annuities, as well as those that could be purchased from other insurance companies. In the sections that follow, I discuss what I learned about a number of the issues that arose during my investigation and the decision I eventually made. In light of the amount of information and options covered, I close the chapter with a summary and suggestions for implementing this decision in the event you choose to purchase a payout annuity with some of the money you have invested in TIAA Traditional.

Safety of Principal

Although TC carries the top ratings from four major rating agencies for life and health insurers (A.M. Best, Moody's, Fitch, and Standard & Poor's), I remain uneasy, especially since Fitch and

Standard & Poor's revised their outlook from stable to negative. A negative outlook reflects concerns of these two rating agencies "about potential investment losses and impairments, as well as economic conditions" (June 19, 2009, announcement on TC's website).

With this recent change in outlook in mind, I decided to search the TheStreet.com Ratings website. This independent rating agency lists the strongest and weakest life insurers. When I discovered that TheStreet.com assigns a rating of A+ to TIAA of America and places it first on a rather short list of strong insurers, I breathed a sigh of relief. TIAA appears to be one of the strongest, if not the strongest, insurance company among its peers.

By nature and training, I am a card-carrying skeptic from the "show-me" state. Acting on my skepticism, I decided to purchase the detailed rating analysis report prepared by TheStreet.com. Much to my surprise, a complimentary, one time–only, copy arrived the next day. This independent rating agency provided detailed ratings of TIAA using five major indices: capitalization, investment safety, profitability, liquidity, and stability. Because users agree to keep this report confidential, I urge you to order a copy and review it thoroughly before deciding to annuitize a portion of your retirement account. TheStreet.com provides a much more informative, nuanced, and unbiased analysis than the ratings reported on TC's website. Even though TIAA appears to be a strong company, I turned my attention to the *I* word—*insolvency*.

Insolvency

Because TIAA appears to be a financially strong company, no one expects it to file for bankruptcy. However, with a sizable portion of my retirement account invested in TIAA Traditional, I wanted to know what would happen if TIAA failed and declared bankruptcy. More specifically, was a TIAA Traditional Payout Annuity covered by the state organization of the Life and Health Insurance Guaranty Association? If it were, I could recover some of my money. If not, we would be in serious financial difficulty if TIAA could not honor its commitment.

The answer appears on page 1 of my TIAA Traditional Payout Annuity Contract Two-Life Annuity with Full Benefit to Survivor; it states,

Payments under agreement are not protected or otherwise guaranteed by any government agency or the California Life and Health Insurance Guarantee Association.

Moreover, on the last page (page G1) appears the following statement in large black boldface letters:

Notice of Non-Coverage
California Life and Health Insurance Guarantee Association Act
THIS POLICY IS NOT COVERED BY THE CALIFORNIA
LIFE AND HEALTH INSURANCE GUARANTEE ASSOCIATION

Because my contract issued on January 1, 2008, clearly states **No Coverage,** I assume that no Life and Health Insurance Guaranty Association covers holders of income annuities issued by TIAA. I can only speculate about the reasons behind this lack of coverage. As the largest pension fund in the United States and the insurer with the most financial strength, it probably opted not to participate to avoid the assessments imposed to cover the failures of companies with lower ratings. Another possibility I considered has to do with the features of TIAA's immediate annuities. The annual payments for its income annuities include a guaranteed payment plus additional amounts. Although a dividend has been paid annually since 1948, TIAA could reduce or eliminate the dividend during hard times to avoid bankruptcy and then restore it when prosperity returned. Moreover, a guarantee seems of limited value because the California Guarantee Association does not cover "any portion of a contract that provides dividends or experience rating credits" (source: *Your Service Directory* provided by TIAA-CREF). In my case, dividends account for roughly 40.75% of my annual payout. Because my assumption may not hold for every State Life Insurance Guaranty Association (LGA), potential annuitants should request a copy of the Immediate Annuity contract prior to annuitizing and check with the State LGA if the contract does not disclose what the State LGA covers.

As I pondered my decision to annuitize, I also weighed the likelihood of running out of money if I invested the money in bonds instead of a TIAA Traditional Payout Annuity. I assumed the same rate of withdrawal and discovered using the Vanguard lifetime spending analyzer that there was a 49% probability of exhausting my resources at age 89; however, there was a 54% probability that either my wife or I would be alive at age 90. Given the constraints I faced, I somewhat reluctantly annuitized the money I had invested in TIAA Traditional, even though it lacked the state guaranty backing.

Type of Annuity Contract

With the money you have invested in TIAA Traditional, you have two major lifetime income annuity options—the standard plan and the graded plan. As I explained in an earlier chapter, these two plans differ in important ways. Under the standard plan, the annuitant receives an annual income that initially is higher than the income from the graded plan. After 8–10 years, the annual income from the graded plan matches the standard plan. In subsequent years, the graded payments outstrip the standard payments. The *cumulative payout* of the graded plan usually catches up to the standard plan in approximately 18 years.

Regardless of the plan you choose, the money you have accumulated in TIAA Traditional has earned the crediting rate that prevailed in the year in which you invested your money. As a result, when you start receiving benefits, they reflect in part the interest rate environment that prevailed when TIAA applied the crediting rates to your contributions. In my case, that has been a distinct advantage because I invested nearly half of my money in this account during a period of high interest rates. For example, I, along with other TIAA Standard Payment annuitants, received a payment "based on interest rates ranging from 4.0% to 9.5%, depending on when the underlying funds were applied to TIAA and when you began lifetime income" (2008).

Payout Differentials

To obtain a clearer picture of the initial payout differential between the standard and graded plans, I secured the data for seven different time periods between 1970 and 2009. The most dramatic differences occurred for those retiring in 1970 and 1975. Those who retired in 1970 and elected the graded plan received 15.8% less than the recipients under the standard plan whereas those retiring in 1975 received 72.5% less. *Initial payout differentials between the two methods are higher when interest rates are high than when they are low* (King, 1995).

Purchasing Power

The graded plan offers the hope of retaining its initial payout's purchasing power while the standard plan is destined to lose it. How does the graded plan manage to provide some protection against inflation?

> Initial income is based on a 4% interest rate (2.5% guaranteed plus 1.5% from additional amounts). If the total payout interest rate exceeds 4%, the amount over 4% is reinvested, adding to your guaranteed income and to the base on which future income will be calculated. The result is that payments are likely to increase throughout your retirement to help protect against inflation. When the guaranteed interest plus the additional amounts exceeds 4%, your income will increase the following year. If these factors add up to less than 4%, your income *could decrease*. Income changes become effective on January 1. (*Outreach*, 2008).

To obtain an estimate of how each plan's initial purchasing power fares in the real world, I used data from King's study of these two plans (King, 1995) to track the initial payouts for five different time periods, 1970 through 1990. In all the five time periods, the standard payout lost its purchasing power and the loss increased as the length of the time period increased. The losses ranged from 15% to 62%. The graded plan payout actually increased its purchasing power in four of the five periods; moreover, in two of the time periods (1980–1994 and 1985–1995) the increase was substantial, 46% and 43%, respectively. During the 1970–1989 period, the graded plan lost 12%.

According to the December 2008 issue of *Outreach*, a TIAA publication, recipients of lifetime income under the graded payment method before 2007 received an average increase of 3% in 2008. In the 1970s, 1980s, and 1990s, the graded payment annual increases hovered around 4% with some even much higher. TIAA has increased the graded payments every year since it introduced the method in 1982. As I stated earlier in this chapter, TIAA does not guarantee annual increases in the graded payments.

Choosing Between the Two Methods

In choosing between the standard and graded payment methods, you may find it useful to consider the three issues that I did. They included the following:

1. Can we maintain our current standard of living and lifestyle if we choose the graded plan?
2. Does it make sense for us to create a diversified retirement portfolio that meets our *fixed expenses* (such as our mortgage payment and life insurance premiums) with the standard plan, our *essential expenses* (such as food, electricity, and water) that are subject to inflation with the graded plan, and our *desirable expenditures* (such as vacations and entertainment) with the minimum distribution option for our nonannuitized assets?
3. Is it wiser to choose the standard plan and save the difference between the payments for the standard and graded plans to be used to offset the effects of inflation? If the U.S. government increases income taxes, this option makes sense, if we resist the temptation to spend the money, rather than save it.

More Options and More Decisions

Each payment plan offers guarantees; these guarantees come with a cost—reduced payouts. I have posed each guarantee as a question requiring a decision.

1. Should you choose a one- or two-life annuity? If you have a partner or spouse as I do, you probably will select a two-life annuity that continues payments for your spouse or partner, whatever is the case. A one-life annuity requires the approval of your spouse if you are married.

2. Should your partner or spouse receive 100% of your benefits, two-thirds of your benefits, or half of your benefits? In choosing among these options, you might find it helpful to consider the factors identified in Table 23.1 by Schloss and Abildsoe (2000).

Although our expenses will drop a bit upon my death, I chose full benefits for my wife. During the 56 years of our marriage, she has been a full partner in our household and deserves a full share of what we have accumulated. Moreover, I doubt that she would feel comfortable with a lesser amount.

3. Should you select a guaranteed period of 10, 15, or 20 years? If you and/or your annuity partner die before the guaranteed period expires, payments continue to your heirs for the remainder of the guaranteed period. In effect, you are trading some retirement income for the *possibility* of leaving some money to your heirs. As you consider the tradeoffs, consider health, longevity history of family, own income needs, and desire to have all the money you have paid for the annuity paid to you and your survivors. Because I attach considerable importance to leaving a legacy for our heirs, I lean toward the 20-year guaranteed period. In our case, choosing the 20-year guaranteed period entails little sacrifice in income because we also are choosing a 100% survivor benefit. Given the long

TABLE 23.1
Benefit options

Options	Factors to Consider
One hundred percent to Survivor	Age and health: If 10 or more years younger and in good health, option appropriate.
Two-thirds to Survivor	No matter who dies first, payments are reduced by one-third! Provides higher payout than other two options. Appropriate if both of you in good health and about the same age with good prospects of living a long time given family history.
One-half to Annuity Partner	If you die first, annuity partner's benefit reduced by 50%. If annuity partner dies first, you continue with no loss of income. Probably makes sense only if annuity partner has much poorer health relative to yours, is comfortable with the arrangement, and has other assets on which to live.

life expectancy of TIAA annuitants, it is more likely than not that one of us will live nearly 20 years.

One additional decision remains: Should you choose to receive your income monthly or annually? Most people prefer monthly because that simplifies the budgeting process and lowers the risk of running through the money before year's end. I plan to choose annual payments, however. Several years ago, my wife and I remodeled a large bedroom on the first floor of our home, so it better fits our needs as we grow older. To finance this remodel, we opened a home equity line of credit. If we take our annuity payment in early January, deposit it in our home equity line of credit account, and draw on it monthly, we can save a considerable amount of interest that can be used to reduce the principal on our loan.

It should be clear from the discussion, thus far, that one's objectives and income needs exert considerable influence over the choices inherent in the decision to annuitize all or a portion of one's TC accumulations.

Flexible Though Irrevocable

As I underscored earlier, the decision to annuitize is irrevocable. Having made the decision, you cannot terminate the contract, change the survivor, modify your survivor's benefits, or alter the guaranteed period if you have elected one. The decision prevents you from tapping additional amounts to cover emergencies.

Despite the restrictions and the irreversibility of the decision, you retain some flexibility. If you decide to change from monthly to annual income payments or vice versa, TC allows the change for the standard and graded payment plans. Moreover, TC permits annuitants to change their source of income. The permissible changes appear in Table 23.2.

The graded method provides greater flexibility than the standard method. You can switch from the graded to the standard method, but you cannot switch from the standard to the graded method. Both methods allow you to shift money to the CREF equity accounts; however, TC limits switches to no more than 20% per year or 100% in equal installments spread over five years. If you transfer from either the TIAA Traditional graded or standard payment methods to CREF equity accounts, you cannot

TABLE 23.2
Income flexibilities for standard and graded methods

Transfers From	Transfers To
TIAA Traditional Graded Payment Method	a. TIAA Traditional using the standard payment method (likely to increase income) b. Any of the CREF equity accounts (likely to decrease the stability of your income stream) *Note:* Transfers back to TIAA Traditional and transfers to TIAA Real Estate, Money Market, and Bond accounts prohibited.
TIAA Traditional Standard Payment Method	Any of the CREF equity accounts (likely to decrease the stability of your income stream) *Note:* Transfers back to TIAA Traditional and transfers to TIAA Real Estate, Money Market, and Bond accounts prohibited.

transfer back to TIAA Traditional. In other words, no round-trips allowed.

Payouts From TIAA and 11 Other Fixed-Income Providers

In my final evaluation of the income options offered by TIAA, I obtained quotes from TC and 11 other providers on two different options: (a) a fixed payment plan with a 20-year guaranteed period and full benefit for my spouse and (b) a payment plan with a 3% annual cost of living adjustment (COLA), as well as a guaranteed period of 20 years and a full benefit for my wife. Bear in mind that TC's graded plan carries no guaranteed annual increase although it has provided an increase every year since it began in 1982. Moreover, the increase may be greater than 3%, especially if interest rates rise.

Income Under Standard Plan

TC's quote for a TIAA Traditional Payout Annuity under the standard plan surpassed the quotes from Vanguard and 10 other providers. In fact, TC's annual payout exceeded the other 11 by 10%–16% (see Table 23.3).

TABLE 23.3
Fixed-income annuity annual payouts for 12 insurers

Insurers	Annual Payouts (%)
TIAA-CREF	8.8
Vanguard	8.0
Ten Other Insurers (Obtained Through Webannuities.com)	7.4–7.7

Although TC offers me a higher payout, it comes without a guaranty by any State Guaranty Association or government agency. As a result, I wondered if TIAA would decrease my 2010 annual payout, given the woeful state of the economy. The answer appeared on December 10, 2009, when TC posted the following announcement on its website:

> In 2010, participants who receive TIAA Traditional lifetime annuity income will receive at least as much total income (guaranteed income plus additional amounts) as in 2009. TIAA's financial strength underpins the company's claims-paying ability and enables it to maintain lifetime annuity income payments at the same level as in 2009 notwithstanding an uncertain economy. Participants who receive lifetime income from the TIAA Traditional Annuity rely on its stability to help protect their finances from financial market volatility.

From time to time, TIAA also increases the payout when it has unneeded reserves.

> A calculation by TIAA actuaries shows that a hypothetical 65-year-old participant who annuitized in 1995 after 30 years of participating in the TIAA Traditional Annuity through an RA contract would have received annuity payments in 2008 that were 17.6% larger than the initial payment as a result of the gradual return of unneeded contingency reserves. (*TIAA Traditional Annuity: Adding Safety and Stability to Retirement Portfolios*, August 2008.)

Income Under the Graded Plan

The graded plan, as you may recall, pays a lower initial rate the first year and increases every year in varying amounts. The other 11 plans with which I compare it grant an annual cost of living

TABLE 23.4
Graded payout rates for TIAA and 11 other insurers

Insurer	Initial Payout (%)	Annual Increases (%)
TIAA-CREF	6.7	1.8–4+
Vanguard	6.0	3
Ten Other Insurers (Provided Through Webannuities.com)	5.7–6	3

adjustment of 3%. All of the plans carry a 20-year guarantee and a full benefit for the spouse.

As expected, all of the plans, including TC, quoted a lower initial payout rate. TIAA offered the highest initial payout rate. The payout rates for TIAA Traditional apply only to funds that are subject to the 10-year withdrawal restriction, not money invested in TIAA Traditional for the short-term. Its initial payout rate was 6.7% versus the lowest, 5.7%—a difference of 17.5% (6.7 divided by 5.7). The graded payout rates, along with the annual increases, appear in Table 23.4.

Although none of the insurers carries a stronger rating than TIAA, the State Guaranty Association affords annuitants of these other insurers some protection against loss of their principal. The amount of the protection depends on the coverage offered by the state in which the annuity was issued. Unlike the members of its comparison group, TIAA has the potential to increase the payout substantially when needed the most, a period of high inflation. TIAA can also reduce the size of annual increases as it plans to do in 2010. The rate of increase for graded plan participants will be roughly 1% less than the one granted the previous year.

The Choices I Made

After weighing our financial needs, the desire to leave a potential legacy to our heirs, the need for long-life insurance, the desirability of adopting a safe withdrawal rate, the need to protect ourselves against inflation, and the likely safety of our principal, we decided to create a retirement portfolio with the following components:

1. A TIAA Traditional Payout Annuity under the standard plan to cover our fixed expenses

2. A TIAA Traditional Payout Annuity under the graded plan, Social Security, and rental income to cover most of our essential living expenses that are subject to inflation
3. A safe withdrawal plan (minimum distribution) from our nonannuitized assets to cover a portion of our essential living expenses, as well as our desirable expenses

If we confront an unexpected large expenditure, we have a cushion built into our withdrawal plan from the nonannuitized assets. We annuitized slightly more than half of the total assets in our retirement accounts. Furthermore, we chose two options—full survivor benefits and a guaranteed period of payments ranging from 15 to 20 years.

Revisiting What We Have Learned

In case you find yourself bewildered by all of the information and options we have discussed in this chapter, let me highlight the most important points for you to consider as you ponder this important decision (Table 23.5).

Looking in the Rearview Mirror

In retrospect, I realize that my decision to annuitize so much money in TIAA Traditional exposed me to more risk than necessary or desirable. Knowing what I do now, I would prefer to be in a position where I could purchase lifetime income annuities from several strong insurance companies in addition to TIAA to diversify my risk and ensure that some of my annuities were backed by my state's Life and Health Insurance Guaranty Association. Despite my reservations, I also realize that my investments in TIAA Traditional protected me against substantial losses during the two bear markets I have experienced since retiring in 2000. It is quite possible that these losses might have devastated my standard of living in retirement. Furthermore, given the structure of the TIAA Traditional Payout Annuities, if TIAA runs into financial difficulty, the most likely outcome for annuitants is a reduction in dividend payments. Even that outcome should be temporary.

TABLE 23.5
Features of TIAA traditional payout annuities

1. The TIAA Traditional Payout Annuity protects you against longevity risk, the risk of going broke.
2. **The decision to annuitize is irrevocable.**
3. **A TIAA Traditional Payout Annuity does not provide fixed-income payments.** You receive a guaranteed amount subject to the claims-paying ability of TC plus additional amounts.
4. The insurance company that backs TIAA Traditional Payout Annuities is financially strong and has strong ratings from five rating agencies, including an agency with no apparent conflicts of interest.
5. **No government agency or State Life and Health Insurance Guaranty Association provides any protection against insolvency by TC.**
6. Individuals who purchase TIAA Traditional Payout Annuities are much less likely to exhaust their nonannuitized assets.
7. Individuals who purchase TIAA Traditional Payout Annuities will receive higher payouts from their retirement accounts than those who do not annuitize.
8. The payouts from TIAA Traditional Payout Annuities are likely to exceed those paid by other insurers.
9. TIAA-CREF offers TIAA Traditional Payout Annuities under two plans—standard and graded.
10. The graded plan offers the investor somewhat more flexibility than the standard plan.
11. The standard plan has a much higher initial payout than the graded plan.
12. Payouts under the standard plan remain relatively level whereas the graded plan payouts increase.
13. **The standard plan payouts lose their purchasing power over time** whereas the purchasing power of the payouts under the graded plan generally increases.
14. Each plan offers a number of options and guarantees that affect your payouts.
15. The Internal Revenue Service taxes payments under the standard and graded plans as regular income.

Note: Boldface features represent possible drawbacks.

Let buyers beware; your choice is not straightforward. You would be well advised to consider the wisdom of investing in TIAA Traditional early on in your career, especially if you think annuitization represents a viable option in retirement.

> An immediate annuity from TIAA-CREF, "arguably, is better described as a cross between an immediate life annuity and a medieval tontine given the fact that longevity risk is shared by the pool, as opposed to borne by the insurance company." (Milevsky & Young, 2002, p. 35).

CHAPTER TWENTY-FOUR

Should I Incorporate a TIAA-CREF Variable-Income Annuity Into My Pension Plan?

If a variable income annuity appeals to you, there is no value in delaying this option to a later age according to Milevsky (2009), an annuity specialist.

During the past few years, I have read dozens of highly critical articles about variable annuities—insurance products that provide retirement income based on the performance of the underlying investments. Most articles highlighted the excessive costs of these insurance products—sales commissions, annual operating expenses, management fees, and insurance charges. The National Association of Securities Dealers cautioned retirees to avoid them. Occasionally, but not always, writers singled out Teachers Insurance and Annuity Association-College Retirement Equities Fund (TIAA-CREF) as an exception to the rule. They praised TIAA-CREF (TC) for its low costs, even when compared with mutual funds. With the criticisms of variable annuities and the positive comments about

TC in mind, I set out to determine for myself whether a variable-income annuity belonged in my retirement portfolio. My quest led me to investigate the purchase of this investment vehicle in the same way I have done all of my life when shopping for the family car. I conducted extensive research, and as you will learn in this chapter, I discovered how dramatically annuity payments can vary, sometimes to the benefit or detriment of annuitants.

Variable-income annuities, like the TIAA Traditional Payout Annuities discussed in the previous chapter, represent an irreversible decision. I learned that I couldn't cancel the contract; I also discovered that I would have limited control over the money I used to purchase the annuity. I could choose the variable annuity accounts in which the money was invested and switch among the available choices from time to time. If I decided to take my payouts monthly or annually and later changed my mind, I could do so. However, I could no longer elect to withdraw any amount of money I might need should an unexpected large expenditure appear on the financial horizon. The performance of the variable annuity accounts I had chosen would determine my payouts. As I had concluded after examining the TIAA Traditional Payout Annuities, the decision to set aside some of the money in my retirement account was a consequential decision, not to be taken lightly.

If TC runs into financial difficulty, your variable-income annuity contracts should not be affected. Your money is invested in one or more "subaccounts," similar to stock or bond mutual funds. TC segregates these investments from its assets, and neither TC nor its creditors may tap your investments in these subaccounts.

The Variable-Income Annuity Options

TC offers nine different variable-income annuities. Much to my surprise, I discovered that my TIAA Traditional Transfer Payout Annuity (TPA) contracts restricted my investment in these variable annuities in three ways. First, I had to annuitize my TPA contracts in the standard plan, graded plan, or some combination of the two before annuitizing them in the variable annuities because I had no money in my 403(b) accumulation invested in a variable annuity account. Second, any money I transferred from TIAA Traditional could only be used in the equity annuities

TABLE 24.1
Variable annuities and their holdings

Variable Annuity	Holdings
1. Stock	75% domestic, 25% international; large-cap stock emphasis
2. Global Equity	Typically at least 40% international and at least 25% domestic; large-cap stock emphasis
3. Growth	Invests at least 80% of assets in equity securities presenting opportunity for growth; may invest up to 20% of its assets in foreign securities; large-cap emphasis
4. Equity Index	Invests in stocks represented by the Russell 3000 market index; large-cap stocks predominate
5. Social Choice	47% domestic stocks, 13% international stocks, and 40% bonds, mostly long-term; stocks mostly large-cap with socially responsible emphasis
6. TIAA Real Estate	Invests 70%–90% of its assets directly in real estate or real estate–related securities; Currently holds nearly 20% in short-term investments
7. Bond	Mortgage-backed securities, corporate bonds, U.S. government securities, and other asset-backed securities with average maturity of 6.92 years and average credit quality of AA1
8. Inflation-Linked Bond	Mostly U.S. Treasury inflation-indexed securities with nearly three-quarters of them having a maturity of 2–10 years
9. Money Market	Money market instruments with average weighted maturity of 90 days or less; account not insured by any government agency

(numbers 1–5 in Table 24.1). Third, I could only move 20% per year into the equity-only annuities.

If you have invested some of your 403(b) money in CREF or TIAA Real Estate, you can use any of the nine options listed in the table depending on the provisions of your employer's plan.

If you have already annuitized your money, you now may have access to a highly diversified TIAA Lifecycle Retirement Income Fund (TLIRX). This option became available in June 2009. It has a target allocation of 40% stocks and 60% bonds spread across a wide array of TC funds. According to Morningstar, the five largest holdings include TC Bond, TC Short-Term Bond, TC Enhanced Large-Cap Growth Index, TC Enhanced Large-Cap Value Index, and TC Inflation-Linked Bond. Despite the broad diversification represented in the Retirement Income Fund, it behaved rather poorly during the recent market crash losing −17.88% in one year, slightly worse than its benchmark of −16.19% but slightly better than its Morningstar category (−18.31%).

Although its current expense ratio of 0.63% is below the average expense ratio of a similarly weighted hypothetical portfolio (1.09%), the projected expense ratio is substantially higher. If not for the fee waivers through January 31, 2010, the expense ratio would be 2.19%. When, and if, the waivers are lifted, the Retirement Income Fund must earn 2.19% before the retiree earns a dime making this particular fund highly expensive. If the market gains 8%, the Retirement Income Fund will take around 25% of these gains in fees.

The Payouts From Variable-Income Annuities

Because the performance of the market determines annual payouts from variable-income annuities, my curiosity led me to examine how CREF calculates the payouts and how they vary from year to year. My inquisitiveness uncovered several surprises.

Payout Calculations

Initial payments from a TC variable-income annuity depend on a specific mortality table and an assumed investment return (AIR) of 4%. According to TC's own publication, *Receiving Your Retirement Income from TIAA-CREF* (2006), "making an initial assumption about future earnings enables us to pay you a higher amount initially than if we did not assume future growth; and the 4% rate is low enough, at least for the equity accounts, that performance over time might likely be greater, and therefore increase your future payments." TC will provide information about initial payouts upon request.

After the first year, the payment changes based on the actual return of the underlying investment as compared to the AIR. Because TC assumes that a variable-income annuity account generates a 4% positive return, your income will increase only if the actual return exceeds 4%. For example, if your return is 8%, your income will increase only by the amount that exceeds your AIR of 4% [8% − 4% (the assumed AIR) = 4%]. If your return is 4%, you will receive no increase in income [4% − 4% (the assumed AIR) = 0%]. Your income will decrease if your return is less than 4%; for example, if your return is a negative 4%, your income will decrease 8% [−4% − 4% (your assumed AIR) = −8%]. The precise formula appears in Appendix L. Here's an example of how I simplified the calculation to estimate the annual changes in income.

1. Assume that the actual return of the underlying fund or account is 10%.
2. Subtract the AIR of 4% from 10%; your income will increase by approximately 6%.
3. Assume that the following year the return from your account is −10%.
4. Add the AIR of 4% to the −10%; your income will decrease by approximately 14%.

The changes that I estimated are vividly illustrated in Figure 24.1.

This example underscores two features of variable-payout annuities that were not immediately evident to me when I first examined them. First, the AIR of 4% is subtracted from the actual return when it is positive and added to the actual return when it is negative. In effect, the use of the AIR increases the losses and decreases the gains, compared with the actual returns of the account. Second, income can fluctuate; in this hypothetical example, it increased 6% one year and dropped 14% the following year.

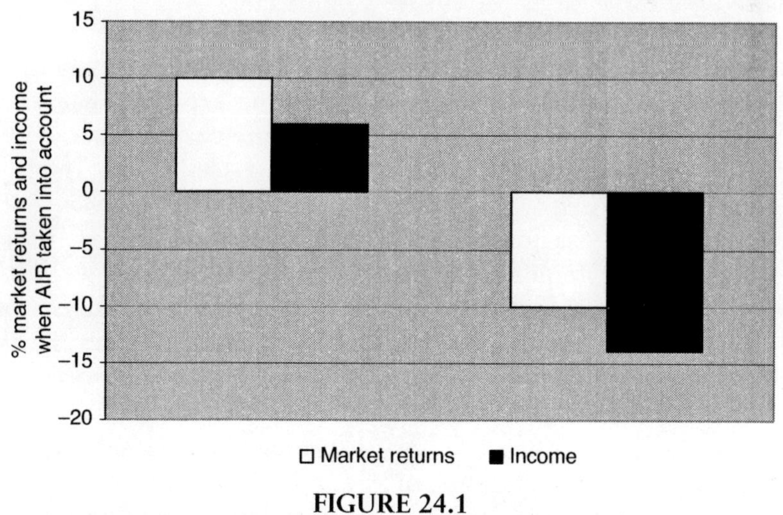

FIGURE 24.1

Income changes relative to changes in market returns.

The real situation, as you will see, reveals even more pronounced swings in income.

Actual Income Changes

Using data I obtained from various TC sources, I examined income changes for holders of the CREF Stock variable-income annuity during bull and bear markets. The results astounded me, as they may you.

Periods of prosperity (1980–2000 and 1990–2000). Take for example income changes for 65-year-old retirees who purchased a $100,000 single life CREF Stock annuity in 1980 (Walsh, 2002). From 1980 to 2000, their annual income rose from $8,163 to a whopping, unbelievable $93,560. Moreover, their income increased every year during this period with the exception of 1982 (14.8% decline) and 1988 (11.1% decline).

If we take another set of 65-year-old retirees who purchased a similar single life variable annuity and began receiving income in 1990, the resulting payouts through 2000 also reveal a rosy picture. Over this period, retirees saw their annual income from CREF Stock skyrocket from $7,159 per year to $23,387, an increase of more than 300%! Their increases in income averaged 13.04%; moreover, their annual income never declined. The smallest increase was 1.5% while the largest was 38.5%.

A period of wild swings (1996–2005). When I examined income changes for the CREF Stock annuity during a period that contained both bull and bear markets, the picture changed markedly. Between 1996 and 2005, CREF Stock variable-income annuity holders experienced a 38.51% increase in income one year and a 28.86% decrease in another. During this same period, these variable-income annuity holders averaged an 8.04% per year increase in income, demonstrating the often misleading nature of averages. (See Appendix N for the annual income changes for all of TC variable-income annuities.)

A period of prolonged declines in income (2001–2003). When I looked at the performance of the equity accounts during the 2000–2002 bear market (see Appendix O), I understood why some annuitants had complained about the declines in their annual income. Annuitants in the Stock Account experienced three consecutive years of declining income: −26.79% in 2001, −5.01% in 2002, and −28.86% in 2003. Unless they could compensate for the three-year decline in their income by tapping other sources of income, they experienced a major drop in their standard of living during this period.

A dramatic one-year drop in income (2009). Following the devastating 2008 bear market, holders of the CREF Stock equity variable-income annuity again suffered a substantial drop of −44.46% in income. Other variable-income annuity holders experienced declines in income ranging from 29.26% (Social Choice) to 47.23% (Global Equities). Even safe havens like CREF Bond Market, CREF Inflation-Linked Bond, and CREF Money Market generated less income for its investors, −4.48%, −7.30%, and −2.53%, respectively (*TIAA-CREF Outreach Newsletter*, April 2009).

Payouts With Different Allocations to TIAA Traditional and CREF Stock

Most TC participants who purchase variable-income annuities combine this type of annuity with a lifetime TIAA Traditional Payout Annuity. To examine the monthly income of participants with various combinations of these two types of income annuities, I relied on data supplied by TC in its April 2009 issue of The *TIAA-CREF Outreach Newsletter* mailed to its participants. In this publication, TC reported how $2,000 in initial monthly income fared during the period 1999–2009 for the following allocations between TIAA Traditional and CREF Stock: 75% TIAA/25% CREF Stock, 50%TIAA/50% CREF Stock, and 25% TIAA/75% CREF Stock. During this unfavorable period for stocks and bonds,

1. Participants, irrespective of the TC Stock allocation (25%–75%), received less total monthly income in 2009 than in 1999.
2. Participants with the *greatest allocation to TIAA* (75%) experienced the lowest drop (from $2,000 monthly to $1,870) while those with the *lowest allocation to TIAA* (25%) experienced a much larger decrease (from $2,000 monthly to $1,329).
3. CREF payouts after 1999 were less, sometimes much less, in 8 of the following 10 years.

4. TIAA payouts *exceeded* the 1999 payout every year for the next 10 years though by small amounts; in 2009 they were 7% higher than in 1999.

Note: TC reports all income data in nominal dollars.

When we examine a period much more favorable to stocks and bonds, the picture improves for annuitants with either 100% TIAA Traditional or 50% each in TIAA Traditional and CREF. According to data reported by John Biggs, TC Chief Executive Officer, in a 1997 open letter to TIAA-only annuitants,

1. Participants who invested $200,000 in a TIAA Traditional lifetime annuity under the standard plan received $456,982 from 1977 to 1996, an average of $22,849 per year. The annual payouts ranged from $19,870 to $24,432.
2. Participants who chose to split the $200,000 evenly between a TIAA Traditional lifetime annuity under the standard plan and CREF fared even better. They received $557,669 in payouts over the same 20-year period and averaged $27,883 per year. The annual payouts ranged from $15,619 to $45,328.

Note: TC reports all income data in nominal dollars.

Biggs's data assumed that the participant was a married man with a spouse of the same age (65) who had elected a 100% survivorship annuity.

Lifetime Payouts From TIAA Traditional and CREF Stock

After reading an earlier draft of my book, a friend of mine, a retired rocket scientist, shared with me some interesting data that he had painstakingly collected over the years. From March 1, 1952, to September 30, 1956, he and his employer contributed a total of $7,008—54% to TIAA and 46% to CREF. Twenty-eight years later, he annuitized his accumulation with two-thirds going to the survivor. From 1984 through December 2009, he had received $182,250 in payouts—$99,428 from CREF and $82,822 from TIAA Traditional. His experience shows the power of compound interest, bull markets in stocks, and annuitizing. He and his wife remain in good health and continue to receive these payouts from his original investment of $7,008.

My friend's annual payments from CREF started at $1,200 annually in 1984 and exceeded that amount every year through December 2009. His highest annual payout was $7,680 with his latest payout less than half that amount ($3,252) but still two and one-half times his starting payout.

The TIAA Traditional annual payouts paint a somewhat different picture. His starting annual payout of $3,612 in 1984 proved to be the high point. His payouts never exceeded that amount and began to decrease in 1988. In fact, his payout was actually one-sixth less in 2009 than when he began in 1984.

Major Features of Variable-Income Annuities

Let me highlight the main features of variable-income annuities as a means of summarizing what we have learned.

1. A variable-income annuity protects you against longevity risk, the risk of going broke.
2. The decision to annuitize is irrevocable.
3. CREF decides how much income you will receive each year from your variable-income annuity based on the performance of your investment and an AIR (assumed investment return).
4. The AIR of 4% adds to your investment losses and subtracts from your investment gains.
5. Income from a variable-payout annuity can fluctuate substantially from one year to the next or one decade to the next depending on the performance of your annuity.
6. If you need extra income from a variable-payout annuity to cover emergency expenses, the insurer/provider prohibits you from withdrawing additional amounts, no matter the severity of your need.
7. You can change your investments using the options offered by TC if your employer's plan permits.

My Take on TC Variable Annuities

TC variable annuities provide insurance against going broke, as well as some protection against the devastating effects of a bear market during the first few years of retirement. This insurance and protection must be weighed against the uncertain flow of income from this source. One cannot control the ebb and flow of the market; it has a collective mind of its own. If you are fortunate enough to withdraw money during an extended bull market like the one that occurred from 1980 to 1999, you will enjoy major increases in your income year after year. If, as I was, you are less fortunate and retire in a period such as we have experienced from 2000 to 2009, you will experience wide swings in your income and actually suffer a substantial loss of purchasing power during this period.

To me the lesson is clear; unless your total financial situation enables you to weather a period of disappointing market returns, you probably should eschew a variable annuity based solely on the CREF Stock Account. To reduce the fluctuations in your retirement income while protecting yourself against longevity risk, you might consider two options:

1. Limit your allocation to variable-income annuities to 20%–25% of your total retirement account.
2. Build a diversified portfolio of variable-income annuities that includes Social Choice, TIAA Real Estate, and Inflation-Linked Bonds. Although this portfolio will reduce your annual income and upside potential, it should enable you to have a smoother ride and a somewhat more stable flow of income. Moreover, it should provide you with a measure of protection against inflation.

Due to the restrictions of my employer's plan and TC, I could not invest in the diversified portfolio described in option 2. Because I was reluctant to base a portion of my retirement income on the unpredictable returns of the CREF Stock variable-income annuity, I opted instead for a somewhat smoother stream of income using the TIAA Traditional standard and graded methods, along with minimum distribution of my nonannuitized assets invested with Vanguard. By taking the income from my retirement account in these ways, I sought to limit the wide variations in my annual income and reduce the risk of exhausting my nonannuitized assets. If unexpected expenses occur, I can cover them.

CHAPTER TWENTY-FIVE

Should I Use Systematic Withdrawal as a Major Source of My Pension Income in Retirement?

Systematic withdrawal can be used only with Teachers Insurance and Annuity Association-College Retirement Equities Fund's (TIAA-CREF) variable annuity accounts, not TIAA Traditional. This approach to withdrawal appeals to many retirees because it allows them maximum control of their assets. Retirees can choose their asset allocations, their investments, and their withdrawal amounts, as long as they comply with the Internal Revenue Service (IRS) minimum distribution requirement, when they reach 70.5. Therein lies the danger. Unless they choose a safe withdrawal rate, they risk going broke. If they lack an understanding of investments and withdrawal strategies, they are further at risk.

Despite the inherent dangers, many retirees, I suspect, will choose systematic withdrawal for a portion of their TIAA-CREF retirement assets. Prior to retiring, I intended to rely heavily on systematic withdrawal for my income from CREF. However, as I delved more deeply into the research on investing and retirement planning, I acquired a more fine-grained understanding of the

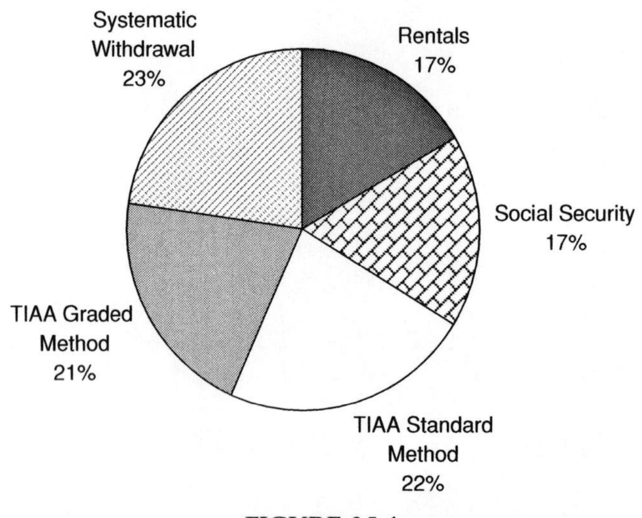

FIGURE 25.1

Percentage of my total income by source.

financial perils inherent in retirement and how to combat them. This added knowledge tempered my enthusiasm for systematic withdrawals.

To explore how systematic withdrawal might figure in my retirement plans, I inventoried my various income sources and how they might insulate me against two of the major risks confronting retirees, namely, longevity risk (exhausting my assets) and inflation risk (losing my purchasing power). In Figure 25.1, I show my five sources of income and how each contributes to my total income. In Table 25.1, I identify how, if at all, each income source mitigates inflation and longevity risk. When I examined how much

TABLE 25.1
Risk protection by income source

Source of Income	Protection Against Inflation Risk	Protection Against Longevity Risk
Rentals	Y	Y
Social Security	Y	Y
TIAA Standard Method	N	Y
TIAA Graded Method	Y	Y
Systematic Withdrawal	Y	N
Total	77.2%	77.3%

of my total income supplied some protection against inflation risk and longevity risk, I came up with totals of 77.2% and 77.3%, respectively. You may find it beneficial to use a table like this to assess your own vulnerability to inflation and longevity risk (see "Worksheet: Systematic Withdrawal" at the end of this chapter).

With a sense of my potential income sources and how they might protect me and my wife against inflation and longevity risk, I turned my attention to the decisions inherent in using systematic withdrawal.

1. What should be my mix of investments (e.g., stocks, bonds, cash, and other) in retirement?
2. What investment vehicles (mutual funds or annuity accounts) should I choose?
3. How do I implement my asset allocation in retirement?
4. What should be my initial withdrawal rate?
5. What should be my decision rule(s) for granting subsequent annual increases?
6. How should I harvest the withdrawals from my investment portfolio?
7. How should I monitor the progress of my portfolio?

You can choose to make these seven decisions by accident or design. I prefer to approach them systematically and draw on the best thinking and empirical evidence available.

The discussion that follows draws on research and insights rooted in the prevailing view about risk management, namely, diversification with non- or low-correlated asset classes.

Asset Mix or Allocation

As we have stated on several occasions in this book, asset allocation (i.e., mix of stocks, bonds, and cash) ranks as the most important investment decision you make. Many investors work from the bottom up and begin with decisions about mutual funds. Important as these mutual fund selections might be, they pale in significance to asset allocation. Your asset allocation decisions represent your first line of defense in risk management. By allocating money to bonds and cash, you lower your risk; the more you allocate to them, the more you lower your risk.

Otar (2001) has conducted the most comprehensive study of asset allocation that I could locate. Using 100 years of market history, he determined that the optimum asset allocation for most retirees is 60% in bonds and 40% in equities. His study points to taking less rather than more risk in retirement if you want to extend the life of your retirement portfolio. Being aggressive with your investments in retirement does not seem to pay off because you may be forced to sell when the market has declined. This phenomenon has been termed *reverse dollar averaging*.

Bogle (2007), on the other hand, uses the rule of thumb, *age in bonds*, that he often recommends to others.

If you dislike a one-size-fits-all approach to asset allocation, let me suggest that you use the 2010 version of the Otar Retirement Calculator (ORC). This calculator provides a user-friendly way to determine an optimal asset mix of investments, variable lifetime annuities, and fixed-income annuities. It will also answer such questions as "When can I retire?" and "How much can I spend?" The author of this calculator has been recognized for his meritorious financial research on retirement and investing. This inexpensive retirement calculator is the most comprehensive one I have tried.

Having determined your allocation to stocks and bonds, you can lower your risk even more by diversifying your stock and bond allocations. There are numerous approaches you can use that range from the simple to the complex (see chapter 8). The simplest approach relies on a single fund that is reasonably well-diversified (e.g., the CREF Social Choice retirement account); a more complex approach might be like the one recommended by Schultheis (2005) in his book, *The Coffeehouse Portfolio*. His recommended portfolio contains seven funds, as opposed to only one. Schultheis allocates 40% to bonds and 10% to each of six other funds (large cap, large-cap value, small cap, small-cap value, international, and REITs or Real Estate Investment Trusts). You would need to modify his allocation to bonds and equities if you followed Otar's (2001) recommendation of 60% in bonds or Bogle's advice (2007), your age in bonds. If you want more information about the Coffeehouse portfolio, simply type "Coffeehouse Investor" in Google and click. His portfolio has averaged 9.1% over the past 18 years and has experienced only three down years—1994 (–0.58%), 2002 (–5.55%), and 2008 (–19.68%).

Regardless of the approach you use, I urge you to try www.riskgrades.com. The tools on this website enable you to evaluate the risk of your investment portfolio, as well as whether you are being fairly compensated for the level of risk you have assumed. These tools cannot be used with your TIAA-CREF annuity accounts. As I explained in chapter 9, these annuity accounts resemble mutual funds but are not; they are insurance products. The website www.riskgrades.com can be used only with stocks, cash, bond funds, and mutual funds.

Investment Vehicles

With your asset allocation in mind, your next step is to choose the mutual funds in which to invest your money. The principles I outlined in chapter 7 should serve you well in making your selections, and I won't repeat them here. The Coffeehouse portfolio that I mentioned in the preceding section meets all of these principles.

I chose mutual funds with low operating costs because they are the best predictor of future returns. According to the Morningstar X Ray tool, a similarly weighted portfolio to mine had annual operating expenses of 1.29% while my portfolio had an average mutual fund expense ratio of 0.25%.

Implementing Your Asset Allocation

As you may recall, a bear market at the outset of your retirement can have devastating consequences for the longevity of your portfolio. If you have chosen systematic withdrawal, you can minimize the effects of an early bear market by using dollar-cost averaging (DCA). Otar (2001) demonstrates empirically how this simple, mechanical method reduces volatility in the early years of retirement and increases the minimum life of the portfolio. Here is how the DCA method studied by Otar works:

1. Purchase bonds or bond funds with the money you have allocated to the bond portion of your portfolio.

2. Take the portion of your retirement portfolio that you have allocated to equities and divide it into four equal parts. Assume that you have allocated $100,000 to equities and divide it into four portions of $25,000 each.
3. Invest $25,000 in equities and the remaining $75,000 in short-term money market funds.
4. In each of the following three years, invest $25,000 more in equities. By the end of the first four years of your retirement, you have all $100,000 invested in equities.

Otar offers a more complex approach to DCA in his book, *High Expectations & False Dreams* (2001), which produces a slightly better outcome. I encourage you to examine it and judge for yourself whether his DCA method using presidential election cycles suits you.

Initial Withdrawal Rate

Most of the studies of withdrawal rates assume that retirees use a systematic withdrawal method for their entire investment portfolio (Bengen, 2004; Cooley, Hubbard, & Walz, 1999). An initial withdrawal rate of 4% adjusted annually for inflation appears "safe," that is, less likely to exhaust one's resources over a 30-year period. "Safe" does not mean a sure thing or a zero chance of going broke. If retirees initially withdraw more than 4% from their retirement assets, they increase the odds of running out of money before running out of breath. When fixed-income annuities are included in the retirement portfolio, the "safe" initial withdrawal rate climbs to 4.5% (Ameriks & Warshawsky, 2001).

When I retired and began withdrawing money from my TIAA-CREF accounts, I opted for a 5% initial withdrawal rate but adopted decision rules for determining my subsequent increases. Guyton (2004) questioned whether the "safe" withdrawal rule was too "safe," and experimented with different decision rules. According to his research, retirees who adopt these rules can safely withdraw 5.8% initially, if they have at least 65% of their portfolio invested in stocks. I opted for a more conservative approach to withdrawal than his research suggested was "safe," and a much lower allocation to stocks.

Having reached 75, I annuitized roughly half of my retirement assets and reset my withdrawal rate to satisfy the minimum distribution requirement of the IRS. These decisions enable me to generate more income with a much lower risk of outliving my money.

Decision Rules

Because inflation seems to increase every year by varying amounts, you and I must decide what rule(s) to use when granting ourselves annual increases to offset inflation. My search revealed several options:

Option 1: *Use minimum distribution.* When retirees reach 70.5 years of age, the IRS requires them to withdraw an amount using their age and a divisor (see Appendix G). This divisor increases with the retiree's age; it has the effect of increasing the percentage retirees must withdraw every year—3.6% at age 70, 5.34% at age 80, 8.8% at age 90, and 12.6% at age 95. By using the minimum distribution rule for annual increases, you are able to offset the effects of inflation and run little, if any, risk of going broke. However, because the IRS bases the percentage on the value of the retirement portfolio at the end of each calendar year, you are likely to experience some modest fluctuations in your income if you designed a portfolio that minimizes volatility.

Option 2: *Increase in line with the Consumer Price Index (CPI).* Most of the studies of initial "safe" withdrawal rates assume that the annual increases correspond to the increases in the CPI. If retirees adopt an initial withdrawal rate of 4%, presumably they can keep pace with inflation by matching increases in the CPI.

Option 3: *Use a fixed withdrawal rate of 5%–6%.* Unless retirees have created a portfolio with low to moderate volatility, this rule can lead to wide swings in income. As long as the portfolio continues to grow in value, the fixed rate of withdrawal will provide some offset to inflation. Moreover, it is unlikely that *the retiree* would ever run out of money.

Option 4: *Use 3.5%, the historical rate of inflation.* Many of the retirement planning calculators ask you for the rate of inflation you intend to use. The historical rate is probably as good an estimate as any because it reflects the actual inflation rates that have occurred over time.

Option 5: *Use decision rules based on market performance and inflation rates.* According to research by Guyton (2004), retirees can "safely" withdraw 5.8% initially with a 65% equity portfolio or 6.2% with an 80% equity portfolio if they adopt the following decision rules:

a. Freeze annual increases following a year when the portfolio's total return is negative.

b. Cap inflation increases at 6%.

c. Do not make up in subsequent years for frozen increases or capped inflation rates.

By following these three decision rules, retirees would have sustained their portfolios for 40 years even though they entered retirement during a bear market, experienced a lengthy period of high inflation, and suffered a second bear market near the end.

If you are interested in learning about even more complex options, google "Bob's Financial Website" and click on "Withdrawal Strategies."

Harvesting Rules

I began the withdrawals from my TIAA-CREF accounts during the third year of the 2000–2002 bear market. At the time, I had roughly 80% of my money in TIAA Traditional, 15% in stock, and the remainder in the Inflation-Linked Bond Account. Realizing after two years of studying investing and retirement planning that I had become too conservative in investing, I decided to withdraw money from TIAA Traditional, first using the Interest-Only option followed by the Transfer Payout Annuity (TPA). I planned to transfer the money from my TPA to Vanguard and use it to increase my investment in stocks while leaving open the option to annuitize my holdings in TIAA Traditional. Nearly 10 years later, I am satisfied with my decision.

Recently, I learned about a study conducted by Spitzer and Singh (2007) to determine the efficacy of different harvesting rules that might be used during retirement. Specifically, they investigated five ways in which money is harvested or withdrawn from portfolios with six different stock/bond mixes and five different initial withdrawal rates. The five ways in which they harvested money from the portfolios are as follows:

1. Rebalancing, that is, withdrawing money from either stocks or bonds and restoring the portfolio to its desired percentage of stocks and bonds
2. Withdrawing money from the asset that had the *highest* return during the year
3. Withdrawing money from the asset that had the *lowest* return during the year
4. Withdrawing bonds first
5. Withdrawing stocks first

Note: Numbers 2–4 do not rebalance, that is, restore the portfolio to its original allocation to stocks and bonds.

Withdrawing *bonds first* minimizes shortfalls for four different time periods—15, 20, 25, and 30—as long as the initial withdrawal rate does not exceed 4% and the stock exposure is less than 70%. Rebalancing consistently produced the worst results. As the money allocated to bonds depletes, some, perhaps most, retirees may grow uneasy with such a high proportion of their money allocated to stocks. A note of caution regarding this harvesting strategy surfaced in more recent research. When the "expected return on U.S. stocks and the equity risk premium are near historic lows," as is the case for retirees in 2008, the bond-first strategy is unlikely to extend the longevity of portfolios as it has done in the past (Weigand & Irons, 2008).

Monitoring Progress

Market returns disappoint, inflation rates soar, and forecasts may miss the target by a country mile. Because circumstances change, you must monitor your progress annually and adjust your withdrawal rate to prevent yourself from going broke. Otar (2001) provides a useful way to estimate the remaining life of your portfolio; he developed this formula based on 100 years of market data.

Remaining portfolio life (RPL) = A/current withdrawal rate

where the value of A is set at

100 = average remaining portfolio life

150 = maximum remaining portfolio life

75 = minimum remaining portfolio life

For example, let's assume that you have $100,000 remaining in your account and that you plan to withdraw 5.5% from your account.

100/5.5 = 18.18 years, the average remaining life of your portfolio

150/5.5 = 27.27 years, the longest you can expect your portfolio to last

75/5.5 = 13.64 years, your portfolio could last as little as this

Combine this information with your age and make an informed judgment about whether you need to consider adjusting your withdrawal rate to increase its life span. If you conduct this simple analysis annually, you will know which track you are on—the right one or the wrong one. By making timely decisions, you can avoid the single biggest fear of retirees, the fear of going broke.

Summary

In this chapter, we have discussed seven major questions facing those who choose systematic withdrawal as the main method of withdrawing money from their retirement account. To assist our readers in using the ideas we have discussed, we have provided a worksheet at the end of this chapter and highlighted the principal ideas in Table 25.2.

TABLE 25.2
Seven elements of systematic withdrawal

1. *Mix of investments*: Age in bonds, remainder in stocks, or determine mix by using the 2010 edition of the Otar Retirement Calculator.
2. *Investment vehicles*: Index mutual funds or low-cost actively managed mutual funds; they are the single best predictor of future performance.
3. *Implementation of asset allocation in retirement*: Use Otar's dollar-cost averaging method to protect self in case of bear market during first five years of retirement.
4. *Initial withdrawal rate:* In the first year of retirement, withdraw 4%, the accepted "safe" rate with a relatively low probability of depleting your income.
5. *Decision rules for granting subsequent annual increases:* You can use 3%–3.5% or one of the more complex set of decision rules proposed by Guyton (2004) (option 5 under discussion of possible decision rules).
6. *Harvesting withdrawals from your investment portfolio:* Many retirees and financial planners rely on rebalancing to restore the desired allocation to stocks and bonds; however, recent research favors withdrawing money from bonds first.
7. *Monitoring progress:* Use Otar's formula to estimate the remaining life of your portfolio.

My Take on Systematic Withdrawal

In this chapter, you have obtained a clearer idea of why I earlier stated that withdrawing money from my retirement account proved a lot more complicated than accumulating it. Adopting the systematic withdrawal method may allow you more control of your funds; however, it also entails a host of interrelated decisions, each with its own perils and possibilities. Perhaps fully annuitizing your retirement assets, as TIAA-CREF required until 1989, seems like a more reasonable option than you may have believed at the outset. By annuitizing a portion (25%–50%) of your nest egg with a 20-year guaranteed period and withdrawing the remainder of your retirement account using minimum distribution, you can simplify your life, minimize your longevity risk, protect yourself somewhat against inflation and the possibility of cognitive impairment, ensure that all of your nest egg will eventually be paid out either to you or your heirs, and enjoy a higher income as an added bonus.

Worksheet: Systematic Withdrawal

1. List your potential sources of income and indicate their vulnerability to inflation and longevity risk with a Y or N.

Source of Income	Percentage of Total Income	Protection Against Inflation Risk	Protection Against Longevity Risk
Rentals			
Social Security			
Fixed-Income Annuity			
Inflation-Protected Annuity			
Systematic Withdrawal			
Total	100%		

2. Specify the percentage of your retirement assets invested in the following:

   Stocks___

   Bonds___ (age in bonds?)

   Cash___

   Other___

3. What investment vehicles have you chosen?

   Index funds___

   Actively managed funds___

   Other___

   Average operating expenses___ versus a similarly weighted portfolio using Morningstar X Ray tool___

4. How have you implemented your asset allocation?
   a. Have you used dollar cost averaging to reduce volatility risk in the early years of retirement
   b. Other

5. What is your initial withdrawal rate?
   a. Four percent (a relatively "safe" initial withdrawal rate)___
   b. Other

6. What is your decision rule for increasing your initial withdrawal rate each year?
   a. Enough to satisfy minimum distribution requirement
   b. In line with increase in CPI

c. A fixed withdrawal rate of 5%–6%
d. The historical rate of inflation (3.5%)
e. Decision rules based on market performance and inflation rates:

e-1. Freeze annual increases following a year when portfolio's return is negative.

e-2. Cap inflation increases at 6%.

e-3. Do not make up in subsequent years for frozen increases or capped inflation rates.

7. What are your rules for taking withdrawals from the mutual funds in your retirement account?
a. Withdrawing money from bond funds first (recommended)__
b. Rebalancing (study shows that this produces worst results)__
c. Withdraw money from funds with highest returns during the year__
d. Withdraw money from funds with the lowest returns during the year__
e. Withdrawing stocks first__

8. How will you monitor the remaining life of your portfolio?
a. Use Otar's formula:

100/current withdrawal rate = average remaining life of your portfolio

150/current withdrawal rate = maximum remaining life

75/current withdrawal rate = minimum remaining life

b. Other

PART FOUR

Remaining Solvent

Hanging on to one's retirement nest egg looms large in the minds of retirees. In part 4, I examine the threat of emotions and con artists to retirees and how to guard against these threats. Finally, I underscore the importance of shifting your mindset in retirement from growth to capital preservation. You will learn four components of a nest egg protection strategy, as well as my approach to avoiding huge losses in my investment portfolio and contingency plans if my best laid plans go awry.

CHAPTER TWENTY-SIX

Mirror, Mirror on the Wall, What Is the Greatest Threat of All?

The fault, dear investor, lies not in our stars, but in ourselves.

Personal greed and fear, the evil emotional twins, threaten the financial well-being of most investors. I know because they have cost me more money than I care to admit. Like most investors in the late 1990s, I abandoned my usual caution and counted on high technology stocks to make me some fast, easy returns. Alas, I, like countless others, witnessed and suffered from the rise and fall of these stocks. Although I successfully battled the urge to be greedy for several years, I succumbed near the top of this bubble and felt the force of its bursting.

At other times, fear has overtaken me, and I sold when I should have been buying. Unable to control my emotions and being ignorant of stock market history, I committed the common mistake of buying high and selling low. Sometimes, instead of selling and waiting until the market began its ascent, I switched to other funds. In these cases, I experienced the result others have. The funds I switched to actually returned less than the ones I sold. As I have learned through my study of investing, this sad result is consistent with what others have experienced.

Unfortunately, emotions aren't the only culprit triggering self-defeating investment behavior. According to a survey by the Consumer Federation of America, around 70% of the people who buy mutual funds through their work plan or a financial professional never ask about costs (Simon, 2006), a serious oversight as we discussed in chapter 3. Moreover, when given an opportunity to invest in a company plan that matches their contributions, many people fail to take advantage of the opportunity to obtain free money that works its compounding magic in a tax-deferred account.

Even when a company offers guidance on how to allocate portfolios between stocks and bonds and what funds to choose among the investment options, a vast majority of 401(k) investors don't take it (Lim, 2006). The small percentage of investors who request the advice ignore it. Taken together, only 7% of the investors who had access to advice actually used it. Those investors who eventually chose a mix of stocks and bonds didn't rebalance their portfolios annually. As we pointed out in chapter 7, this failure reduced the value of their portfolios over time by anywhere from 7% to 11%.

Given the ubiquitous role of self-defeating emotions in investing plus the failure to consider costs, to seek the advice of financial professionals, to follow it when given, and to rebalance their portfolios, it should come as no surprise that investors generally haven't done well in the market. As we pointed out in the Introduction, studies by Bogle (2005) show that many investors received only a small fraction of the annual returns generated by the stock market.

Of the numerous contributors to the poor performance of individual investors, I suspect that the self-defeating emotions of greed and fear play the biggest role. To minimize their role, if not completely eradicate them, an investor must take steps to combat them, and it is never too late to do so. I was nearly 70 when I managed to get these emotional demons under control. I did it by carefully choosing my allocation to stocks and bonds. When selecting how much to allocate to bonds and stocks, I considered volatility, as well as expected returns. As I described in an earlier chapter, your possible loss increases rather substantially as you stretch for returns. Therefore, I asked myself: "What is my *panic point*, the point at which fear may overwhelm me, and I sell when I should be buying?" Sometimes I have misjudged my emotional tolerance for loss, and when the bear raised its ugly head, I panicked and sold some of my stocks when I should have been buying them on sale. Then I compounded my error by buying back into the market after it had risen substantially.

Now that my asset mix reflects my panic point, I have taken other steps to deal with greed and fear. The media in all its forms has triggered my self-defeating emotions countless times. Echoing the admonitions of financial experts, I cancelled subscriptions to financial publications, avoided newsletters that claim to predict what the stock market will do and which stocks to buy, and tuned out any television stations/programs that tout the advice of the latest hot fund manager. If you follow my lead, you will save yourself lots of money and be more likely to maintain your asset mix. Wall Street and its handmaidens, the financial news media, profit from giving advice that if taken seriously will fatten their Individual Retirement Accounts, not yours. Readers and listeners beware.

If you have a complex portfolio, rebalancing to restore its original asset mix will test you. It means selling the best of the litter and buying more of the sick puppies. You might alleviate your uneasiness as I do, reminding yourself that you are following a winning strategy—selling high and buying low.

CHAPTER TWENTY-SEVEN

How Can I Protect My Nest Egg Against Huge Losses?

The first rule of investing is not to lose money, and rule number two is not to forget the first rule.

—Warren Buffett

Avoiding large losses during retirement should be your highest priority.

—Israelsen, 2008

When you have forged your lifetime investment strategy and withdrawal plan, you need to take steps to protect your nest egg in and near retirement. In this chapter, we will discuss why protection of your nest egg from huge losses assumes such prominence during this period of your life. We will elaborate on the steps I took and explore the steps you might take. Because the best laid plans often go awry, we also need to develop a contingency plan in case we suffer greater losses than we anticipated. I close with several approaches that you might use.

According to Milevsky (2009), a bear market in the years just before and soon after retirement threatens the longevity of your retirement portfolio. This comes as unwelcome news to me and others who retired in early 2000. Since that time, we have suffered not one, but two bear markets. The Standard & Poor's (S&P)

500 stock index plummeted 50% from January 1, 2001, through October 2002. In 2008–2009, the bear roared again; in less than 10 months the S&P 500 stock index dropped nearly 40%. No one knows whether the recent market gains represent a temporary rally before the market resumes its decline.

During this turbulent eight-year period, the value of my total retirement portfolio has *increased 15%* despite making withdrawals for more than six years from TIAA Traditional and losing some money in the second bear market. I attribute my good fortune to several reasons. For the first two and one-half years of my retirement, my wife and I managed to live off my early retirement bonus from Stanford University and other sources of income. Of equal importance, most of my money was invested in TIAA Traditional. During this eight-year period, TIAA Traditional never faltered. Like a Timex watch, it kept on ticking; it never lost value and continued to pay the guaranteed interest rate plus dividends. Using money from my Transfer Payout Annuities, I invested in mutual funds near the end of the first bear market and took advantage of the lower stock prices and subsequent rise in the stock market.

Protecting My Own Nest Egg

As I look to the future, I have taken several steps to safeguard my retirement assets against a possible lengthy stretch of poor returns and market turbulence. In December 2008, I decided to:

1. annuitize all of my remaining money in TIAA Traditional,
2. withdraw only the required minimum distribution from my nonannuitized assets,
3. place enough of my nonannuitized assets in cash and bonds to provide us the additional income we need to live during the next 10–12 years,
4. invest the rest of my nonannuitized assets in a low cost, low turnover, multiasset, globally diversified stock portfolio, and
5. reinvest the dividends from my stock portfolio over the next 10–12 years.

My resulting safety net of investments includes these components:

Annuities (53%)

1. Immediate income annuities using TIAA Traditional standard and graded plan for steady income, protection against longevity risk, and some protection against inflation.

Nonannuitized Assets (47%)

1. Cash and bonds for income, maximum safety, and some protection against inflation
   (a) TIPS (Treasury Inflation-Protected Securities)
   (b) GNMAs (mortgages backed by the U.S. government)
   (c) Foreign government inflation-protected bonds
   (d) Money market
2. Multiasset, globally diversified stock portfolio for growth and income and some protection against inflation
   (a) Dividend paying stocks
   (b) Domestic growth stocks
   (c) Small-cap value stocks
   (d) International growth and value stocks
   (e) Real estate
   (f) Commodities

If the 25% of my nonannuitized retirement savings that are invested in a multiasset, globally diversified stock portfolio performs better than expected over the next 12 years, we benefit from the capital gains, as well as the dividends, that accumulate during this period. (Unless you have steeped yourself in the literature on investing, a less complex portfolio seems advisable. As I pointed out in chapter 8, excellent opportunities are available.)

Our approach to risk management doesn't completely eliminate risk. TIAA may become insolvent. Although we regard this event as highly unlikely, the possibility remains. Black swans do happen; in fact, one may have occurred in 2008 when nearly all asset classes fell 40% or more. If the unthinkable occurs, it will be a sorry day in the Bridges's household and thousands of other retirees as well. I am counting on TIAA's independent risk management group to avoid a financial Armageddon. Reducing the dividends and refunds from contingency reserves seems a bit more likely in troubled times.

If these reductions were temporary, we could weather the storm and not be devastated by it. In view of TIAA's financial strength, the diversification of its investments in TIAA Traditional, and the proven effectiveness of its risk management team, I am reasonably confident that major reductions won't be necessary.

During the latest bear market my *nonannuitized* investments suffered a loss of less than 15%. According to the research conducted by Israelsen (2008), a somewhat similar portfolio's worst loss from 1970 to 2007 was only 2.23%. The discrepancy serves as a vivid reminder that past performance is not predictive of future performance, especially when asset bubbles develop and burst in all asset classes.

Recovering from a loss in the value of your investment portfolio requires a much more substantial five-year annualized return for postretirees than preretirees (see Figure 27.1). To recover from a 15% loss, my postretirement portfolio will need to earn a 10.9% annualized return over the next five years. If I were in the buy-and-hold, preretirement wealth-building stage, my portfolio would fully recover from the 15% loss by earning only a 3.3% annualized

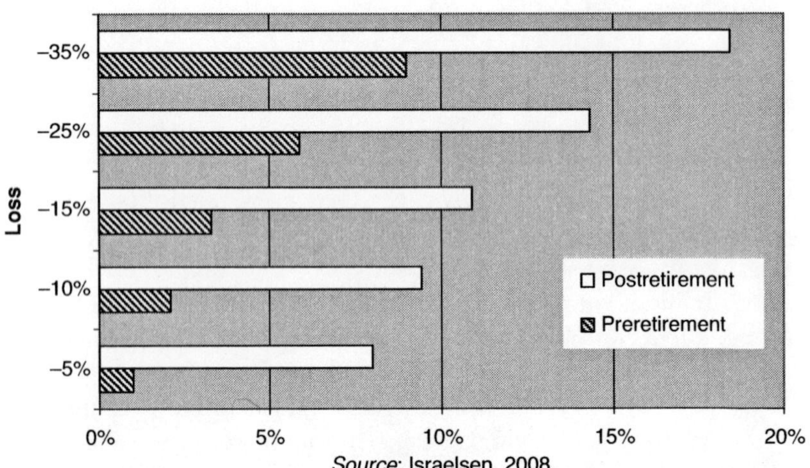

Source: Israelsen, 2008.
Assumptions: $500,000 initial balance with first year withdrawal of 5% and a 3% annual increase.

FIGURE 27.1

Five-year annualized return needed to recover from a loss for pre- and postretirees.

return. Note the striking contrast between preretirees and retirees in how much they need in annualized returns over a five-year period to recover from a loss. The differences arise in part due to a retiree's reverse-dollar cost averaging, that is, selling, as opposed to buying stocks, when they have declined, as well as spending dividends instead of reinvesting them.

This recent bear market taught me a valuable lesson: take no more risk than necessary. In my case, I tried to boost my returns by investing a portion of my retirement account in a multiasset, globally diversified stock portfolio. Like many others, including numerous financial experts, I learned that investors can suffer large losses in the short run that are especially difficult to recover from in retirement. In the future, I may follow the safe assets approach recommended by Bodie and Clowes (2003) and invest all of my nonannuitized assets in Treasury Inflation Protected Securities (TIPS).

Protecting Your Own Nest Egg

As you near retirement, you must alter your mindset. For most of your working life, you focused on growth. *Now you must begin to concentrate on capital preservation.* Bear markets happen with a lot more frequency than we ever imagined. To protect your nest egg, you need a capital preservation strategy that limits your vulnerability to three major sources of risk (Milevsky, 2009): (a) longevity (outliving your nest egg), (b) inflation (loss of purchasing power), and (c) market crashes (bear markets immediately before and after you retire).

Preserving Your Capital

Let me be so bold as to offer three possible capital preservation strategies:

1. *Safe assets.* You can protect yourself against all three of the aforementioned risks by investing your retirement account in TIPS (Bodie & Clowes, 2003). Use the Otar Retirement

Calculator to obtain a preliminary estimate of this approach to funding your retirement over a minimum of 30 years.

2. *Safe assets plus a fixed lifetime income annuity*. If you discover that TIPS will not provide sufficient income, consider creating a retirement portfolio with TIPS and a fixed lifetime income annuity purchased from one or more financially strong insurance companies. Limit the amount used to purchase the annuity from a single insurer to what is guaranteed by the state organization of the Life and Health Insurance Guaranty Association. (See www.nolhga.com for the amount covered in your state.)
3. *Safe assets combined with a fixed lifetime income annuity and a globally diversified portfolio*. Perhaps, you might feel more comfortable with your future prospects if you added a diversified mix of international and domestic stocks to the second strategy described in the preceding paragraph. If you decide to make this addition, consider using the minimum distribution option to extend the life of your stock portfolio and leave open the possibility of a financial legacy for your heirs or favorite charity.

The particular strategy that you eventually choose depends on a number of factors, including your living expenses, the amount and location of your various investments, the provisions of your employer's plan, your legacy motives, and health situation. If you have a wealth management advisor, you can rely on him/her for assistance in choosing the appropriate strategy.

Performing a Stress Test

As a confirmed belt and suspenders investor, I wholeheartedly subscribe to Pascal's law: "the *consequences* of decisions and choices should dominate the probabilities of outcomes" (Peter Bernstein). After enduring two severe bear markets, many investors likely embrace Pascal's law as well. To examine the consequences of investment decisions, as well as the probabilities of outcomes, I have found it useful to perform a stress test. Perhaps, a detailed example will show you the value of such a test.

Let's assume that you are 65 years old with a nonworking spouse and have not adopted one of the three strategies I suggested. You have accumulated $500,000 in your retirement account and plan to withdraw $1,641 a month. Moreover, you have invested 40% in stocks, 40% in bonds, and 20% in cash.

As a first step in performing your stress test, you focus on the probability that your retirement account will last until you reach age 95. You switch on your computer and log into the T. Rowe Price Retirement Income Calculator. After inputting the assumptions listed in the above paragraph into this calculator, you push the Submit button. The results bring a smile to your face.

You would like to spend $1,641 a month; there is a 90% chance that your retirement portfolio will last until age 95.

With these reassuring results in mind, you proceed to the second step of your stress test, focusing primarily on the consequences of this decision. Your particular asset allocation (40% stocks, 40% bonds, 20% cash), according to Vanguard's historical data on portfolio allocations (see Appendix M), suffered a loss of −18.4% in 1931. The probability of a similar loss is quite low; however, the consequences of such a large drop in the value of your investment portfolio could be disastrous. To examine the consequences, let's assume that the market drops −18% in the year just prior to your retirement. Instead of beginning with $500,000 in your retirement account, you start with $410,000. You now run the T. Rowe Price Retirement Income Calculator again with all the same assumptions you made in the first step of your stress test with one exception—the reduced value of your retirement account balance. The results bring a frown to your face.

You would like to spend $1,641 a month during your retirement; unfortunately, there is only a 61% chance that your portfolio will last until age 95. If you want a 90% chance of your portfolio lasting until age 95, you should reduce your spending by $321 a month. You can safely spend $1,345 a month.

TABLE 27.1
"Safe" monthly withdrawal amounts relative to amount allocated to equities

Allocation to Equities (%)	"Safe" Initial Monthly Withdrawal Amount (90% Probability of Retirement Account Lasting Until Age 95)
40	$1,345
50	$1,324
60	$1,292
70	$1,255

By performing this two-step stress test, you now have a more realistic picture of what you can spend from your retirement account if you want to protect yourself from a worst case scenario. Should you choose to ignore this scenario and it actually happens, you will need to obtain around a 12%–13% annualized return over the next five years to recover from this loss (see Figure 27.1).

Discouraged by what you have learned, you decide to explore on the T. Rowe Price Retirement Income Calculator what would happen if you invested more aggressively. Much to your surprise, you discover that increasing the amount of money you invest in stocks actually lowers your "safe" withdrawal rate. For example, if you increased your stock allocation to 70% with the remainder in bonds and short-term investments, your "safe" withdrawal rate drops from $1,345 per month to $1,255 (see Table 27.1). Moreover, as you increase your allocation to stocks above 40%, you reduce your monthly income. Believe it or not, reducing your stock allocation from 40% to 30% actually increases your monthly income from $1,345 to $1,362. This analysis shows one reason why it is important for you to shift your mindset during and near retirement from growth to capital preservation.

Monitoring the Remaining Life of Your Portfolio

As I suggested in chapter 25, Otar (2001) proposes a useful technique for estimating the remaining life of your portfolio. It is advisable to conduct this remaining portfolio life (RPL) test annually. If you discover that your RPL has entered a danger zone, move to your contingency plan.

Creating a Contingency Plan

Cautious investors, especially in retirement, have a Plan B, a just-in-case or contingency plan to deal with plans that go awry. In my situation, I have considered not one, but two contingency plans. The first centers on increasing my income, whereas the second focuses on adjusting the withdrawal strategy from my retirement account.

We are fortunate enough to own a large, historic home with seven bed rooms on the Stanford University campus. As empty nesters, we now have five empty bedrooms on the second floor. In case our financial plans flounder, we intend to rent the two largest bedrooms, each with its own private bath. That constitutes Plan B.

If Plan B doesn't cover a possible shortfall, we plan to adjust our withdrawal strategy to avoid exhausting our retirement account prematurely. Research conducted by T. Rowe Price offers three possible options to ensure the longevity of one's retirement portfolio (Greene & Tergesen, 2008):

1. Grant yourself no cost-of-living increases for the next five years.
2. Retain your current withdrawal rate (e.g., 4.5%), base it on the new balance, not the original balance, and continue the future cost-of-living increases of 3%.
3. Take a slightly higher percentage of your new balance and freeze it for the next five years.

Frankly, I hope that we never have to consider Plan C. I am unsure which of the three options we would choose. Nonetheless, I offer them as a possibility to consider as you plan your future with the goal of remaining solvent in retirement foremost in mind.

If neither of these contingency plans appeals to you and you haven't purchased a lifetime income annuity, now may be the time for you to consider one. In a recent article, Lankford (2009b) showed how a 65-year-old man could actually receive more money annually even though his retirement portfolio had declined 30%. The key to increasing his annual income flow was purchasing a lifetime income annuity with half of his remaining investment portfolio. You can log onto AnnuityShopper.com to determine whether this plan works for you.

Summary

We have underscored the importance of shifting your mindset from growth to capital preservation near and in retirement. The more aggressively you invest near and in retirement, the greater the likelihood that you will suffer huge losses from which you will never recover. I discussed my approach to avoiding such losses and closed with components of a nest egg protection strategy you might tailor to your own needs and circumstances. It emphasized four components: (a) the composition of an investment portfolio geared to protect you from going broke, (b) a stress test to estimate your ability to weather a major market decline, (c) a technique for monitoring the remaining life of your portfolio, and (d) a set of possible contingency plans in case your best laid plans run awry. May the odds be with you!

Managing finances . . . before and during retirement, is like being the Captain of a ship. You have to have a map and a set course, but you do also have to adapt to changing weather and sea patterns, including the occasional hurricane.

—Diehard conversation #53439, entry number four, Morningstar website under Discuss.

CHAPTER TWENTY-EIGHT

How Can I Protect My Nest Egg Against Fraud?

To obtain a crude estimate of the pervasiveness of senior fraud, I typed "senior fraud" into Google. I obtained 33,400,000 hits.

Seniors walk around with a bull's-eye on their backs. They have the unenviable distinction of being the con artists' number one target. Moreover, these con artists can be financial advisers, relatives, friends, or the Internet thieves. There are so many ways in which these con artists can bilk us that the list of possibilities would fill the Yellow Pages of our local telephone book. I am not suggesting that we stay awake at night worrying about who has taken aim at the bull's-eye on our backs. However, I am proposing that seniors consider some protective measures.

Garden Variety Con Artists

Historically, con artists have appealed to greed, fear, and our desire to be liked. To protect myself against these predators, I intend to consult an attorney or a trusted, long-time friend when anyone asks me to commit some or all of our resources to them. In addition, I plan to ask myself:

1. How much of my nest egg am I likely to lose if I have misplaced my trust in this person? (A question that Madoff's investors should have asked.)
2. How badly would I feel if I have misplaced my trust in this person? (The heartrending stories of Madoff's investors foreshadow how you are likely to feel.)
3. What are the worst things that could happen to me if I have misplaced my trust in this person? (You could lose everything as did Madoff's investors.)
4. Do I fully understand the contents of this document or proposal? (None of Madoff's investors understood how his fund worked.)

An acquaintance of mine failed to ask questions like these and act on what he would have forecast. The result devastated him and his wife. When he retired, he and his wife decided to leave the country to do volunteer work for several years. Having made this decision, they sold their home and put their life savings in the name of their only child. When they returned from overseas, they discovered that their loved one had squandered their money to feed a drug habit.

Recently I read about an elderly couple who signed up for a reverse mortgage in 1988 that paid them $312 a month (Harney, 2006). Eighteen years later the wife had to sell the home when she moved into a nursing home. To her dismay, she learned that 100% of the gains in her home's market value belonged to the bank. The bank had paid out $67,586.01 in monthly payments and walked away with $416,500. Sadly, the couple had signed a contract, which they didn't fully understand, and the surviving wife has nothing left but a major heartache and an empty bank account. They failed to ask question 4 in the previous paragraph, to seek independent counsel, and paid a heavy price for their oversight.

Con artists are clever, ingenious, inventive people who devote their lives to cheating others. We seniors head the list of targets for these con artists, and we should all resolve to answer the questions I listed previously before signing any documents that may jeopardize our financial and emotional futures.

Internet Thieves

The World Wide Web is a mixed blessing. On the one hand, we can keep in touch with friends and relatives wherever they may be, conduct business over the Internet, locate information in seconds that years ago would have taken weeks or months, and entertain ourselves with podcasts, music, and movies. On the other hand, we become vulnerable to thieves who prey on us to steal our identities and our money. Phishing, pharming, and spoofing are among their favorite tactics (see http://www.homestreet.com/security/email.aspx), and we need to protect ourselves against the nefarious activities of the Internet predators. Users of MS Windows operating systems are especially vulnerable to the attacks of hackers.

Like many others, I check my accounts at banks, credit unions, and companies holding my retirement investments. To safeguard my nest egg, I take the following measures:

1. I check only my accounts from my home computer and never from another computer or a public wireless network.
2. I use a firewall to block others from accessing my computer and an antivirus program to protect my computer from virus attacks.
3. I also use antispyware to detect unwanted spying on my computer usage.
4. I always verify the security and authenticity of a website that handles my financial affairs by looking at my web browser window to see whether the address begins with https:// (note the s attached to http) and there is a padlock image. Moreover, I double-click on the padlock image to verify that the SSL security certificate is for the company I am accessing.
5. I prefer to conduct my financial affairs with firms that use multiple levels of security such as security images that I have selected. These security images appear once I log onto the website and enter my user name. In addition, the website asks

me to answer one of several personal questions if I or anyone else tries to access my account from another computer.

6. I always close my web browser after logging out of my accounts.
7. I never answer e-mails requesting account or personal information no matter how genuine the request appears to be. I notify the firm that supposedly requested the information.
8. I never act on get-rich schemes that arrive in my mailbox.
9. I use lengthy passwords with small and large cap letters and numbers and change them regularly.

Out of curiosity, I checked four websites to see how they dealt with security. Here's what I learned about them:

- All displayed https://, a padlock image, and an SSL security certificate.
- Two used security images after I entered my user name.
- One required me to answer a personal question when I accessed it from other than my home computer.
- One offered a Customer Protection Guarantee that reimbursed the customer for any losses due to unauthorized activity. The fine print disclosed conditions under which the guarantee did not cover losses. My reading of these conditions left me uneasy about the guarantee; it certainly wasn't ironclad.
- One limited its discussion of security to what customers should do to protect their accounts and nothing about what the company was doing.

If the above security measures don't alleviate your concerns, consider using a spare computer with only Internet Explorer or Safari installed on it; use this computer to access financial account information and nothing else.

My limited search led me to conclude that you should examine how a firm handles security. Armed with this information you can decide whether you want to do business with the firm and/or take steps to protect yourself if you do. Don't hesitate to suggest ways to improve the website of any firm that currently handles your financial affairs.

Finally, if you suspect that you are a victim of fraud, place a fraud alert on your credit file with the three major credit bureaus: Equifax (1-800-525-6285), Experian (1-888-397-3742), and TransUnion (1-800-680-7289).

TIP!

If you feel that you are drowning and someone offers to throw you a rope, make certain it's not a snake.

Worksheet: Protection Against Fraud

If you use the Internet to access your accounts, you should consider what you are doing to protect your nest egg. Examine the list below, check the steps you have taken, and establish goals for increasing your protection.

__1. I only check my accounts from my home computer and never from another computer or a public wireless network.

__2. I use a firewall to block others from accessing my computer and an antivirus program to protect my computer from virus attacks.

__3. I also use antispy software to detect unwanted spying on my computer usage.

__4. I always verify the security and authenticity of a website that handles my financial affairs by looking at my web browser window to see whether the address begins with https:// (note the s attached to http) and there is a padlock image.

__5. I double-click the padlock image to verify that the SSL security certificate is for the company I am accessing.

__6. I prefer to conduct my financial affairs with firms that use multiple levels of security such as security images that I

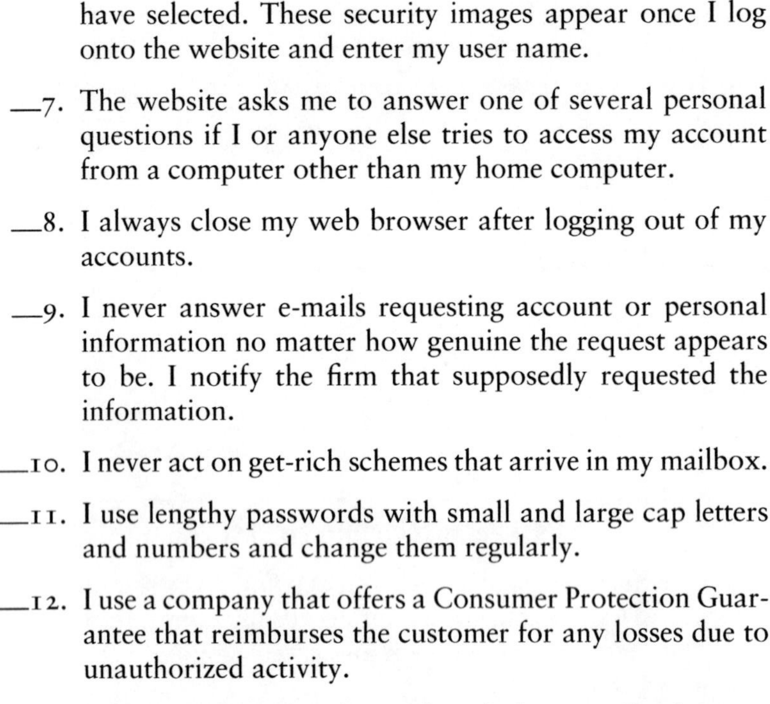

have selected. These security images appear once I log onto the website and enter my user name.

__7. The website asks me to answer one of several personal questions if I or anyone else tries to access my account from a computer other than my home computer.

__8. I always close my web browser after logging out of my accounts.

__9. I never answer e-mails requesting account or personal information no matter how genuine the request appears to be. I notify the firm that supposedly requested the information.

__10. I never act on get-rich schemes that arrive in my mailbox.

__11. I use lengthy passwords with small and large cap letters and numbers and change them regularly.

__12. I use a company that offers a Consumer Protection Guarantee that reimburses the customer for any losses due to unauthorized activity.

__13. I use a spare computer with only Internet Explorer or Safari installed on it to access financial information on my accounts and nothing else.

Goals for change: Review the above list, star (*) the items you want to implement, and implement them.

PART FIVE

Beyond Retirement

Most of us desire to leave this world in the black. If we do, a host of decisions arises. I discuss seven decisions that I anticipated and how to resolve them. Some decisions were easy, like how to reduce the taxes on our estate and how to prepare our heirs for a possible windfall. More difficult ones centered on how much money to leave each of our four children and who should serve as trustee for money left in trust.

CHAPTER TWENTY-NINE

What If I Finish in the Black?

Where there's a will, there are relatives.

When you are laid to rest, you may be fortunate enough to have some money left. Unless you have planned for this eventuality, the Internal Revenue Service (IRS), your state government, and assorted attorneys may wind up with more of this money than your heirs. Even if your heirs receive most of your inheritance, potential problems loom beyond the grave that can be minimized, if not avoided, by planning for them. Risk management extends to the hereafter unless you are someone determined to spend every last dime before greeting St. Peter at the Golden Gate.

As I pondered the future and the possibility that our four children may inherit some money from us, seven questions arose:

1. How can we reduce the state and federal taxes on our estate?
2. Who would serve as the successor trustee?
3. How can we protect the inheritance from the risk of loss?
4. How much do we leave each of our four children?
5. Who should serve as the trustee for money left in a trust?
6. How do we reduce the likelihood of sibling conflict?
7. How can we prepare our heirs for a possible windfall?

Reducing Estate Taxes

I discovered that there are several ways to reduce estate taxes: establishing charitable trusts, gifting tax-free money each year to our children and grandchildren, paying educational expenses of grandchildren directly to the educational institution, and creating an A/B Trust. Given our circumstances, we settled on an A/B Trust. Our attorney charged us around $3,500 to create this trust and saved us several hundred thousand dollars in estate taxes. In addition, we established a revocable living trust, which, unlike a will, avoids probate, ensures that there will be little, if any, delay in settling the estate, and eliminates attorney fees associated with probate. If you anticipate having a sizable estate, a revocable living trust and A/B Trust are certainly worth consideration. Whether you leave a small or a large estate, it is critical for you to have a will. We have both; our family attorney who specializes in estate planning prepared them for us.

Choosing a Successor Trustee

A critical decision everyone must make is who will serve as the successor trustee of the living trust. We considered two possibilities: (a) appointing one or more of our children and (b) appointing a third party like an attorney or a trust officer at a bank. In the end, our decision was influenced by the experience of my wife's aunt who named her attorney as the executor of her will. When the aunt died, the attorney turned to a trust officer at the local bank to perform this function. Between the two, they walked away with 25% of the estate. In addition, her aunt, a former member of the Women's Army Corps, left $25,000 to the federal government to pay down the national debt. The heirs needlessly paid state estate taxes on this bequest.

Protecting the Inheritance

My wife and I lived through the depression and have been frugal throughout our lives. Having saved and done without, we don't want our money squandered. Nor do we want it to wind up in the hands of a nonfamily member like a creditor or a litigant. If our children choose to conserve some of their inheritance for their own children, we want to ensure that happens. After reading *Beyond the Grave* (Condon & Condon, 2001), we settled on Protection Trusts for each of our children. We feel reasonably confident that our money will remain in our bloodline and not wasted. Anyone planning to leave an inheritance could profit from reading *Beyond the Grave*. The authors of this book, both inheritance-planning attorneys, share with their readers the array of problems they have encountered in their practice and how to leave money to your children the right way. Their book is an interesting and entertaining read filled with real-life stories and a minimum of legalese. Read and reap!

To underscore the need to protect an inheritance, let me relate the sad tale told to me recently. This person confided in me that he had inherited a sizable amount of money from his parents. He held the inheritance in his name for several years. During this time his wife badgered him to put this money in a joint account. Tired of hearing, "You don't love me, or you would place my name on this account along with yours," he finally capitulated. Five months later, his wife filed for divorce and walked away with half of his inheritance. With more than half of all marriages ending in divorce, one should not overlook this possibility when leaving an inheritance.

Slicing the Inheritance Pie

When we created our revocable living trust, we agonized over how much to leave each child. Should it be equal shares regardless of need, or should it be unequal shares determined by need? For those of you who are wrestling with this decision, let me share what I have learned during my consideration of this issue. Financial circumstances are never chiseled in stone; they can change either for better or worse. Children who are well-off today may not be so tomorrow; children who are struggling currently may experience good times later. No one can predict the future. We also came to recognize that money has symbolic significance; children may equate their share of an estate with how much their parents love them. Though this may not be the case, their perception is their reality. Finally, a child who has done well in life may be thinking, "Why am I being penalized for working hard and being successful?" When we considered all of these factors, we decided on equal shares even though there is unequal need. Whatever choice you make may leave you with lingering doubts. We have ours.

Trustees

Since we decided to leave our money in trust for each of our children, we faced another decision: Who should serve as trustee—the heir, a sibling, or a third party? In the best of all possible worlds the heirs should be able to control their inheritance. Not all of us live in such a world. You may have children who are unable to manage their money due to financial immaturity or a disability. What to do? If you select a sibling to serve as the trustee, you can reduce the annual administration costs. But, the sibling will be saddled with a burdensome, time-consuming responsibility. Moreover, when a child serves as a trustee for a sibling, there is the potential for problems that have an everlasting destructive impact on their relationships with one another. If you want to obtain insight into the forms these problems can take, read the book by Condon and Condon that I mentioned earlier. After reading their riveting accounts of mankind at its worst, I thought that appointing a child as a trustee for a sibling belonged in the garbage can of bad ideas.

Sibling Conflict

Sibling strife does not stop at the bank vault. Although money can be the source of sibling conflict, enduring problems can arise around the distribution of your possessions. As children grow up, they often develop emotional attachments to one or more objects that you own. Upon the death of you and your spouse, siblings may become eternal enemies in disputes over something like a treasured figurine with little or no monetary value. The myth of "one happy family" comes to light on the death of the last parent. All of the underlying resentments present since childhood surface when siblings are least able to handle them. Irreparable harm results. We realize that it is our responsibility to develop a plan or process for distributing our possessions to avoid exacerbating the emotions that may arise upon our deaths.

Preparing Our Heirs for a Windfall

This writing project began with a desire to teach our children about investing because I wanted them to invest our hard-earned money wisely. Successful investors, as I have learned, understand the emotional aspects of investing, as well as the fundamentals of investing. With this knowledge, I have sought to teach our children and grandchildren some of the basics of behavioral finance and investing.

Behavioral Finance

Simply stated, behavioral finance has to do with the psychological aspects of investing. Each investor has two inner demons: greed and fear. Greed impels us to chase the hot performers in order to beat the market and demonstrate how smart we are. We witnessed the greed demon during the dot-com era; nearly everyone, including me, my wife, and three of my children, rushed to purchase technology funds or stocks. When the bubble burst, we all lost money, some lots of it. The fear demon strikes when the market falls and we panic. We sell when we should be buying or standing pat. As a result, we lose money by committing the classic error—buying high and selling low. If investors expect to battle these demons successfully, they face a formidable task. The financial news media and your fellow investors constantly bombard you with hot tips and urge you to join the gold rush or get out of the market because it is overheated. Resisting them is virtually impossible unless you have a strategy in place and the resolve to implement it even when your inner demons whisper otherwise.

Investment Basics

Let me play Johnny One Note. It bears repeating: keep it simple, limit investment costs, and diversify. Although the Coffeehouse portfolio (chapter 8) represents a sensible choice, the easiest way to achieve near market returns at a reasonable cost is to invest in a highly diversified target-date retirement fund from either Vanguard or T. Rowe Price (Morningstar). Either strategy works fine in tax-sheltered accounts. As for taxable accounts, it makes sense for California residents to invest in a Vanguard tax-managed balanced fund, a tax-managed international fund, tax-exempt California money market fund, and a tax-exempt CA intermediate bond fund. Residents of other states might substitute the Intermediate Term Tax-Exempt bond fund for the CA tax-exempt bond fund. If our children resolved to invest their inheritance using these investments or something along these lines, I would rest in eternal bliss.

Not being content with educating our children about investing, I embarked on a more challenging task—teaching our grandchildren about the importance of saving. On my 70th birthday, I presented each of our four grandchildren with an envelope containing $70 and how much this would be worth if they saved it until their 65th birthday. Our two granddaughters expressed surprise, "Papa, you gave us presents on YOUR birthday." Then they compared their amounts at age 65. Erica, the oldest, wanted to know why her younger sister, Jamie, had more money. I tried to explain as simply as I could why one amount was larger than the other though I must confess that I am not sure whether I succeeded. Each year on my birthday I give each of the grandchildren a similar envelope with an amount equal to my age and use this occasion to teach an investment concept. On my 75th birthday, I presented each grandchild with a chart showing the importance of starting a savings plan early. By investing only $2,000 a year for five years beginning at age 13, they would accumulate one million dollars by age 65. This will bear repeating in future years because one of them thought that she was NOW a millionaire. Striving for simplicity, I included a dime, along with $76, on my most recent birthday. Puzzled by the dime, they asked, "Grandpa, what's the dime for?" I responded, "Every time you receive a gift or earn some money, put aside ten cents of every dollar; someday you will have lots of money." I look forward to my birthdays and am comforted by the knowledge that they want their grandpa around for many years to come.

TIP!

If you are interested in teaching your children or grandchildren personal financial skills, try these websites for ideas:

TheMint.org

The Jump$tart Coalition

The National Association of Personal Financial

Advisers (NAPFA)

Afterword

Retirees want to live happily in retirement and feel fulfilled. If you have enough money, you may enjoy peace of mind. To be happy and fulfilled are just as challenging to achieve as financial security. In chapter 30, I discuss ways to use your mind and body so that you won't lose either prematurely. Finally, I recount how my friends and I have found fulfillment by making ourselves useful in a variety of ways.

CHAPTER THIRTY

Money, Happiness, and a Fulfilling Retirement

You can't buy happiness.

With age 95 looming far into our future, most of us worry more about outliving our nest eggs than about leading a happy, fulfilling life. Now ten years into my retirement, I realize that focusing solely on financial planning is myopic. If you manage to save a lot of money for retirement, you may later discover that money can't buy happiness or a fulfilling life unless you have planned for it. Achieving happiness and a fulfilling life in retirement isn't easy. I know because I didn't plan for it, and I have only been partially successful.

Use It or Lose It

Shortly after I retired, I listened to a lecture by my former internist, now a gerontologist. He underscored what he termed the "two keys to a long life." The first was, "Use it or lose it." The word "it," made infamous by former president Clinton, refers in this case to the mind and the body. According to Dr. Walter Bortz, research suggests that watching television is not the way to use your mind. Studies of brain waves show that TV viewing produces the same brain wave activity as staring at a blank wall. Unfortunately, I watch more TV than is mentally healthy because I enjoy watching movies, sporting events, and the news. Breaking this viewing habit remains a challenge for me.

For mental stimulation, I solve puzzles, read about politics and investing, and write books. In my first year of retirement, I wrote a memoir which I titled, "Looking in the Rearview Mirror." Wishing that I had known more about the lives of my father and mother, I thought my children and grandchildren would appreciate learning about mine. After my daughter read a draft, her only comment was, "Dad, it's all about *you.*" Maybe, just maybe, she and her three brothers will some day come to appreciate that it was all about me. My next writing project focused on retirement planning and investing, topics that I thought might be beneficial to my children, grandchildren, and friends. Reading and trying to learn about topics that were foreign to me proved challenging and stimulating. My third book, *A Problem-based Approach to Management Education,* was written with a former student, Philip Hallinger, and built upon our previous work. I haven't yet decided on my next writing project.

To keep physically fit, I walk daily—usually 30–40 minutes, sometimes longer. Most of the time my companion is a Sony Walkman tuned to National Public Radio (NPR). Several years ago my wife and I hiked a lot, but her arthritis and bad feet limit her physical activity. Occasionally, I walk with a friend or a former student. Although I enjoy listening to NPR, I find it more enjoyable to walk and talk with someone else. Recently, I began to supplement my walking with a 25-minute exercise program, *Sit and Be Fit,* which I recorded on my digital video recorder. Together, the walking and additional exercise have improved my emotional and physical well-being.

There are countless ways in which one can use it rather than lose it. I chose activities that I enjoy. To live a fulfilling life to 95, choose activities that you enjoy and provide a workout for your mind and your body. Spending all day in front of a TV screen does not fit the bill.

Make Yourself Useful, or What's the Job Description for the Rest of Your Life?

To drive home the second key to a long, fulfilling life, Dr. Bortz recounted an experience he had as a young lad. His grandfather owned a grocery store in rural Pennsylvania. From time to time young Walter visited the store and stood around hoping for some candy from his beloved grandfather. One day his grandfather looked at him and said, "Walter, make yourself useful." That comment stuck with him and has become a mantra for living his life.

To make yourself useful, consider volunteering. There is ample research evidence demonstrating the value of volunteering in promoting happiness, health, and longevity (see Harris & Thoresen, 2005). Serving others brings meaning to your life and rewards you with the "Helper's High." You can serve others through formal or informal volunteering. Apparently greater benefits occur to those who volunteer formally rather than informally. If this is the case, several of my friends have an edge on me. They are formal volunteers, whereas I am an informal one. A friend of mine grew up on a farm and developed a useful set of carpentry skills. When he retired from his professorship, he volunteered to build homes for Habitat for Humanity. Each year he supervises the construction of six to eight homes for the less fortunate. Another friend runs a men's group at his church and pursues his academic interests in health and psychology at a local university. A third is a retired college president who chaired a national campaign to raise money for cystic fibrosis, a disease that afflicted his two granddaughters. He also chairs the board of an art institute.

As for me, I never developed the habit of becoming a formal volunteer. For much of my life, I devoted my time to work and family. When I was 36, my concern for family heightened during a taxicab ride from O'Hare airport in Chicago. I engaged the cab driver in a conversation. He talked about his life. I learned that he had worked three jobs so that he could buy a home on Lake Michigan and cars for his wife and children. As a result, he spent little time with his family. In the end he was estranged from his kids, and his wife divorced him. His final comment had a profound effect on me, "I lost what I had, and what I had was more important than what I wanted." From that moment on I decided to devote even more time to my family. Consequently, I have a reasonably good relationship with my four children and have been happily married for more than 55 years. As my wife said on our Golden Wedding Anniversary, "We like as well as love each other." By emphasizing work and family, I neglected those activities that might have stood me in good stead as a retiree, namely, volunteering and becoming active in social and church groups.

My sense of usefulness derives mainly from helping former colleagues, friends, and my children with financial decisions that face them. Occasionally I speak to a group about retirement planning and work with individuals who are contemplating retirement. Though I feel reasonably competent to help others in making decisions about investments and retirement, I have discovered that many are reluctant to discuss their financial affairs with someone whom they know. From time to time former students come by my home and seek advice as they cope with a range of problems. Others phone me from distant places and use me as an executive coach. Still others drop by to talk and share what is going on in their lives. These activities nourish my spirit and afford me a taste of the "Helper's High."

If formal volunteering appeals to you, I suggest you develop the habit years before you retire. The transition to retirement will be easier. According to what I have learned, your skills and wisdom will more likely be welcomed if you have cemented yourself in the volunteer organization before you retire. Three good starting points for finding volunteer opportunities are listed below:

Administration on Aging http:www.aoa.gov (202) 619-0724. (Help older people in need.)

The National Retiree Volunteer Coalition (800) 899-0089 ext. 5091 (Work with universities and local governments.)

Senior Corps (800) 424-8867 (Helps seniors find volunteering opportunities in their local community.)

Additional Keys

My former internist overlooked two additional keys to living a happy, fulfilling, and long life in retirement: being socially connected and religiously involved. Putting all of your emotional eggs in one basket can be dangerous to your physical and mental well-being (Coontz, 2006). Retirees especially need to broaden their social connections, people whom they enjoy and in whom they confide. If your spouse is the only one with whom you discuss important matters, you will become socially isolated when that person dies or becomes incapacitated. That happened to a friend of mine's father; having no one else can be devastating. It is important to establish close social and emotional ties beyond your nuclear family. I am fortunate that I have several friends with whom I share my fears, concerns, and matters of personal import. Though I believe in God and try to lead a Christian life, I do not attend church regularly. Some of my friends have an edge on me because they attend church regularly, and regular churchgoers tend to live longer than those who do not.

As you think about retirement, factor into your thinking the need to plan for a long, happy, and fulfilling life. If your financial house is in order, you could benefit from adopting the philosophy of Milton W. Garland, an active centenarian and inventor. He said, "Live like you're going to live forever, not like you're going to die tomorrow."

TIP!

If you want to learn more about how to live a happy, fulfilling life, read *Get a Life: You Don't Need a Million to Retire Well* by Ralph Warner (2004). It will help you prepare for retirement better than any book that I have read.

APPENDIX A

Illustration

THE ELDER FAMILY INVESTMENT AND WITHDRAWAL PLAN FOR SIMPLE PORTFOLIO

Note: When you reach retirement age, you will need to make decisions about the following:

- Asset allocation and composition of your investment portfolio
- Lower and upper limits of your target (initial) allocation
- Initial withdrawal rate
- Subsequent increases in your withdrawal rate
- Treatment of your dividends (reinvest or use for living expenses)
- Sale of shares to cover a shortfall in your living expenses
- Time to restore your allocation to its original target

If you are interested in seeing how decisions about these matters might be implemented, we encourage you to study the following example. I based the example on an Individual Retirement Account (IRA) balance of $100,000 for a 65-year-old retiree who invested in three mutual funds (Total Bond Index, Total Stock Market Index, and Total International Stock Index).

To begin . . .

1. Starting portfolio balance: $100,000 + $4,000 in Money Market Fund
2. Asset allocation: 35% stocks/65% bonds (age in bonds)
3. Investment portfolio

	Lower Limit %	Target %	Upper Limit %
Mutual Fund			
Total Bond Index	55	65	75
Total Stock Market Index	20	25	30
Total International Stock Index	8	10	12

4. Initial withdrawal rate: 4% ($4,000); taken from Money Market Fund
5. Increase withdrawal amount each year: 3%
6. Reinvest dividends (capital gains and income)

Decision Rules: End of Each Year

1. Increase living expenses by 3% (from 4% to 7%)
2. Sell shares in gaining stock funds to cover next year's living expenses and set aside in a money market fund
   a. If a shortfall remains after selling the gains in the stock funds, sell enough shares in the bond fund to cover the shortfall
   b. If there are no gaining stock funds, sell shares in bond fund to cover living expenses
3. If any stock or bond funds fall outside the upper and lower limits, rebalance to target allocation

Illustration Using the End of Year Portfolio Balance and Decision Rules

Mutual Fund	End of Year Value
Total Stock Market Index	$38,000 (32.2%)*
Total International Stock Index	$14,000 (11.9%)
Total Bond Market Index	$66,000

* Fund that falls outside its upper or lower limits.

1. **Next year's living expenses = $4,120** (an increase of 3% over previous year which was 4% or $4,000).
2. **Sell enough shares in gaining funds (Total Stock Market Index) to cover living expenses.**
3. **The new total balance after selling the shares in Total Stock Market Index to cover living expenses is $118,000–$4,120 = $113,880.**
4. **Restore portfolio to original targets (65% of new total balance in the Total Bond Market Index, 25% in Total Stock Market Index, and 10% in Total International Stock Index).**

Total Bond Index	$74,022 (65% of $113,880)
Total Stock Market Index	$28,470 (25% of $113,880)
Total International Stock Index	$11,388 (10% of $113,880)

Note: See Appendix D for access to a portfolio rebalancing tool.

APPENDIX B

Possible Questions to Ask When Seeking Financial Advice

Financial planners are fond of saying, "Clients don't want plans; they want answers to their questions." That observation certainly applied to me. However, in retrospect, I realize most people aren't sure of what questions might be asked, and they don't fully understand how to evaluate the answers.

Possible Questions to Be Answered by Your Financial Planner

Note: If you are a do-it-yourself investor or are inclined to work with or assess the recommendations of a financial planner, you may find it helpful to use these questions as a guide. Select those questions that apply to you. I have organized these questions under the following topics:

- Readiness to retire
- Investment advice
- Taxes

- Managing my investment portfolio
- Contingency plans
- Making sense of financial planner's recommendations

Note: In the bracket after each question, you will find either **Ch**, an abbreviation for chapter, or **Ap**, an abbreviation for Appendix. For example, [Ch-1] means that you will find the question discussed in chapter 1; [Ap-B] means that a discussion of the question appears in Appendix B.

Let's get started with the topic facing those considering retirement:

Readiness to retire

1. How ready am I to retire? [Ap-D]
2. How much do I need to save to retire__years from now to retire with__% of my income? [Ap-D]
3. How much can I withdraw from my IRA in the first year? [Ch-25 & Ap-D]
4. How much can I increase my subsequent yearly withdrawals? [Ch-25]
5. How long is my IRA likely to last? [Ap-D]
6. What is the probability that my money will last that long? [Ap-D]

Investment advice

1. What percentage of my savings for retirement should I invest in cash, bonds, and stocks? Why? [Ch-5 & Ap-D]
2. What mutual funds would you recommend I invest my savings in? Why? [Ch-4 & Ch-8]
3. Are these index or actively managed funds? [Ch-4] If managed funds, how long have the fund managers been in the driver's seat? How have these funds performed in bear and bull markets? How have they performed relative to their benchmarks? [Ch-4]

4. What are the operating expenses and other costs for using these funds? [Ch-3 & Ap-D]
5. How diversified is the portfolio that you are recommending? [Ch-6 & Ap-D]
6. Does it make sense for me to purchase a fixed income annuity with some portion of my retirement savings? Why? Why not? If so, who is a low-cost provider of immediate fixed income annuities that has a strong credit rating? [Ch-12, Ch-23, & Ch-24]
7. Should I convert all or a portion of my IRA into a Roth IRA? Why? [Ap-D]

Taxes

1. What can I do to reduce my estate taxes? [Ch-29]
2. How can I reduce my income taxes? [Ch-29]

Managing my investment portfolio

1. What would a rebalancing table look like for the investments in my taxable and tax-deferred accounts? [Ap-A]
2. Will you provide me with a cash flow analysis for my retirement? [Ap-B under "Making Sense of Recommendations"]

Contingency plans

1. If I have insufficient funds to retire, what are my options? [Ch-11]
2. If a bear market occurs at the outset of my retirement, what should I do? Why? [Introduction & Ch-21]
3. Do I need long-term care insurance? If so, how much do I need? Why? [Ch-14]

So that I might make sense of your recommendations

1. What type of analytic tool(s) will you be using? (linear, Monte Carlo, or historical back testing)?

Note:

a. Linear (uses a uniform rate of return and inflation year after year) [least useful]
b. Monte Carlo (uses sequences of random rates of returns to determine the probability your investment portfolio will last for 20, 25, 30 years)
c. Historical back testing (assumes different retirement dates, e.g., 1960, 1961, 1962 using subsequent market returns and inflation rates to determine the percentage of times your portfolio is depleted)

2. What rate(s) of return will you use?
3. What inflation rate will you use? Why?
4. What assumption will you make about life expectancy in your analysis?
5. How will you take income taxes into account in your analysis?
6. How did you take investment costs into account when estimating the expected returns?

Bear in mind that the answers to these questions are based on a number of assumptions about returns, inflation, spending patterns, life expectancy, and the like. Because these assumptions may not hold in the future, you need to monitor your situation annually. One way to do this is to examine the *cash flow* projection if the planner provides one. This projection likely shows your expenses, income, and portfolio balances on an annual basis. You can use this cash flow projection to monitor your financial picture, to determine if the projections are on track, and to reduce your spending if necessary. Alternatively, you can request an annual projection that takes into account new information such as an increase in your life expectancy, your returns, the previous year's inflation rate, your withdrawals, and unanticipated events that affect your financial status.

Now that your consultation with a financial planner is over, what have you learned?

Based on what I now know, I would feel that I had received my money's worth if when finished:

1. I had a clear sense of how long my investment portfolio would last under a variety of conditions, namely, my current and the planner's suggested asset allocation, different rates of return, different initial withdrawal rates, and different market conditions (seven to be exact, including withdrawals starting with a bear market). Moreover, I knew the probability of success for many of these conditions. The financial planner generated these projections using Monte Carlo, historical back testing, or both.
2. I understood the planner's investment philosophy, the reasoning underlying it, and his/her recommendations for investing my money in specific mutual funds that together produced a well-diversified portfolio.
3. Finally, I knew what the total costs were for the investments being recommended and some guidance on how to manage my investment portfolio.
4. I had a means for monitoring the state of my financial health over time and a contingency plan for dealing with any situations that might develop, which posed serious threats to my financial future.

Question: What would it take for you to feel that you received your money's worth?

APPENDIX C

Experiences With Vanguard's Financial Planning Services

In 2002, I switched most of the assets that I had invested in College Retirement Equities Fund (CREF) to Vanguard, the low-cost king of mutual funds. During most of the time, I was accumulating my retirement money. Because I have nearly eight years of experience with Vanguard, I would like to share with you what I have learned about this client-centered financial services organization. Perhaps, my experience and assessments will be of value to you if either of these options becomes available to you and you decide to use a financial planner.

Vanguard

If you want low-cost mutual funds, Vanguard is the leader. Its founder, John Bogle, has long been a critic of the mutual fund industry and led the way in creating index funds which historically have consistently outperformed the average actively managed fund. Bogle developed the Cost Matters Hypothesis and urged investors to create a low-cost, simple investment portfolio. Although he strongly endorses index funds, his former company also offers some actively managed funds that follow a strategy that emphasizes low turnover, stable management, low operating expenses, and a particular investment style. When the assets of these actively managed funds reach a certain level, Vanguard either closes the fund to new investors or adds another investment manager who adheres to the same investment style but uses a different approach. These practices reflect the client's, not the investment manager's, interests. When you buy mutual fund shares from Vanguard, you become a partial owner of the fund as well. Any cost savings fatten your IRA, not the owners of the company as is the case with a number of commercial mutual fund companies.

Investment Options

Vanguard offers over 100 investment options and a wide selection of bond funds, equity funds, and hybrid funds containing stocks and bonds. Moreover, it has a definite investment philosophy that it advocates and follows. This strategy stresses asset allocation and diversification by investment approach (indexed and actively managed), geography (domestic and international), style (value and growth), and market capitalization (large, mid, and small). The goal is to increase returns and reduce volatility. One can implement the Vanguard philosophy with only three index funds (Total Stock Market Index, Total International Stock Index, and Total Bond Index). A 50% stock and 50% bond portfolio might look like the following:

Total Stock Market Index (40%)

Total International Stock Index (10%)

Total Bond Index (50%)

If investors prefer to use a mix of indexed and/or actively managed funds, they confront a formidable task that many people feel ill equipped to handle. In this event, investors can opt for the Coffeehouse portfolio (chapter 8), the all-weather portfolio (chapter 8), or a portfolio recommended by Bernstein (chapter 8). If none of these appeals to you, rely on a Vanguard financial adviser who provides this service for a reasonable fee. Those investors who have sufficient assets invested at Vanguard can obtain this service free.

Guidance In Retirement Planning

If you have sufficient funds with Vanguard, it will provide you with a Personal Financial Report at no charge; otherwise, you will be charged a reasonable fee. This report has two primary objectives:

1. Analyze your current portfolio and supply recommendations for a long-term investment strategy appropriate for your risk tolerance and goals and
2. Analyze your current and projected expenses, income, and assets, and the sufficiency of your resources to meet your retirement goals and needs.

Prior to preparing this report, Vanguard requires you to complete a questionnaire. When your Personal Financial Report has been prepared, you receive a copy and are encouraged to study it and make a list of the questions you wish to ask your adviser. Subsequently, you spend an hour discussing this report with your adviser over the phone.

Here's my take on the strengths and limitations of the Report that Vanguard provided me.

Principal Strengths

a. Detailed description of Vanguard's investment approach

b. Examined my portfolio balance using different historical starting dates, including the worst (1965) and the best (1982).

c. Examined the probability of my portfolio lasting over an extended period using varying rates of return and initial withdrawal levels.

d. Suggested a strategy for rebalancing and spending from the portfolio.

Principal Limitations

a. The Vanguard software program could not take into account my intention to transfer money from another company to Vanguard over the next nine years.

b. The software program could not take into account my decision rules for withdrawing funds after the first year.

c. Vanguard assumed a much higher level of risk in my portfolio than I was willing to take. They chose to include my investments kept at TIAA-CREF and treat the investments at these two companies as one portfolio. This made logical sense to me but not psychological sense. With a substantial sum of my money at Vanguard allocated to stocks, I certainly wouldn't sleep well and might panic, rather than stay the course, if the market dropped more than 20%.

d. One of the funds recommended by Vanguard was, in my judgment, among its worst performing funds.

Vanguard, unlike TC, recommended a specific set of mutual funds and a different asset allocation. Although TC advised me to place 60% in equities, Vanguard recommended that I invest 40% of my total portfolio in equities until age 80 and 30% afterward. Vanguard, like TC, recommended a complex portfolio containing the following seven funds using the money I had invested with them:

Dodge & Cox Balanced Fund*	18%
U.S. Growth Fund	18%
Total Stock Market Index Fund	30%
Extended Market Index Fund	3%
Strategic Equity Fund	5%
Explorer Fund	5%
Total International Stock Index Fund	21%

* A holding I wanted to retain at the time but have since sold.

In addition to this Personal Financial Report, Vanguard provides an impressive array of investment information, retirement guidance, and planning tools on its website. Most questions that retirees have can be answered by using their website. Anyone can use the information, guidance, and planning tools provided on this website free of charge. Moreover, the material is clearly and briefly written and quite informative.

If it is important for you to meet face to face with your financial adviser, Vanguard may not be suitable for you. The representative of this company visits my employing institution several times a year, but I haven't found it easy to schedule a visit when I needed it. As for me, I am comfortable talking with advisers over the phone as long as I am confident that they are working for a client-centered organization.

Summary Comments

Let me reiterate, I felt fortunate to have access to the low-cost variable annuities at TC during the time I was employed in higher educational institutions. After retiring, I was grateful to have access to the array of low-cost indexed and actively managed funds at Vanguard. Since 2002, I have exploited the strengths of both companies in creating my pension plan.

APPENDIX D

Planning Tools & Calculators

1. **Am I ready to plan my retirement?**
   http://www.moneycentral.msn.com: Under the planning section of this site, look for the Retirement IQ Test to obtain an idea of how ready you are to plan your own retirement. The 25 questions will take you roughly 15 minutes to complete.

2. **Am I ready to retire?**
   http://yourretirementyourway.com/quiz.php: Readiness to retire involves more than whether you have enough money to retire. Take the Retirement Readiness Quiz to assess your progress in preparing for retirement. Covers important issues that affect one's ability to thrive in retirement. Targeted to Canadians but useful for U.S. residents as well.

3. **Can I afford to retire?**
   Otar Retirement Optimizer
   http://www.retirementoptimizer.com/: I consider this retirement calculator the most comprehensive and powerful one available. It is fully worth the price of $99.99 and can be downloaded from his website. See discussion in Chapter 11.

4. **What is my net worth?**
http://www.Kiplinger.com.personalfinance/tools/networth.html?: Prior to retirement you may want to assess your financial situation. This user-friendly planning tool asks you to supply information about your financial assets and liabilities. Once you have entered this information on the worksheet on Kiplinger's website, you simply click "Calculate your net worth." Voila, in an instant you know your net worth.

5. **How much do I need to save for retirement?**
www.ChoosetoSave.org: Click on "Ballpark Estimate."

6. **How much can I withdraw from my retirement account?**
www.vanguard.com: Once on the Vanguard website, click on "Planning and Education" followed by "Planning Tools" and "Retirement Planning." Scroll down the page until you see "Determine how much you can withdraw." You will be asked for your portfolio balance at retirement, your asset allocation (conservative, moderate, or aggressive), and time to be spent in retirement. Click on "Calculate"; it will provide you with your withdrawal rate and initial monthly withdrawal. Before using this tool, read the detailed assumptions. This calculator is easy to use and relies on historical data regarding returns and inflation for the period 1960 to 2005. The monthly withdrawal represents the highest level of spending in which 85% of the historical paths left you with a positive balance at the end of your selected length of retirement.

7. **How long will my retirement account last?**
T. Rowe Price.com: Click on "Retirement Planning," then "Tools & Income" and "Retirement Income Calculator." Read Tutorial before using the calculator. It uses Monte Carlo simulations and allows you to test the success rate of seven different asset allocations and portfolios.

   Vanguard.com: Click on "Planning & Education" followed by "Retirement Planning," "Retirement Planning Tools & Calculators," and "Lifetime Spending Analyzer." Uses historical back testing to determine the longevity of various retirement portfolios under different return and inflation conditions between 1960 and 2003. Also, provides information about your life expectancy.

8. **How much of my income can I replace if I retire?**
ChoosetoSave.org: Click on "Ballpark Estimate." This calculator is easy to use; it enables you to include other income sources (e.g., an annuity or rental) and to specify your rate of return (suggest that you be conservative and use 6.5%) and life expectancy (suggest that you use 93 to 95). The calculator will let you know if you have saved enough to replace whatever percentage of your final wages you desire. Be sure to read the FAQ before providing the information requested.

9. **Should I convert my IRA to a Roth IRA?**
CalcTools.com: Before calculating whether it makes sense for you to convert your IRA to a Roth IRA, click on "click here for important information" to learn what assumptions the calculator makes about life expectancy, IRA distributions, and federal tax. Although this calculator does not determine your eligibility for converting an IRA to a Roth IRA, it does suggest where you can obtain more information about Roth IRAs.

10. **What should my asset allocation be?**
Easyallocator.com: Uses Modern Portfolio Theory to create an investment portfolio that reflects your risk preference. Suggests low-cost Exchange Traded Funds and Index Funds for your taxable and tax-deferred accounts. Indicates your expected return rate and suggests an initial withdrawal rate.

11. **How can I narrow the universe of mutual funds to a manageable number that match my selection criteria?**
Vanguard.com: Once you enter the Vanguard website, type "Mutual Fund Screener" in the window at the top right of the home page. The Screener has two sets of criteria: basic and additional. Before using this tool, you will find it helpful to decide on your asset allocation and how you intend to further diversify your investment portfolio. You can use the mutual fund screener free of charge to search the entire universe of mutual funds. This tool is useful in narrowing your choice. Based on what I have learned about investing, it makes sense to include the following in your criteria: cost, turnover, managerial longevity, investment style, and total returns (five years or ten years). You can do additional research on the funds identified by your criteria to see how each fund performed during bull and bear markets (available on Yahoo.finance)

and whether the manager sticks with his/her investment style (check strategy discussion provided in mutual fund screener and Morningstar.com)

12. **How diversified is my investment portfolio, and what are its operating expenses?**
Morningstar.com: Click on "Tools" and then "Instant X Ray." This tool enables you to check how costly your portfolio is relative to its category and how it is allocated across the three major asset classes: cash, stocks (domestic and international), and bonds. You can also see how your portfolio is diversified in terms of size (large-, mid-, and small-cap) and style (value and growth) and whether you are making too large a bet on different sectors of the market. If you subscribe to Morningstar, you can obtain a written explanation of what is noteworthy about your portfolio (e.g., whether it is overweighted or underweighted in terms of size, style, and market sectors).

13. **Am I being adequately compensated for the risk I am taking?**
RiskGrades.com: Enter your investments in stocks and mutual funds, and assign a name to your portfolio. In addition to evaluating whether you are being adequately compensated for the risk you are taking, the RiskGrades tool will supply valuable information about your portfolio, including its RiskGrade, the risk profile of the portfolio, and the impact of individual assets on overall portfolio risk. When I evaluated the risk of the Coffeehouse portfolio using the RiskGrades tool, I learned that it has a RiskGrade of 35, qualifies as a *conservative plan investment strategy*, reduces the risk of the portfolio by 18% through diversification, is 0.76 times as volatile as the Standard & Poor's (S&P) 500 Index, is less risky than 97% of the sampled portfolios, and provides more than an adequate return for the risk being taken. There is no charge for using the RiskGrades tool. For a lucid discussion of the RiskGrades website, see "RiskGrades: Getting a Handle on Volatility," *Computerized Investing* (May/June, 2003), pp. 21–26.

14. **How well is my investment portfolio doing?**
http://www.financialwisdom.com/fwonline/java/IRRCalc.html: To use this calculator, you will need to have the following information: beginning and ending balance of your

portfolio, as well as the additions and withdrawals for each month of the year. The calculator then performs a "time weighted, internal rate of return calculation."

15. **How can I easily rebalance my portfolio?**
www.bee-man.us/finance/portfolio_rebalance.htm: When you arrive on this website, click on "Finance" (right-hand side of page). To use this nifty calculator, you will need the symbols of your investments, the number of shares, and your target allocation (percent). Enter the data, and voila the answer appears. Read the instructions before entering the data.

16. **How can I obtain answers to specific questions about retirement and investing?**
Morningstar.com: Click on "Discuss" and then "Vanguard Diehards." Other users will respond to your questions and are likely to provide you with thoughtful answers. Check it out before posting your question(s). Morningstar charges a $5 fee for the right to post questions.
AARP.com: Type "Financial Planning and Retirement" into the Search window on the AARP website. You will discover help on a wide array of topics dealing with financial planning and retirement.

17. **What is a comprehensive source of free financial calculators?**
www.Dinkytown.net: This website features 300 financial calculators. You can use these calculators to estimate your income taxes, prepare a loan amortization schedule, develop a college savings plan, or solve other financial problems of interest to you.

APPENDIX E

Special Issues for Women

Women, whether single or married, are especially vulnerable to a number of the risks discussed in this book. This vulnerability stems from the following differences between men and women:

- Women, on average, work 12 fewer years than men.
- Women earn less than men; on average, they earn about three-quarters of what men do.
- Women live longer than men—three years on average.
- Older women are much more likely to be widowed, divorced, or never married with no one to care for them.

The increased risks for female retirees that arise from these differences include

- Outliving their assets (see chapters 12 and 21)
- Loss of ability to care for themselves or to be cared for by spouses (see chapters 14 and 16)
- Inflation (see Introduction, chapters 2 and 23–25)
- Investment risk (see chapters 3–8 and 27)

Those who wish to explore this topic in greater depth should find these online resources helpful:

1. "Making Your money Last a Lifetime" (joint project of the Women's Institute for a Secure Retirement and the Actuarial Foundation)
2. "Longevity: The Underlying Driver of Retirement Risk" (research report of the Society of Actuaries)
3. "The Impact of Retirement Risk on Women" (research report of the Society of Actuaries)

To access these reports, simply type the title of the project/report into Google and press Enter.

APPENDIX F

Must Reading for an Informed Investor

Do yourself a favor and become informed about investing by reading these five books:

Bernstein, W. J. (2002). *Four pillars of investing: Lessons for building a winning portfolio*. New York: McGraw-Hill.

Bogle, J. (1999). *Common sense on mutual funds*. New York: John Wiley.

Malkiel, B. G. (2008). *A random walk down Wall Street*. New York: W.W. Norton & Company.

Swedroe, L., & Hempen, J. H. (2006). *The only guide to a winning bond strategy you'll ever need*. New York: St. Martin's Press.

Ferri, R. A. (2006). *All about asset allocation*. New York: McGraw-Hill.

You will become the most informed investor in your neighborhood and know everything you need to know about investing. I suggest you start reading them in the order listed.

From time to time you will hear or read an investment term and wonder what it means, pick up a copy of *Wall Street Words* written by David L. Scott.

Online Resource on Learning to Invest

Some of you may prefer to learn the basics of investing via the Internet. You can find a free home-study course with unit tests at the following website:

http://www.naoi.org/studycourse/ABasics.htm

It will take you five to six hours to complete. I have tried it and concluded that it will prepare most people to make informed investing decisions.

Useful Resources for Retirement Planning

"Taking the mystery out of retirement planning."

http://www.actuarialfoundation.org

"Spending and investing in retirement: Is there a strategy?" (Simply type title in Google.) Society of Actuaries website

Warner, R. (2004). *Get a life: You don't need a million to retire well.* Berkeley, CA: Nolo Press.

APPENDIX G

Determining Minimum Distribution Requirement

Uniform Lifetime Table

Age of Account Holder	Divisor*	Age of Account Holder	Divisor*
70	27.4	85	14.8
71	26.5	86	14.1
72	25.6	87	13.8
73	24.7	88	12.7
74	23.8	89	12.0
75	22.9	90	11.4
76	22.0	91	10.8
77	21.2	92	10.2
78	20.3	93	9.6
79	19.5	94	9.1
80	18.7	95	8.6
81	17.9	96	8.1
82	17.1	97	7.6
83	16.3	. . .	. . .
84	15.5	115+	1.9

* In general, holders of a 403(b) or an IRA must begin minimum distributions from their accounts when they reach the age of 70.5. (See Chapter 22 for exceptions to this rule.) To determine your minimum distribution requirement, consult the *Uniform Lifetime Table*, identify the divisor for your age, and divide the total invested in your retirement account by the appropriate divisor. If you have a much younger spouse or you inherited an IRA, use other lifetime tables to determine your minimum distribution requirement (appears in Internal Revenue Service (IRS) publication 590). We advise you to obtain the minimum distribution due on your retirement account(s) from your investment company since a heavy penalty must be paid if you fail to satisfy this requirement.

Preretirees and retirees alike often ask these two questions:

1. If I hold a 403(b) *and* an IRA, must I determine the minimum distribution for each type of account separately? The answer is unequivocally "yes."
2. If I annuitize some of my assets, can I also use the annuity payouts to satisfy the minimum distribution requirement for a portion of my nonannuitized assets? No, your annuity payouts satisfy the minimum distribution requirements for your lifetime annuities and nothing else.

There is a penalty for underpaying your minimum distribution requirement—50% of the underpayment. I suggest that you ask your investment company to compute the minimum distribution for you.

APPENDIX H

Operating Expenses for CREF Variable Annuity Accounts, 1997–2008

Variable Annuity	1997 Operating Expenses (%)*	2008 Operating Expenses (%)*
Stock	0.31	0.56
Global equities	0.30	0.62
Growth	0.59 (est.)	0.59
Equity index	0.31	0.50
Social choice	0.38	0.53
Bond	0.29	0.54
Inflation-linked bond	0.33	0.49
Money market	0.27	0.49

*Does not include transaction costs. You can estimate these by multiplying the turnover rate by 1%. Index funds generally have low turnover rates and transaction costs. See Appendix I.

APPENDIX I

Total Investment Costs for the CREF Variable Equity Accounts

Variable Annuity	2008 Operating Expenses (%)	2007 Transaction Costs (est.) (%)	Total Investment Costs (est.) (%)
Stock	0.56	0.49	1.05
Global equities	0.62	1.08	1.70
Growth	0.59	1.27	1.82
Social choice	0.53	0.60	1.13
Equity index	0.50	0.09	0.59

APPENDIX J

Publications

Saving for Retirement

Women should begin with this publication before reading the second group . . .

Charting Your Course: A Financial Guide for Women

I suggest you read the following in the order listed . . .

Building Your Portfolio with TIAA-CREF and TIAA-CREF Mutual Funds: Smart Choices, Smart Investments

Withdrawing Income During Retirement

Must reading in this order . . .

Planning Your Retirement With TIAA-CREF
Living Well in Retirement
Reviewing Your TIAA-CREF Income Choices
Receiving Your Retirement Income From TIAA-CREF
Adjusting Your Annuity Income: Your Payment Flexibilities (request this booklet from TIAA-CREF)

More in-depth reading on topics treated under must reading . . .

A Guide to TIAA-CREF's Minimum Distribution Option
Systematic Withdrawals and Transfers From TIAA Traditional
Transfer Payout Annuities: Making Transfers From TIAA Traditional

Planning ahead for your survivors . . .

Building Your Legacy
After a Loved One Passes Away

N.B.: It is inevitable that some overlap occurs in these publications.

APPENDIX K

TIAA-CREF: Strengths, Shortcomings, and Needed Changes

For all but two years of my career in higher education, I was a faithful contributor to TC. During that period, I saw my nest egg grow from three figures to seven figures. Moreover, I was more than satisfied with the services provided by this nonprofit organization. Things changed when I retired, and my frustrations flowered when I began withdrawing funds from my account.

Planning a withdrawal strategy proved far more complicated and difficult than I had ever imagined. On more than one occasion, I learned that what I planned to do ran contrary to the rules and regulations of TC. Most of these restrictions applied to my largest holding, TIAA Traditional. For example, to rebalance my portfolio after retirement, TIAA required me to use a Transfer Payout Annuity (TPA). After I converted my TIAA Traditional to several TPAs, I learned that the dates for my annual payments could not be changed. Moreover, if I later exercised my option to convert a TPA to a lifetime income annuity, I had to convert the entire amount even if I desired to convert only a portion of it. After converting my TPA to a lifetime income annuity, I could later decide to transfer a portion of this fixed annuity to a variable annuity by means of a TIAA Post Settlement Transfer. If I elected this option, CREF would prohibit me from investing in TIAA Real Estate, the Money Market Account, or any of the bond accounts. All of these transactions involved considerable paperwork and hiring a notary; some required me to obtain Medallion signature guarantees from my credit union. This Medallion guarantee provided a measure of protection to me and TC from losses due to fraudulent signatures. The guarantor becomes liable for any losses if the signature later proves to be inauthentic and money has been distributed to someone other than the person entitled to the payment from TC.

My frustrations did not end there. When I met with my wealth management advisor to discuss my Retirement Review Report, I received no guidance in how to implement TC's recommendations. As I discovered somewhat later, implementation was by no means a straightforward task. When I transferred some funds from my 403(b) to an Individual Retirement Account (IRA), I initially failed to satisfy the minimum distribution requirement for both types of retirement accounts. With the help of my wealth management advisor, I eventually avoided a 50% penalty by making an extra withdrawal from my retirement account.

And then there were the problems with record keeping and processing requests. On a few occasions, TC failed to post transactions, report accurate totals in my investment portfolio, complete requests in a timely manner, and forewarn me of the pitfalls inherent in the options I was considering at the time. When I searched the Internet, I discovered that others had experienced similar problems. At least one university had decided to drop TC as a provider due to these problems and its failure to resolve them.

As you might imagine, I was ready to hang a poster with a giant lemon on TC's headquarters in New York City. All of this reminded me of the fourth home we had purchased in Homewood, Illinois. That home proved to be a lemon, and I told friends with whom I commuted to the University of Chicago that I planned to hang a large sign depicting a lemon over the front door of our new home in a half-completed subdivision. We laughed, but my next-door neighbor, a lineman for the Chicago Bears, preferred more drastic action. He vented his frustrations by using a karate chop to split the contractor's office counter in two and kicking down his office door. After that episode, the contractor became more responsive to all of our requests for assistance.

Now that I have completed my research and listened to other retirees whose retirement accounts have shrunk by 30% or more, I have decided against hanging a lemon on TC's headquarters. TIAA Traditional has performed admirably during the two mega-meltdowns in the stock market that we have experienced since January 1, 2000, the date of my retirement. Through October 2008, long-term corporate bonds declined 18%, on average, a decline not seen since 1926 (Sommer, 2008). During this period, TIAA Traditional never wavered and proved once again that it truly is a *stable value* fund.

If you, as I, have invested a large portion of your retirement account in TIAA Traditional, you have developed a deep appreciation of its value in stabilizing your retirement ship of state when it sails into stormy waters. One can build a fine all-weather portfolio at TC around TIAA Traditional, along with TIAA Real Estate, Inflation Bonds, and the Stock Account. To boost income and protect yourself against the risk of going broke, you might choose to convert all or a portion of TIAA Traditional to a lifetime income annuity when you retire. That is what I did and have been satisfied, thus far, with my decision. The payout rates beat the competition but are not backed by any government agency or state guaranty association.

Despite its service shortcomings, I firmly believe that you can thank your employer for providing this option if it has done so. To be sure TC has undergone a transition and with this transformation has come a host of problems. It has acknowledged these problems and begun to correct them. Nonetheless, some problems remain as I have noted elsewhere in this book.

In my judgment, TC could enhance its reputation and better serve its participants if it made the following changes:

1. *Provide a road map for preretirees and retirees*. Many of my frustrations stemmed from surprises and regulations that I learned about after the fact. TC should spell out in a single resource the steps to be followed and the consequences of making major decisions like using a TPA to withdraw money from TIAA Traditional. If a retiree considers annuitizing a portion of CREF in the Stock Account, (s)he needs to know how much annual income can drop over one-, two-, and three-year periods, not simply that annual income may fluctuate. People who are trying to decide whether to annuitize

TIAA Traditional using the standard or the graded plan need to know what the historical record of payouts looks like for the best, worst, and typical case. It is in TC's best interests to help participants become well informed and subject to fewer surprises and frustrations.

2. *Eliminate the 12b-1 fees.* The CREF Stock Account rakes in more money ($586 million) in advisory and administrative fees than those assessed by other mutual funds (Rottersman, 2009). The Vanguard 500 Index Fund, often the benchmark for judging the effectiveness of mutual funds, charges only $181,000 in advisory fees and $12 million in administrative fees (Rottersman, 2009). In addition to these fees, TC assesses a 12b-1 fee for its marketing efforts to increase its assets. Vanguard, a client-centered company, also markets its products, assesses no 12b-1 fees, and lowers its operating expense charges as assets increase. TC should follow Vanguard's lead. Vanguard's practices seem to me more consistent with TC's motto, "Financial services for the greater good."

3. *Increase the flexibility for those who set up a TPA.* As I discovered, TIAA prohibits one to ladder a TPA. TPA holders face an either–or situation with respect to annuitization. They must either annuitize 100% or 0% of their TPA. Over time, people's circumstances change, and they may find it desirable and necessary to spread out their purchases of a lifetime annuity. I was surprised and dismayed to learn that TIAA would not allow me to stagger my annuitization purchases over several years because I held TIAA Traditional in a TPA. From my perspective, this restriction appears to be a constraint that serves no valid purpose.

4. *Broaden the investment options in its variable annuity accounts.* Participants in the wealth-building stage who wish to build a multiasset, globally diversified portfolio have limited options. I suspect some would welcome the opportunity to invest in retirement accounts dedicated to international and small-cap value stocks. Currently, TC emphasizes large-cap stocks and offers no annuity accounts dedicated to stocks (value and small-cap) that historically have generated higher returns with less volatility than growth stocks, large or small.

Those retirees who desire income and prefer a less complex investment portfolio would, I believe, welcome the opportunity to invest in an equity-income fund that focused on dividend paying stocks, as well as a broadly diversified fund (or account) that did not exhibit such violent swings in annual income. If not for its fee structure and reliance on actively managed funds, the TIAA Access Lifecyle Retirement Income Fund seems like a step in the right direction.

5. *Improve the Retirement Review.* TC currently provides this report to some of its preretirees and retirees. I found this document wanting in several respects. First, it bases the recommended asset allocation on a risk-tolerance questionnaire that has no predictive validity. Moreover, if I had followed the recommendations, my investment portfolio would have been devastated when the stock market collapsed. Second, the recommended asset allocation does not align well with TC's investments. Third, I had allocated much more to TIAA Traditional than the review recommended; yet, the document provided me no guidance in how to implement the revised portfolio. Finally, the analysis relied on a fixed rate of return when, as we have learned recently, returns vary, sometimes by a wide margin. Vanguard uses Monte Carlo and historical rates of returns and inflation to provide more realistic retirement scenarios.
6. *Reduce the complexity that TC participants face when they approach and enter retirement.* We have learned during the current health-care debate how complexity breeds fear, uncertainty, suspicion, and misunderstanding. In my experience, the array of choices and potential paperwork baffle many participants heading into retirement, as well as some of its wealth managers. Given its apparent level of personnel turnover, TC could reduce its training costs and potential for providing erroneous information by simplifying its choices for retirees and those nearing retirement.
7. *Offer a hybrid fund, a new retirement product likely to gain in popularity.* This hybrid fund (see Feldman, 2009) embeds an annuity, TIAA Traditional, in a target-date retirement fund. The annuity replaces the bond portion of the target-date retirement fund with the balance of the fund invested in

low-cost, index funds. By the time you reach retirement age, roughly 50% of your assets are invested in an annuity with multiple vintages, that is, varying interest rates. The annuity and Social Security together provide stable income and minimize the income fluctuations that retirees dread. Moreover, this hybrid fund simplifies the process of accumulating and withdrawing one's money. TC seems uniquely positioned to offer such a hybrid fund.

Until TC makes these changes, I believe it makes sense, if you have the option, to invest in TIAA Traditional and TIAA Real Estate (when the commercial real estate market shows signs of recovering) with the remainder invested at Vanguard. By investing with Vanguard, you can build a multiasset, globally diversified portfolio with an annual expense ratio ranging between 0.14% and 0.20%, depending on how much money you have invested. In a period of low returns, you want to reduce your investment expenses. As John Bogle, Vanguard's founder, has said on numerous occasions, "You get what you don't pay for." I have chosen to follow his advice and have been quite satisfied with Vanguard's service, first-class website, and performance. There have been no surprises and certainly no frustration. If you lack this option, TC remains a satisfactory choice and can become an excellent choice if it returns to the days described so aptly by Jason Zweig in 1998:

> a money management firm focused more on serving its clients than on the profits to be had by attracting new ones ... and reaches out to its customers in a way that puts most of the fund industry to shame.

APPENDIX L

Formula for Calculating Annual Income Increases/Decreases From Variable Annuities

$$(1 + \text{Fund Return}) \text{ divided by } (1 + \text{AIR}), \text{ less } 1$$

Example 1: Assuming an assumed investment return (AIR) of 4% and an actual return of 10%, the *increase* will be

$$(1.10/1.04) - 1 = 0.05769 \quad \text{or} \quad 5.769\%^*$$

Example 2: Assuming an AIR of 4% and an actual return of −5%, the change in payment will be

$$(0.95/1.04) - 1 = -0.08654 \quad \text{or} \quad -8.654\%^*$$

*Examples drawn from Benjamin Goodman and Michael Heller, **Annuities: Now, Later, Never?** TIAA-CREF Institute, October 2006.

APPENDIX M

Historic Returns: Worst Case, One Year*

Portfolio Allocation	Worst Case, One Year
70% bonds/30% stocks	−14.2% (1931)
60% bonds/40% stocks	−18.4% (1931)
50% bonds/50% stocks	−22.5% (1931)
40% bonds/60% stocks	−26.6% (1931)
30% bonds/70% stocks	−30.7% (1931)

**Source*: Vanguard.com (2009). Model portfolio allocations.

APPENDIX N

Annual Income Changes for TIAA-CREF Variable Annuity Accounts, 1996–2005

Account	N	Mean*	Minimum*	Maximum*
Stock	10	8.04	−28.86	38.51
Global equities	10	5.93	−35.39	39.99
Growth	10	6.45	−47.73	42.00
Equity index	10	8.17	−29.67	42.88
TIAA real estate	10	3.98	−0.04	8.05
Bond	9	2.27	−3.58	8.22
Inflation bond	8	3.92	−2.32	13.48
Social choice	10	5.92	−15.64	27.89
Money market	10	−0.374	−3.98	2.33

*All numbers expressed in percent.

APPENDIX O

TIAA-CREF Variable Annuity Income Changes, 2001–2003

Variable Annuity	2001	2002	2003
1. Stock	−26.79%	−5.01%	−28.86%
2. Global equities	−35.39	−10.70	−29.58
3. Growth	−47.73	−8.69	−33.11
4. Equity index	−26.09	−2.90	−29.67
5. Social choice	−13.01	−2.33	−15.64
6. *TIAA real estate*	6.16	1.39	−0.04
7. *Bond*	7.75	0.80	8.22
8. *Inflation bond*	8.05	−0.55	13.48
9. *Money market*	2.33	−1.40	−2.85

Source: TIAA-CREF publication. Your retirement income portfolio (**Chapter** 7) in *Retirement Strategies*, 2006.

APPENDIX P

Annual Review of Your Savings and Retirement Plan

1. Financial goal (how much do I wish to withdraw in current dollars from retirement account when I retire?) ________

2. When can I retire? ________

3. What is the current value of my retirement assets? ________

4. What is my optimum mix of stocks, bonds, and cash? ________

5. What is my current annual income? ________

6. What percentage of my income should I save? ________

7. How much do I wish to withdraw from my retirement assets in current dollars? ________

8. **How much can I withdraw from my current retirement assets? ________**

9. **What is the status of my savings and retirement plan? ________ (excellent, good, adequate, or inadequate)**

10. **If I annuitize a portion of my retirement assets will it improve the adequacy of my retirement plan? ________**

11. **How can I improve my retirement income picture? By**
    (a) Downsizing my home,
    (b) Selling my home and moving to a rental,
    (c) Move in with kids (only if you have to),
    (d) Renting my basement or rooms?

Note: The bold-faced questions can be answered using the Otar Retirement Optimizer. Place a recurring date on your electronic calendar to conduct this annual review.

INVESTING TERMS

Actively managed funds—funds subject to managerial risk because the managers try to beat the market through their stock/bond selection and/or market timing

Annualized returns—returns that reflect the effects of compounding and assume that the investor has used dividends and interest income to purchase additional shares

Annuity—an insurance product that someone buys in exchange for a stream of future income payments

Asset class—usually refers to stocks, bonds, or cash

Benchmark—an appropriate standard for judging the performance of an actively managed fund or portfolio manager. For example, an appropriate standard for judging an asset allocation of 60% stocks/40% bonds would be a *comparable* hybrid index fund that contained a similar allocation. It would be inappropriate to compare the performance of this portfolio with a fund like the Standard & Poor's 500 that contains all stocks.

Blend funds—holds growth and value stocks or stocks with a mix of value and growth characteristics

Cap—the total value of a firm's outstanding shares

Currency risk—fluctuations in the value of the dollar relative to other currencies

Diversification—investing in different asset classes (stocks, bonds, and cash) and subasset classes; (e.g., investment styles like value, growth, and blend; domestic and international; large cap and small cap)

Dollar-cost averaging—investing regular amounts of money, usually monthly, sometimes buying additional shares at higher prices and other times at lower prices

Equity income funds—funds that invest in companies paying dividends; usually such companies are large established ones with a good record of dividend payouts

Equivalent-taxable yield—a pretax yield that equals or exceeds the after tax return

Failure rates—depletion of the nonannuity portion of a retirement portfolio

Fixed annuity—an insurance product that pays a fixed amount of income for life or a fixed length of time

Growth funds—invest in stocks of companies with fast-growing earnings or revenues and the potential for price appreciation

Hybrid funds—invest in two or more asset classes, usually stocks and bonds

Index funds—funds that seek to replicate a particular index like the Standard & Poor's 500 (large cap) and Wilshire 5000 (total U.S. stock market); often referred to as passively managed funds

Investment portfolio—group of investments held by the investor

Longevity risk—the possibility of outliving one's retirement nest egg

Minimum distribution requirement—a federal mandate for retirees who have reached the age of 70.5 to withdraw a minimum amount from their tax-sheltered retirement accounts each year; failure to withdraw the minimum results in a 50% penalty

Rebalancing—periodic buying and selling of stocks and bonds to restore an investment portfolio to its desired percentage in stocks and bonds

Returns—total returns refer to the sum of dividend or interest income and capital gains

Risk—generally used to characterize fluctuations in market returns

Sovereign risk—possible loss due to political instability, war, or default on a foreign country's financial obligations

Value stocks—stocks believed to be worth more than their current price

Variable annuity—an insurance product that pays an amount of income which varies with the performance of the stock market

Volatility risk—the fluctuations in market returns

REFERENCES

Aim, Invesco. (2009, October 20). Rethinking risk: Can the market make you rich? *Morningstar Perspectives* on morningstar.com.

Ameriks, J. (1999). The retirement patterns and annuitization decisions of a cohort of TIAA-CREF participants. *Research Dialogue*, Issue No. 60. TIAA-CREF Institute, New York, NY.

Ameriks, J. R. V., & Warshawsky, M. J. (2001). Making retirement income last a lifetime. *Journal of Financial Planning, 14*, 60–76.

Armstrong, F. (2004). *The informed investor*. New York: AMACOM.

Babbel, D. F., & Herce, M. (2007). *A closer look at stable value funds performance*. Wharton Financial Institutions Center Working Paper No. 07–21. Wharton School, University of Pennsylvania, Philadelphia, PA.

Bengen, W. (2004). Determining withdrawal rates using historical data. *Journal of Financial Planning, 17(3)*, 64–73.

Bernstein, P. L. (2008, June 22). What happens if we are wrong? *The New York Times*.

Bernstein, W. (2001). *The intelligent asset allocator*. New York: McGraw-Hill.

Bernstein, W. (2002). *The four pillars of investing*. New York: McGraw-Hill.

Block, S. (2008, October 5). Low-risk investments: Are they safe? *USA Today*.

Boardman, T. (2007, February 15). *Annuitization lessons from the UK*. Paper presented to the IMF Seminar on Ageing, Financial Risk Management and Financial Stability, Washington D.C. Retrieved 4/18/07 from https://www.imf.org/external/np/seminars/eng/2007/ageing/pdf/boardm.pdf.

Bodie, Z., & Clowes, M. J. (2003). *Worry-free investing: A safe approach to achieving your lifetime goals*. Upper Saddle River, NJ: Pearson.

Bogle, J. (1999). *Common sense on mutual funds*. New York: John Wiley.

Bogle, J. (2003, June 5). *The policy portfolio in an era of subdued returns.* Speech before the Investment Analysts Society of Chicago and The EnnisKnupp Client Conference, Chicago, Illinois.

Bogle, J. (2005, November/December). The relentless rules of humble arithmetic. *Financial Analysts Journal, 61*(6), 22–35.

Bogle, J. C. (2007). *The little book of common sense investing: The only way to guarantee your fair share of stock market returns.* New York: John Wiley.

Brinson, G. P., Singer, L. R., & Beebower, G. (1986, July–August). Determinants of portfolio performance. *Financial Analysts Journal*, 39–44.

Brock, F. (2004). *Retire on less than you think.* New York: Times Books.

Burns, S. (2003, October 26). Heeding advice of an elder. *The Dallas Morning News.*

Charlson, J. (2009, August 10). Frugality pays with target-date funds. *Morningstar Fund Spy*, 1–3.

Charlson, J., Falkof, D., Lutton, L., & Rekenthaler, J. (2009). *Target-date series research paper: 2009 industry survey.* Morningstar. Retrieved July 31, 2010 from http://corporate.morningstar.com/us/documents/MethodologyDocuments/ResearchPapers/TargetDateFundSeries_IndustrySurvey.pdf.

Charlson, J., et al. (2010). Target-date series research paper: Industry survey. *Morningstar.*

Clements, J. (2006, October 18). Curb your enthusiasm: Why investors often lag behind the market indexes. *The Wall Street Journal Online.*

Colman, E. (2008, June 1). Thousands lose out in pensions rip-off. *The Sunday Times.*

Condon, G. M., & Condon, J. L. (2001). *Beyond the grave.* New York: HarperCollins.

Cooley, P. L., Hubbard, C. M., & Walz, D. T. (1999). Sustainable withdrawal rates from your retirement portfolio. *Financial Counseling and Planning,* 10, 39–47.

Coontz, S. (2006, November 7). Too close for comfort. *The Washington Post.*

Creech, D. (2005). *How advisors protect investor returns?* Retrieved August 1, 2010 from http://www.investorresourcesinc.com/filestore/PDF/Dalbar_apir189.pdf.

Crenshaw, A. B. (2006, April 2). Building a nest egg doesn't come with blueprints. *The Washington Post.*

Dalbar, Inc. (2006). *Quantitative analysis of investor behavior.* Boston MA.

Davis, C. (2005, July 21). TIAA-CREF's fees headed in the wrong direction. *Morningstar Advisor.*

Davis, M. H., & Burner, S. T. (1995). Three decades of Medicare: What the numbers tell us. *Health Affairs,* 14(4), 231–243.

Dolan, K. (2009, December 21). The astonishing economics of big funds. *Morningstar.*

Editorial. (2010, January 18). How retirees saved the bank. *New York Times.*

Elliott, S. (2007, August 12). A dot-org stresses that it is no dot-com. *New York Times.*

Ellis, C. D. (1998). *Winning the loser's game.* New York: McGraw-Hill.

Fahlund, C. S. (2006). Juggling competing goals: College vs. retirement planning. *AAII Journal, XXVIII*, 15–17.

Fama, E. F., & French, K. R. (1993). Common risk factors in the return of stocks and bonds. *Journal of Financial Economics, 33(1)*, 3–57.

Feldman, A. (2009, February 5). Can a hybrid 401(k) save retirement? *Business Week.*

Feldman, R. (2008, May 7). *Maximize portfolio wealth by minimizing risk.* Retrieved July 31, 2010 from Investorsolutions.com.

Ferri, R. A. (2006). *All about asset allocation.* New York: McGraw-Hill.

Franklin, M. B. (2008, July 2). Preserve your savings for life. *The Washington Post.*

Gaffney, M. (2008, September 19). Don't privatize Social Security. *The Detroit News.*

Gardner, M. (2006, May 17). *Lessons on retirement from the experts: Retirees.* Retrieved August 1, 2010 from http://www.csmonitor.com/2006/0517/p13s02-lign.html.

Gibson, R. C. (2007). *Asset allocation: Balancing financial risk* (4th ed.). New York: McGraw-Hill.

Greene, K., & Tergesen, A. (2008, October 18). How retirees can ease pain of market rout. *Wall Street Journal*, D1, D6.

Greene, K., & Tergesen, A. (2010, January 10). Medicare costs more—for some. *Wall Street Journal*, D-4.

Greenenough, W. C. (1990). *It's my retirement money, take good care of it: The TIAA-CREF story.* Homewood, IL: Irwin.

Guyton, J. T. (2004). Decision rules and portfolio management for retirees: Is the "safe" initial withdrawal rate too safe? *Journal of Financial Planning, 17P*, 54–62.

Hahn, J. (2008, December 29). *Medicare: Part B Premiums.* Congressional Research Service Report for Congress, www.crs.gov.

Hamilton, M. (2007, October 28). Longevity's evil twin: Inflation. *Washington Post.*

Hammond, B., & Richardson, D. P. (2009, October 1) *Market Monitor.* A publication of TIAA-CREF Asset Management.

Harney, K. R. (2006, May 13). Trying to reverse a raw deal. *Washington Post.*

Harris, A. H. S., & Thoresen, C. E. (2005). Volunteering is associated with delayed mortality in older people: Analysis of the longitudinal study of aging. *Journal of Health Psychology, 10*, 739–752.

Herbert, P. (2007, August 15). Subprime and the impact on bonds. *Morningstar*.

Hulbert, M. (2006, April 9). *Same portfolio, higher cost. So why choose it?* Retrieved August 1, 2010 from http://www.nytimes.com/2006/04/09/business/yourmoney/09stra.html?.

Huxley, S., & Burns, J. B. (2005). *Asset dedication*. New York: McGraw-Hill.

Israelsen, C. (2008, November/December). The benefits of low correlation: Round II. *Journal of Indexes*, 38–34.

Kaplan, R. L. (2008). *A guide to starting social security benefits*. Illinois Law and Economics Research Papers Series, Research Paper No. LE08–025. Retrieved August 1, 2010 from http://ssrn.com/abstract = 1192902.

King, F. P. (1995, December). The TIAA graded payment method and the CPI. *Research Dialogues*, *46*, 1–7.

Kollmeyer, B. (2006, September 19). Benchmarks vs. stock pickers: Stacking up international actively managed funds against index funds. *Market Watch*.

Kristof, K. (2006, December 10). *Some annuities bad for seniors*. Retrieved July 15, 2010 from insurancenewsnet.com.

Lankford, K. (2009, July). Guaranteed income for life. *Kiplinger.com*.

Levitz, J. (2008, July 30). IRA rollover ads criticized by senator. *Wall Street Journal*.

Lieber, R. (2010, January 30). The unloved annuity gets a hug from Obama. *New York Times*.

Lunquist, L. A., & Golub, R. M. (2004, November). Cruise ship care: A proposed alternative to assisted living facilities. *Journal of the American Geriatrics Society*, 52(11), 1951–1954.

Lutton, L. P. (2009, September 9). Vanguard's target-date funds earn top marks. *Morningstar Fund Spy*.

McDonnell, K. (2006, March). Retirement annuity and employment-based pension income, among individuals ages 50 and over: 2004. *EBRI Notes*, 27(3), 6–11.

Milevsky, M. A. (2009). *Are you a stock or a bond? Create your own pension plan for a secure financial future*. Upper Saddle River, NJ: FT Press.

Milevsky, M. A., & Salisbury, T. S. (2006). *Asset allocation and the transition to income: The importance of product allocation in the retirement risk zone*. Toronto, Canada: York University.

Milevsky, M., & Young, V. A. (2002). *Optimal asset allocation and the real option to delay annuitization: It's not now or never*. Toronto, Canada: York University.

Mitchell, O., Poterba, J. M., & Warshawsky, M. J. (1999). New evidence on the money's worth of individual annuities. *American Economic Review, 89(5)*, 1299–1318.

Mont, J. (2009, October 21). Bear markets do wonders for retirement. Retrieved January 15, 2010 from TheStreet.com.

Morris, S. (2006, October). What's the right way to index? Morningstar ETF Investor, 1–4.

Mulvey, J. & Purcell. (2008, December 1). Converting retirement savings into income: annuities and periodic withdrawals. Ithaca, NY: Cornell University ILR School.

Otar, J. C. (n.d.). *Lifetime retirement income: The zone strategy*. Retrieved from http://www.retirementoptimizer.com/articles/Article105.pdf.

Otar, J. C. (2001). *High expectations & false dreams: One hundred years of stock market history applied to retirement planning*. Toronto, Canada: Webcom Limited.

Otar, J. C. (2010). *Unveiling the retirement myth*.

Phillips, K. (2008, May). Numbers racket: Why the economy is worse than we know. *Harper's Magazine*, 43–47.

Poterba, J. M., & Warshawsky, M. J. (1999, January). The costs of annuitizing retirement payouts from individual accounts. Retrieved February 12, 2010 from http://ideas.repec.org/p/

Powell, R. (2009, November 1). *Use retirement planning tools at your own risk*. http://www.marketwatch.com/story/retirement-tools-often-underestimate-risk-2009–11-05.

Richards, L. (2006, February 27). *Fiduciary duty: Return to first principles*. Speech to Eighth Annual Investment Adviser Compliance Summit, Washington, DC.

Rottersman, M. (2009, February 20). *Most profitable mutual funds ever*. Retrieved from http://www.etfguide.com/research/133/16/Most-Profitable-Mutual-Funds.

Ruffennach, G. (2009, November 14–15). Have you learned your lessons yet? *The Wall Street Journal*, R-4.

Scatizzi, C. (2010). "Risk-wise" risk management. *Computerized Investing, XXIX(1)*, 16–19.

Schloss, I. S., & Abildsoe, D. V. (2000). *Understanding TIAA-CREF: How to plan for a secure and comfortable retirement*. New York: Oxford University Press.

Schoen, C., Nicholson, J., & Rustgi, S. (2009, August 20). Paying the price: How health insurance premiums are eating up middle class incomes. New York, NY: The Commonwealth Fund.

Schultheis, B. (2005). *The coffeehouse portfolio*. Kirkland, WA: Palouse Press.

Scott, D. L. (1997). *Wall Street words: An A to Z guide to investment terms for today's investor*. New York: Houghton Mifflin.

Siegel, J. J. (2002). *Stocks for the long run.* New York: McGraw-Hill.

Simon, E. (2006, August 20). Now, you're your own pension manager. *San Jose Mercury News*, 4E.

Sloan, A. (2006, October 31). Cost-of-living increases don't come cheap. *WashingtonPost.com.*

Slott, E. (2003). *The retirement savings bomb.* New York: Penguin Group.

Sommer, J. (2008, November 23). Seeking solace? You'll find little in the bond market. *The New York Times.*

Spitzer, J. J., & Singh, S. (2007, June). Is rebalancing a portfolio during retirement necessary? *Journal of Financial Planning*, 46–57.

Stevens, S. (2001, May 24). Why you need long-term care insurance. Retrieved October 25, 2005 from Morningstar.com.

Swedroe, L., & Hempen, J. H. (2006). *The only guide to a winning bond strategy you'll ever need.* New York: St. Martin's Press.

Swedroe, L. E., & Kizer, J. (2008). *The only guide to alternative investments you'll ever need: The good, the flawed, the bad, and the ugly.* New York: Bloomberg Press.

Swensen, D. F. (2005). *Unconventional success: A fundamental approach to personal investment.* New York: Free Press.

Taleb, N. N. (2007). *The black swan: The impact of the highly improbable.* New York: Random House.

Tergesen, A. (2009, October 17). Test-driving your retirement plans. *Wall Street Journal*, R1, R4.

TIAA-CREF (2006, January). Receiving your retirement income from TIAA-CREF. New York, NY: Teachers Insurance and Annuity Association-College Equities Fund (TIAA-CREF).

TIAA-CREF Asset Management. (2007). TIAA Real Estate account. *Quarterly Analysis.* TIAA website, quarter ending December 31, 2007.

TIAA-CREF. (2008, September). *Minimum distribution: Making it simple.* Publication produced and distributed by TIAA-CREF. New York: New York.

TIAA-CREF. (2008, August 1). *Statement on credit exposure in the TIAA general account and the TIAA-CREF fixed-income portfolios as of June 30, 2008.* Retrieved from http://www.tiaa-cref.org/support/news/articles/gen0712_104.html.

Van Harlow, W., & Milevsky, M. A. (2007, August). *Structuring income for retirement.* Boston, MA: Fidelity Research Institute.

Vanguard.com (2005, Summer). Case study: Two professors take a cram course in long-term care alternatives. Retrieved October 25, 2005 from Vanguard.com newsletter, *In the Vanguard*, 1–3.

Walsh, T. (2002). *Annuities and inflation.* New York, NY: TIAA-CREF Institute.

Warner, R. (2004). *Get a life: You don't need a million to retire well.* Berkeley, CA: Nolo Press.

Webb, A. (2006, January). *Is adverse selection in the annuity market a big problem?* (Issue Brief No. 40). Boston, MA: Center for Retirement Research at Boston College.

Weigand, R. A., & Irons, R. (2008, January). When does a bond-first withdrawal sequence extend portfolio longevity? *Journal of Financial Planning*, 21, 66–77.

Wolf, J. A. (2001, August 22). *Testimony of James A. Wolf, President, TIAA-CREF Retirement Services, before the President's Commission to Strengthen Social Security*. Retrieved March 15, 2008 from http://www.ssa.gov/history/reports/pcsss/Wolf_Testimony.pdf.

Yablonski, P. (2006). Retirement annuity and employment-based pension income, among individuals ages 50 and over: 2004. *EBRI Notes*, 27(3): 2–5.

Zweig, J. (1998, January 1). *Five investing lessons from America's top pension fund.* Retrieved August 1, 2010 from http://money.cnn.com/magazines/moneymag/moneymag_archive/1998/01/01/236875/index.htm.

Zweig, J. (2009, December 19–20). Will "12b-1" fees ever stop bugging investors? *The Wall Street Journal*, B1.

ABOUT THE AUTHORS

Edwin M. Bridges, Professor Emeritus, Stanford University, has an extensive background in higher education. Prior to joining the Stanford University faculty in 1974, he taught at Washington University (St. Louis), The University of Chicago, and University of California (Santa Barbara). He is internationally known for his work on problem-based learning and has worked with faculty from a variety of disciplines in China and the United States. During his 35-year career in higher education, he has consulted with numerous organizations, including the World Health Organization, the World Bank, and the New York City Public Schools. Professor Bridges has received two lifetime achievement awards for his contributions to the field of educational administration.

Since retiring in 1999, Ed lives with his wife, Marjorie, in an historic home on the Stanford University Campus. Six years ago, they celebrated their Golden Wedding Anniversary. In retirement, he has devoted much of his time to activities that he neglected during his career as a professor—investing and retirement planning. After reading hundreds of books and articles on these subjects, he decided to share the lessons he learned with friends, colleagues, family, former students, and others through his writing and public speaking. He brings these lessons to life by drawing on his personal setbacks, mistakes, and triumphs in investing and planning for retirement.

Brian D. Bridges is a registered investment adviser in the state of California and a trained financial planner (University of California, Santa Cruz) with a strong background in counseling (M.A., Department of Counseling Psychology, Santa Clara University).

Prior to entering the fields of financial planning and life-enhancement counseling, Brian provided engineering solutions to IBM, Sun Microsystems, and NASA's Jet Propulsion Laboratory. He graduated summa cum laude in industrial engineering (Cal Poly, San Luis Obispo) and completed an MSIE degree at Stanford University.

INDEX